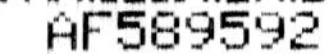

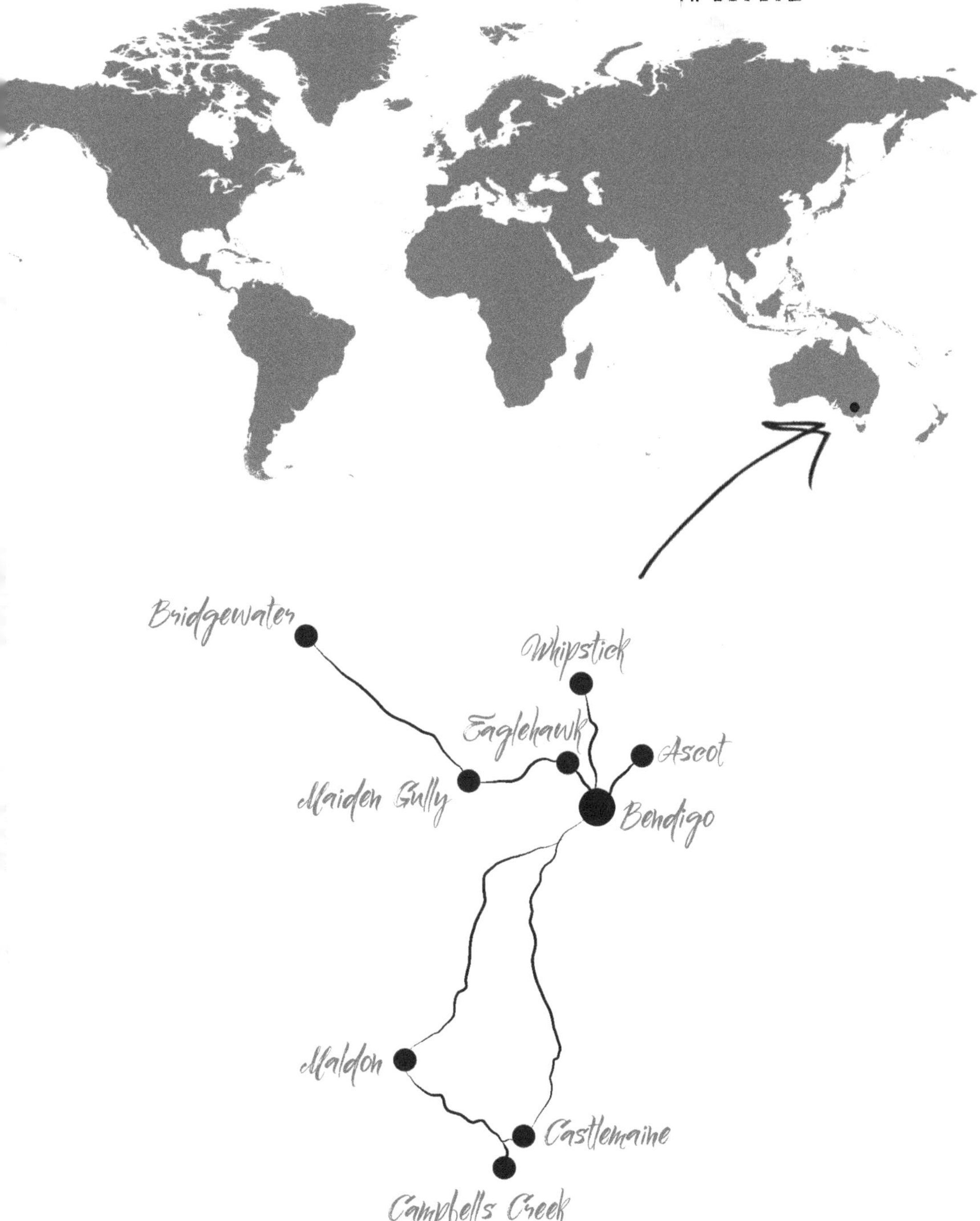

Bridgewater
Whipstick
Eaglehawk
Ascot
Maiden Gully
Bendigo
Maldon
Castlemaine
Campbells Creek

For Sonia, who makes beautiful spaces.
- LM

National Library of Australia Cataloguing-in-Publication entry

Author: Mitchell, Lauren

Photographer: Doak, Amy and McCarthy, Brendan

Title: Artist Spaces Of The Victorian Goldfields

ISBN: 9780994412690

Subject: Interior Decoration, Decoration Of Specific Rooms In Residential Buildings, Art

Dewey Number: 747.7

All images by Amy Doak except for pages 28 - 37 by Brendan McCarthy.

Published by:
Of The World Publishing
PO Box 8070
BENDIGO SOUTH LPO VIC 3550

www.oftheworldbooks.com

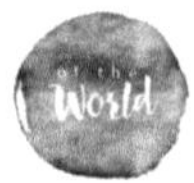

Artist Spaces

of the Victorian Goldfields

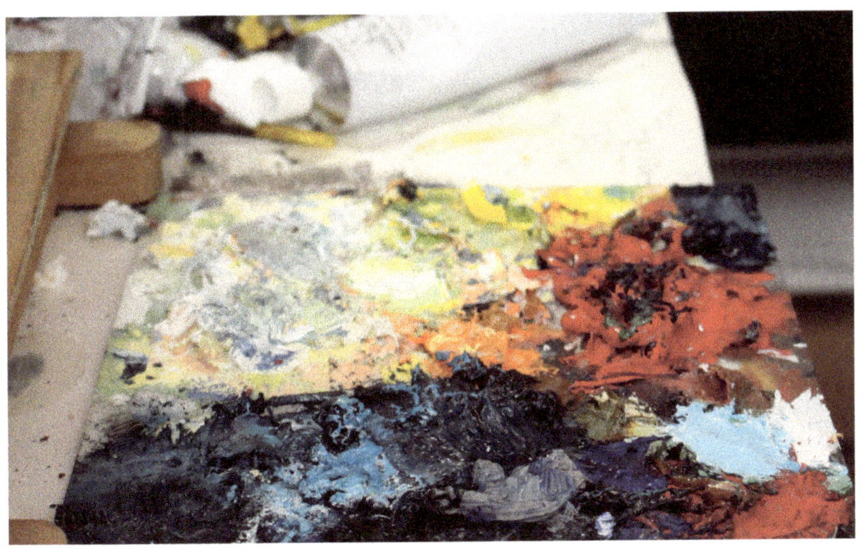

Words by Lauren Mitchell

Images by Amy Doak & Brendan McCarthy

Contents

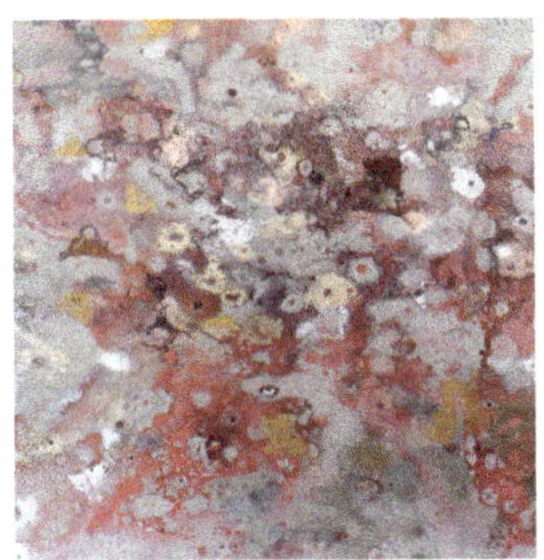

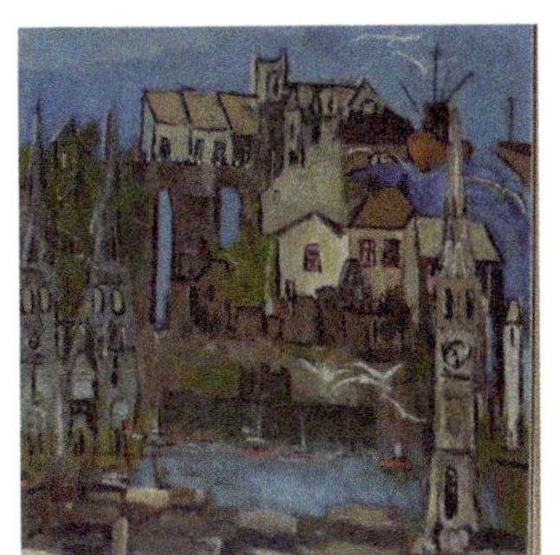

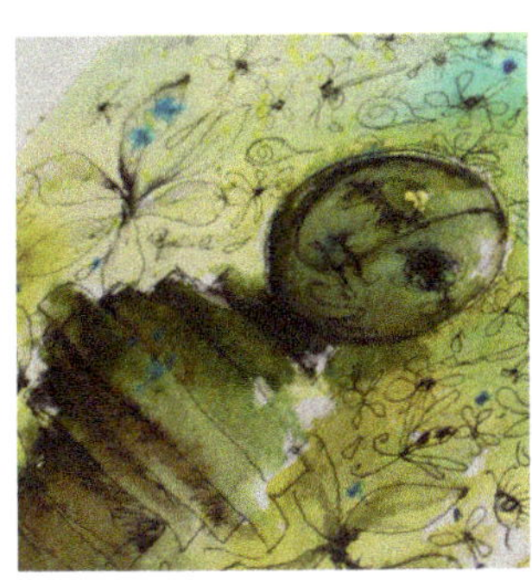

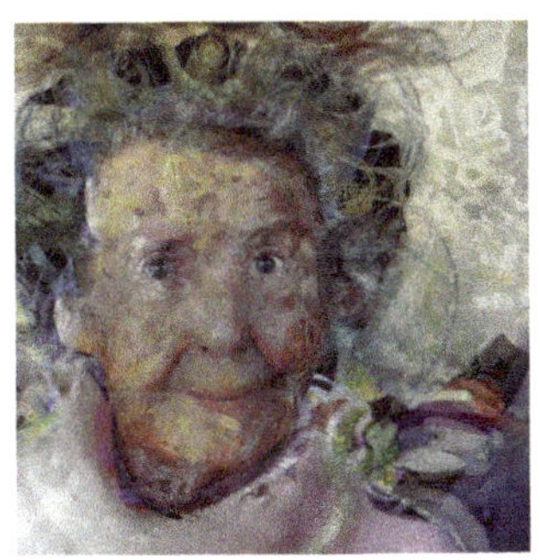

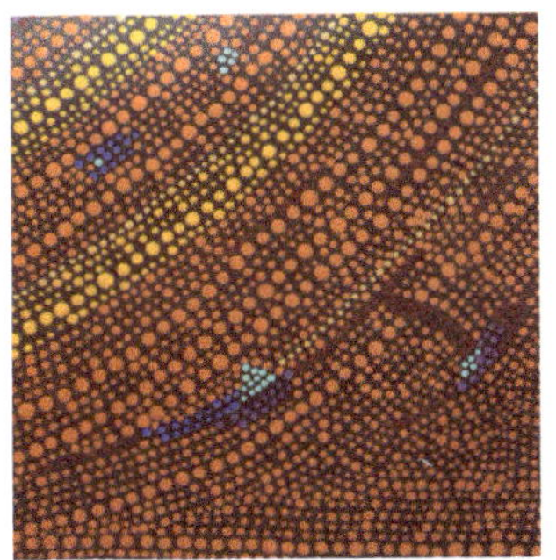

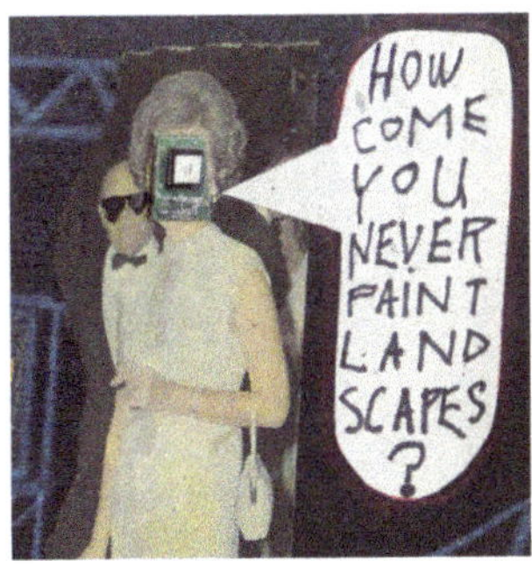
HOW COME YOU NEVER PAINT LANDSCAPES ?

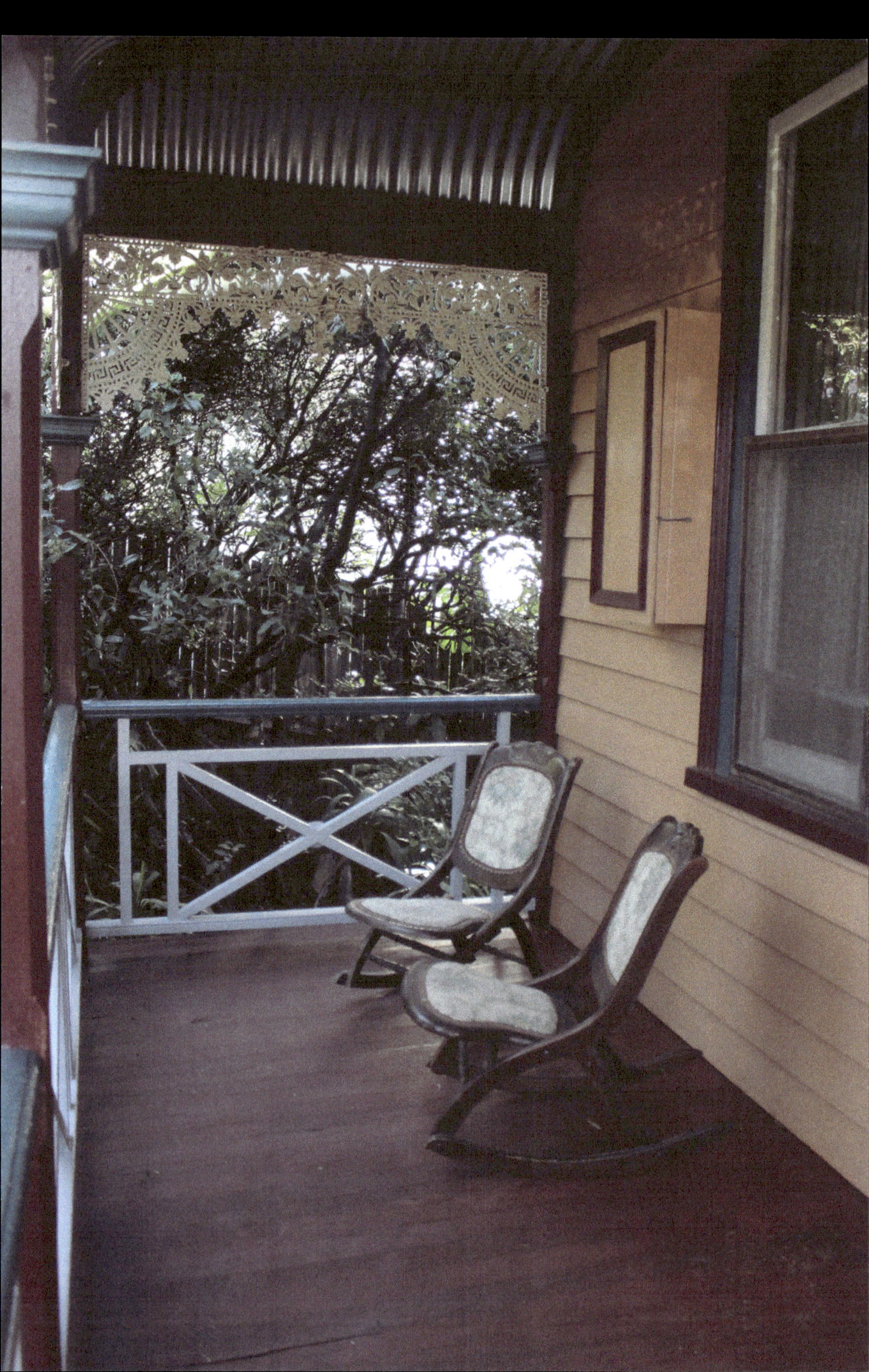

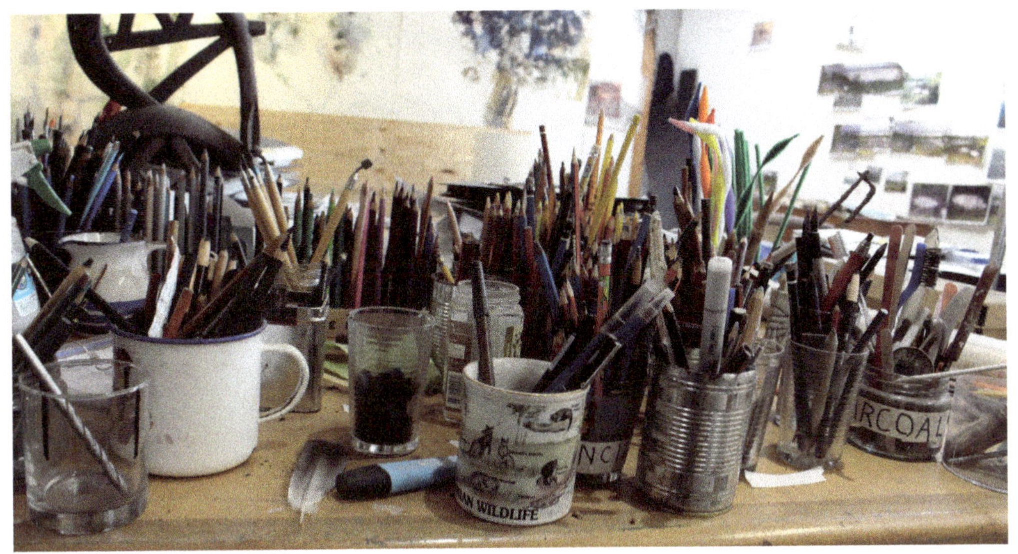

Dear reader,

These stories were gathered as autumn turned to winter. It's a wonderful time to travel around the goldfields region of Victoria, Australia. Cooler weather brings greens and golds back to the landscape. Icy white wattle blooms in the bush. Bare branches are revealed on stately street trees along stretches of historic sandstone and timber buildings.

As such, the seasons came to characterise this book. The photographs revealed white skies and warm interiors. Leaf litter and winds of change. These are the stories of a time and place, made interesting by the people who live here. In this case, the artists.

From the mid-1850s the world's richest goldfields lured people the globe over. Many and varied nationalities came to shed the skin of former lives and live as equals among mud and canvas huts, if only until riches were found. And once they were, much wealth was pumped back into the grand cities and tiny towns, leaving a legacy of great architecture. Of foresight and creativity.

Today this area still attracts people seeking to build a home and life on their own terms. Central Victoria is considered one of the most affordable places to live, in terms of lifestyle and amenities. Think top-class hospitals and education, sport, art and cultural offerings, without the city price tags.

The 13 artists featured here are all linked by humble ambition; to live simply and sustainably with the freedom to go on making great art, regardless of life's pressures. They have engineered their lives, homes and studios to achieve this. As such, each artist's space is a true reflection of the person within.

Each story is also, somehow, linked to the facts of living on the goldfields. They are vehicles to tell a wider tale. This is part travel book, part history book, part celebration of life and art, goldfields-style.

Lauren Mitchell

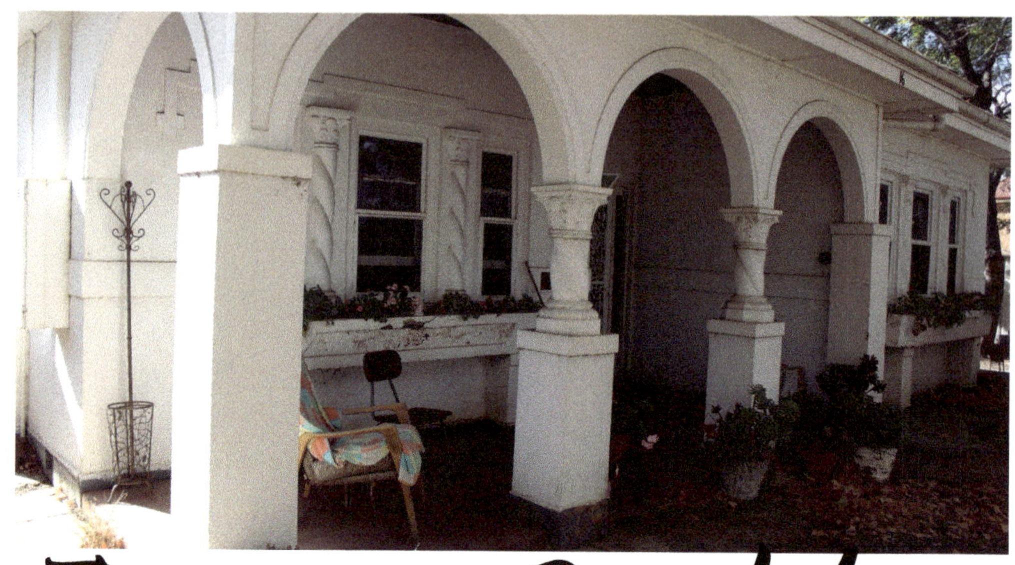

Jessica Spalding

Winds of change

For everything there is a season. Highs, lows, grief, success. It all eventually falls away and makes space for what's next. Like the autumn leaves out the front of Jessica Spalding's house. The palest yellow star-shaped leaves, swirling in an early May wishy-washy wind.

They're sticking to soles, they're sneaking into the entrance hall as Jess opens a white framed fly-wire door. "We moved here just over 12 months ago, just before the leaves started falling," she says. "If I had have known how bad it was we might not have." She curses the leaves. For now.

"I chose this house because I like the angles. Because it's right in town and has lots of nice light." Jess makes mugs of peppermint tea under a kitchen skylight. Up, up it reaches through the high Californian bungalow ceiling, offering a glimpse of sky, cloud and TV antennae.

We're in inner-city Bendigo. At one end of Jess' street is the city's main drag. At the other is the tram depot, and running the length are steel tracks on which tourists trundle in vintage carriages. Trams have characterised Bendigo since 1890. Until 1972 they served as public transport, and since then, a tourist attraction.

In recent years the trams have been further revived to reflect Bendigo's growing creative culture. There's the blues tram, the restaurant tram, the Art Series Hotel tram adorned with the work of Mark Schaller. And then there's the Jimmy Possum tram. Which brings us right back to Jess' place.

As the in-house artist for furniture and design house Jimmy Possum, Jess' job was to fill nine stores around the country with her paintings. Her work can

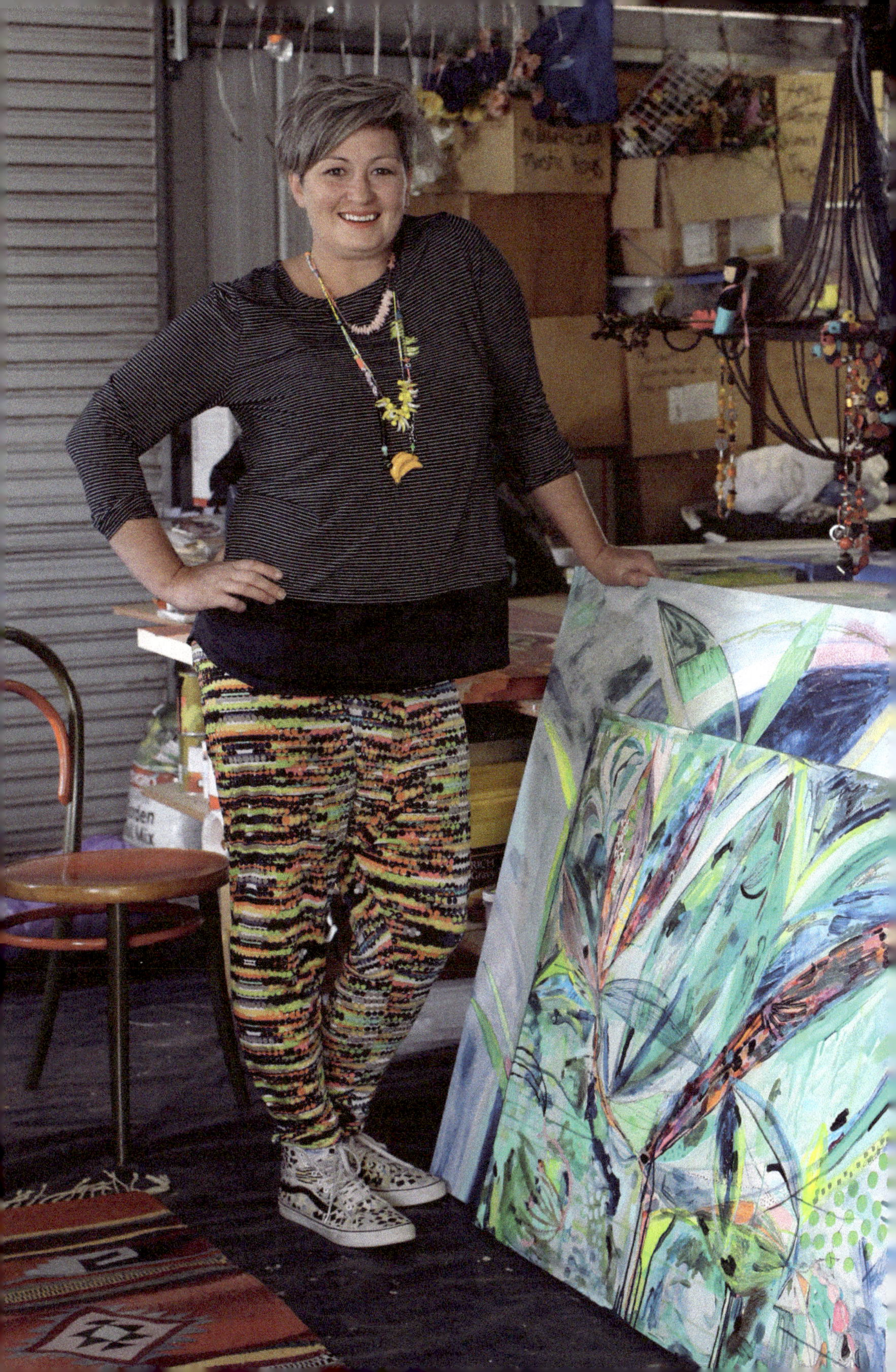

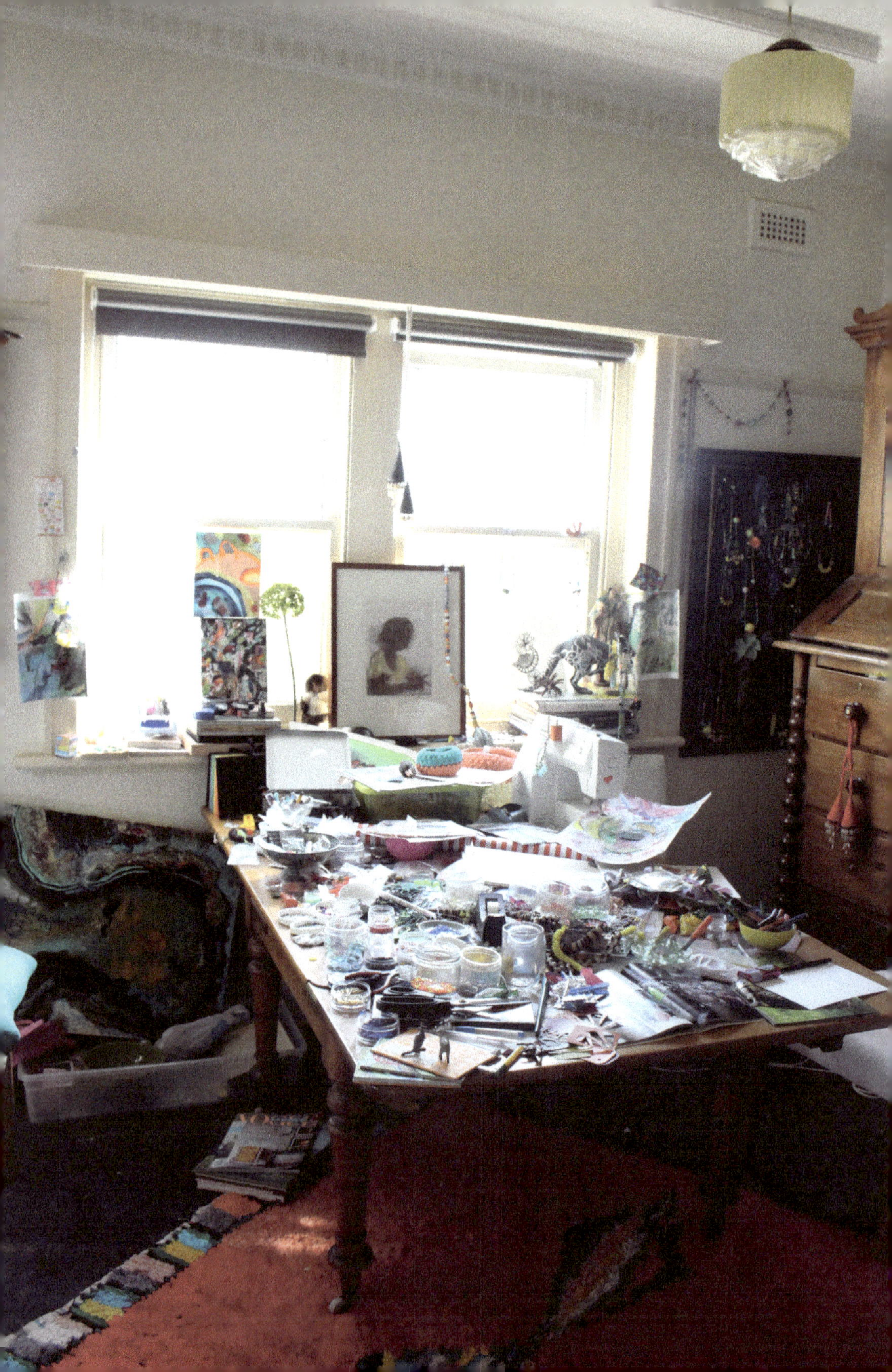

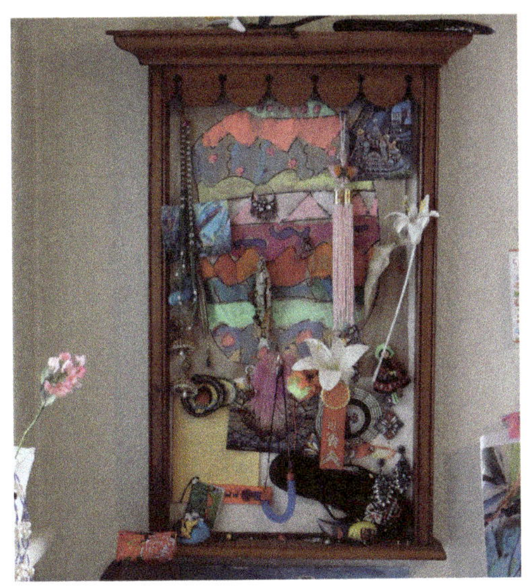

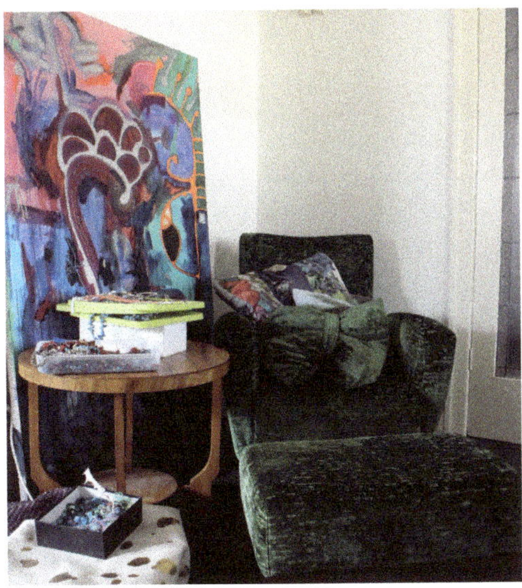

also be found onboard said tram, in Bendigo Health's oncology room, the Otis Foundation's retreat for breast cancer sufferers, and Eaglehawk's arthouse Star Cinema. And it can be found in abundance in every crack and crevice of this house.

The bungalow is a mishmash of clustered, glittered, glorious clutter. It reveals a collector's affection for the small stuff. For beads and bottle tops, tiny toys and a ten-year-old's drawings. The latest project hides the Jimmy Possum timber tabletop. It's the perfect metaphor for Jess, who says there is no distinction in her life between art and sustenance.

Making things is so important that Jess says for a long time, art was the one thing that kept her going. "I lost the plot there for a little while," she says. "It was sort of good research, makes for great art."

Much of Jess' 20s were spent in inner-Melbourne suburbs, in a string of share houses and squats, dangerously blurring the lines between fun and freedom, addiction and despair. "I had a misspent youth and they weren't always good years," she says. "Art was the only thing that kept me going. Making things for no reason. Like a meditation. I used to make little brooches out of bits of rubbish and sell them on the street. Bits of computers. Debris. I'd walk on the beach and collect things and put them all together. I still make them sometimes. I find them quite therapeutic. Little bits of rubbish. Rubbish put in a nice context is beautiful."

Even in her darkest times, Jess sought colour and light. Then, ten years ago, along came the shiny, shiny beacon between that life and this; Jess' son Louis. "I wanted things to change. I felt like he was a little gift from God. I don't think I knew how to change otherwise, without that red hot poker."

When Louis was six months old Jess moved back to her childhood home city of Bendigo to put some distance between her past and to join the family business. She says, at first all she wanted to do was make a machine-embroidered chair. After ten years at Jimmy Possum, there was never time for that. Jess was too busy painting. The thousands of paintings she completed made her arguably Bendigo's best-selling artist.

In the autumn of 2016, as Jess shares her story here, news breaks that after 21 years Jimmy Possum will close by winter. It's the end of an era for Bendigo; the business took locally-made furniture – and the city's name – across Australia.

"I'm sad that the furniture, the fabric, the design aspect of my life will be gone because I love it," Jess says. "I love all aspects of design, and the people working at Jimmy Possum. They are amazing, but they leave with exceptional training, so it will be exciting to see where they take it."

She says she has mixed emotions about her job coming to an end. But mostly, she's ready for change. "It has been a huge responsibility to fill all those stores with paintings. It wasn't ever about having one idea and seeing it through to the end, it was constantly having ten ideas and working through all of them. I was never short on ideas and part of me thrives on that, but having an obsessive nature means other aspects of your life get left behind. It was such an all-encompassing job... certainly not a nine-to-five. I think all artists can relate to that, you just never switch off."

Those paintings will keep coming, long after the JP factory doors close. In Jess' backyard is a massive shed – another selling point for the house. It's a woman's-own domain of paint cans and more collections, oddities and inspiration. Canvases carry a whiff of the sea roads Jess has recently travelled on. "I'll never stop painting," she says. "It's not a choice I have. Right now I'm working on some mural ideas with local businesses, doing some different things out of the studio and some collaborations. I'm working with the community to spread some serious art about, so that will be awesome."

In 2015 Jess joined 40 other iconic Australian artists and designers in adorning larger than life-sized kangaroos with their art as part of the Hop for Hope project. The 40 roos were auctioned to raise more than $160,000 for the Alannah and Madeline Foundation, which works to keep children safe from violence. It's projects like these that will continue to drive her.

Jess often thinks of the people who have bought her paintings. Sometimes, she hears their stories, of her work becoming a loved fixture of a family home. "Or about fights within families of who's going to inherit that big yellow painting they've all grown up with," she says. "It's fascinating to hear what they mean to their owners."

Jess has a theory as to why people respond to her work with such warmth. "My job taught me that you can't just slap a bit of paint about and think someone will buy it," she says. "People respond to integrity and ideas and all the things they can't explain about an artwork.

"Sometimes in life it's not how well you do something, it's the passion and striving to authentically express yourself that matters and I believe that's what people respond to. People can relate to that and that's why my paintings have been popular. Not because they're good. But because they cling to a dream. They are hope."

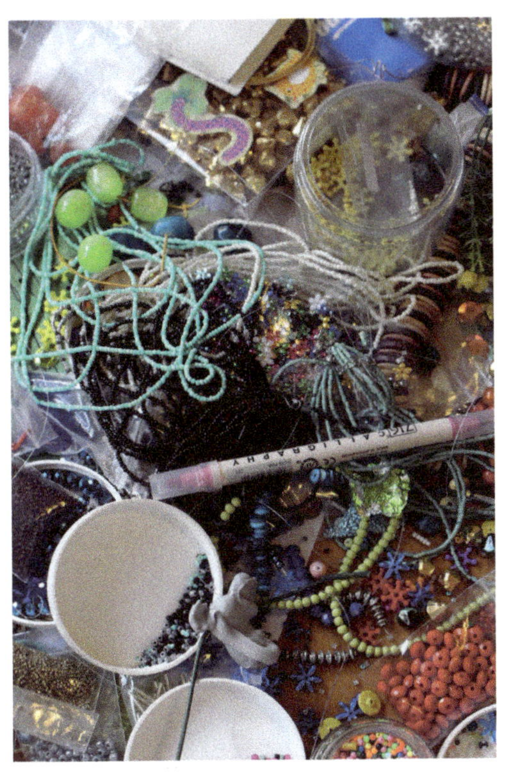

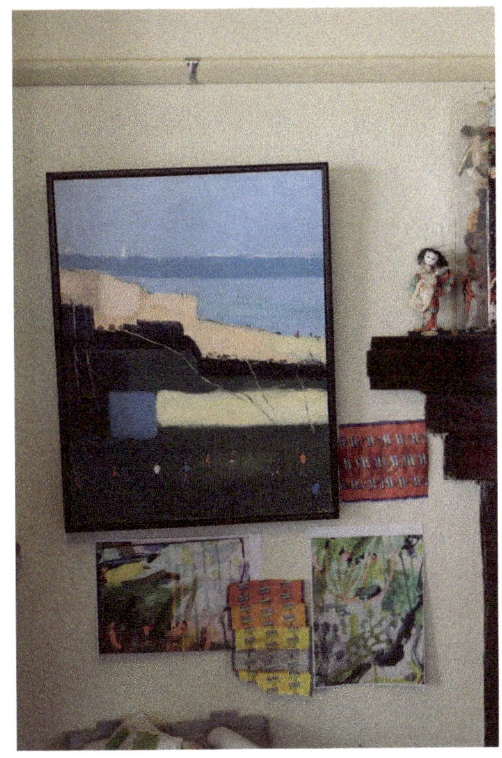

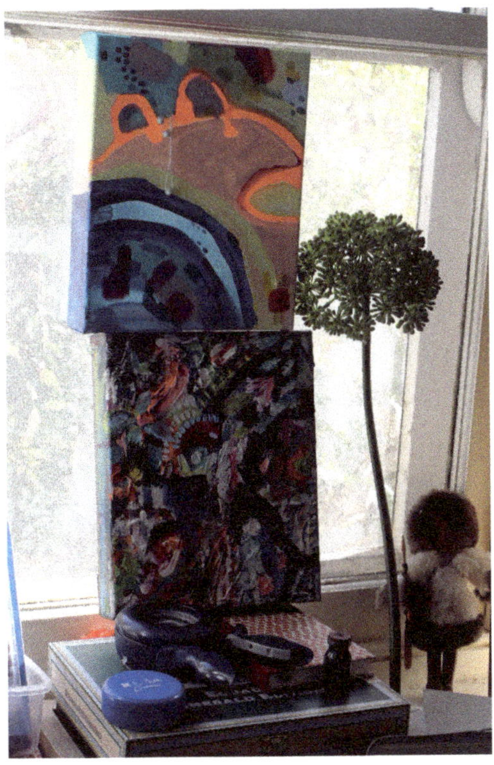

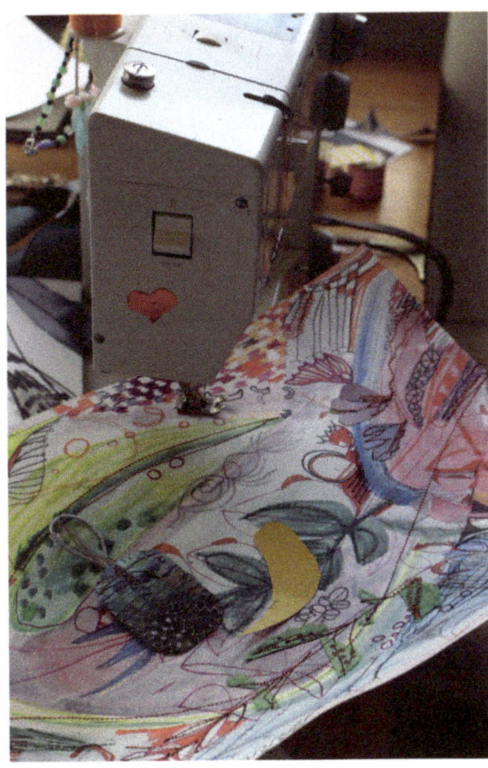

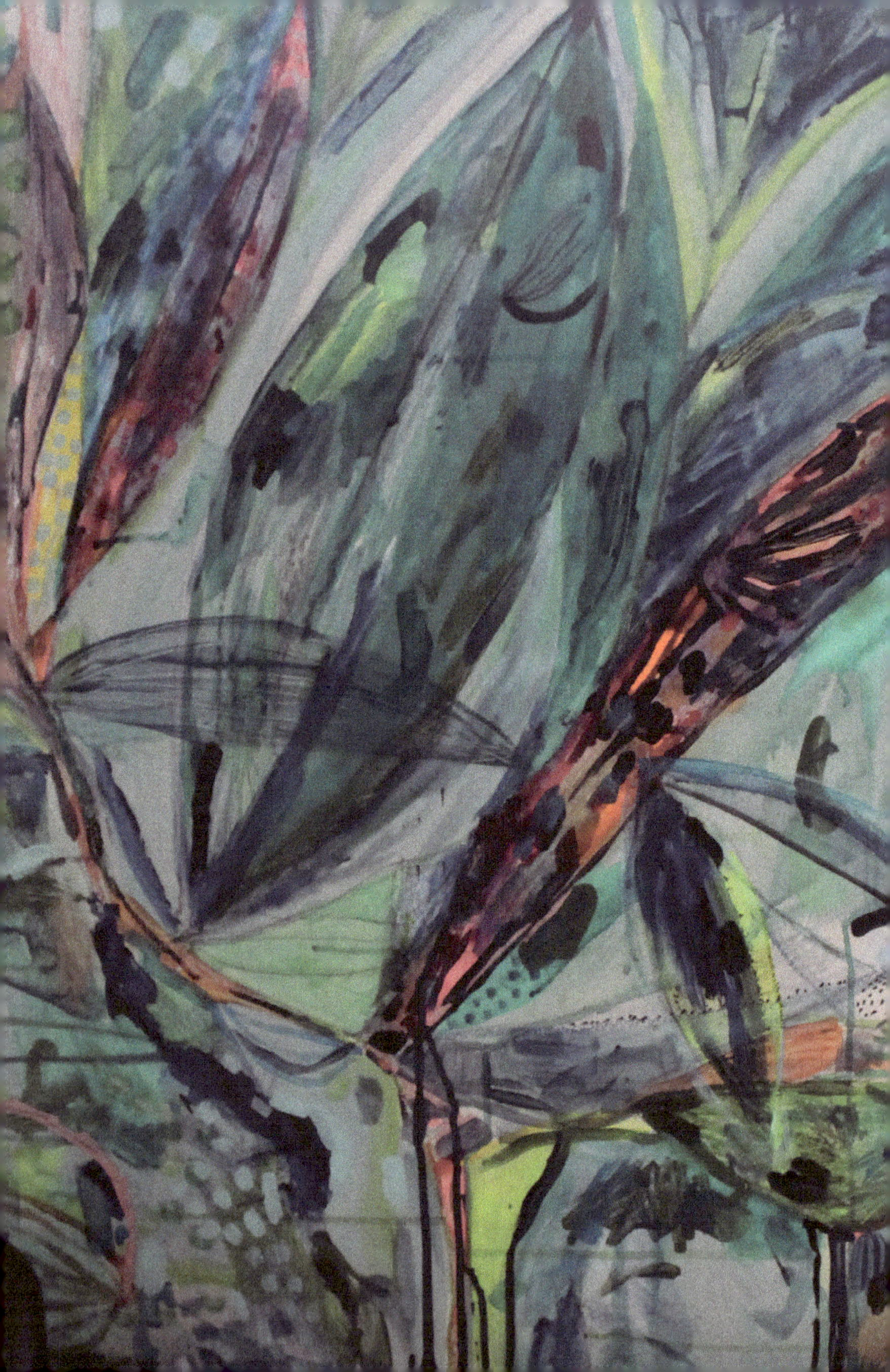

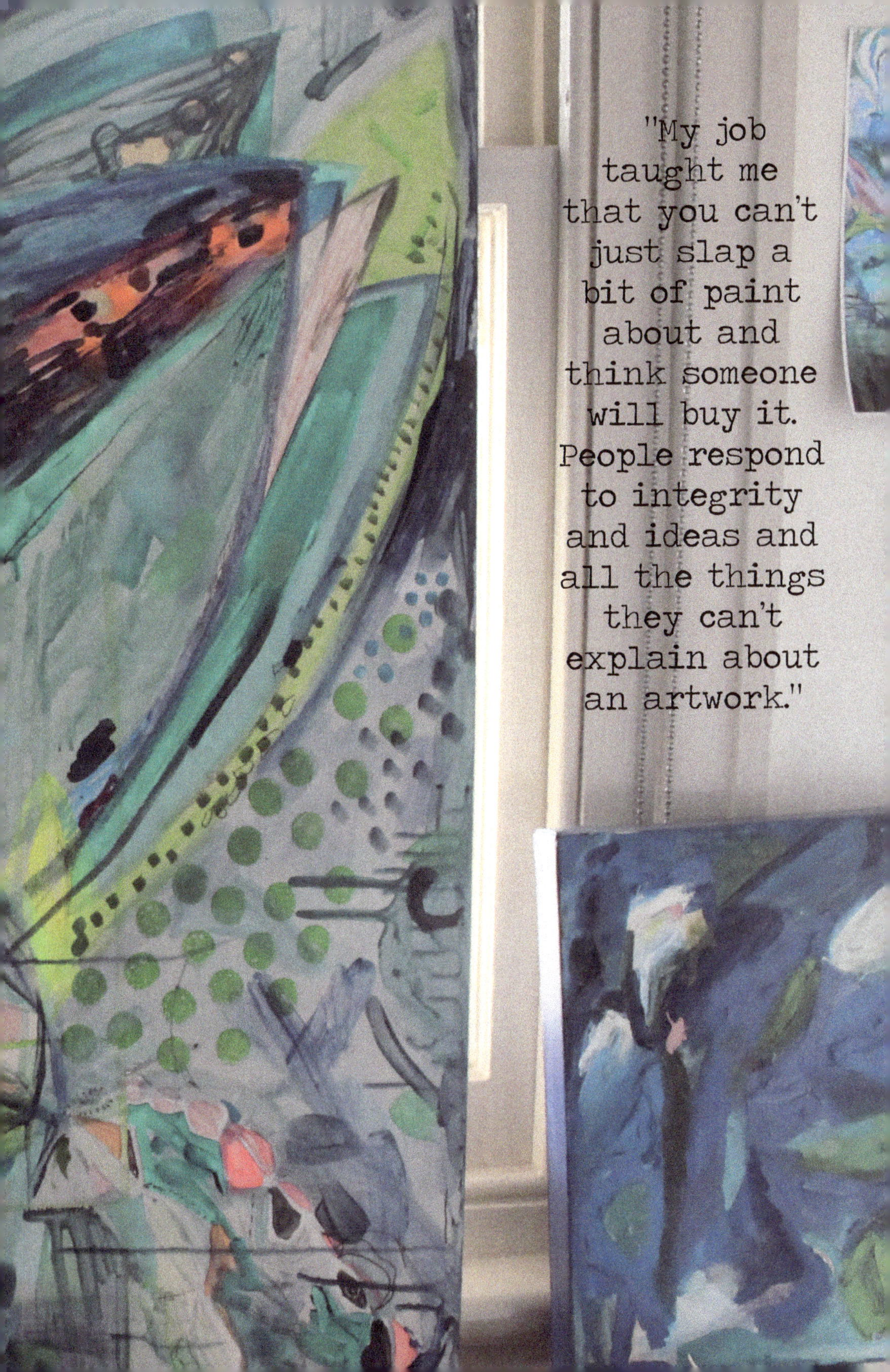

"My job taught me that you can't just slap a bit of paint about and think someone will buy it. People respond to integrity and ideas and all the things they can't explain about an artwork."

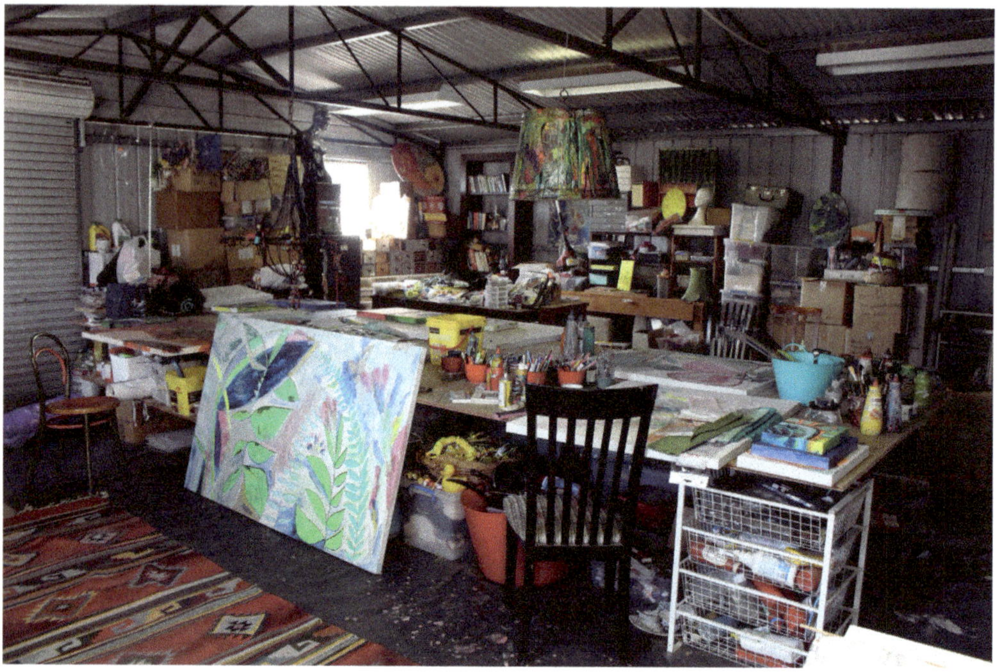

Canvases carry a whiff of the sea roads Jess has recently travelled on.

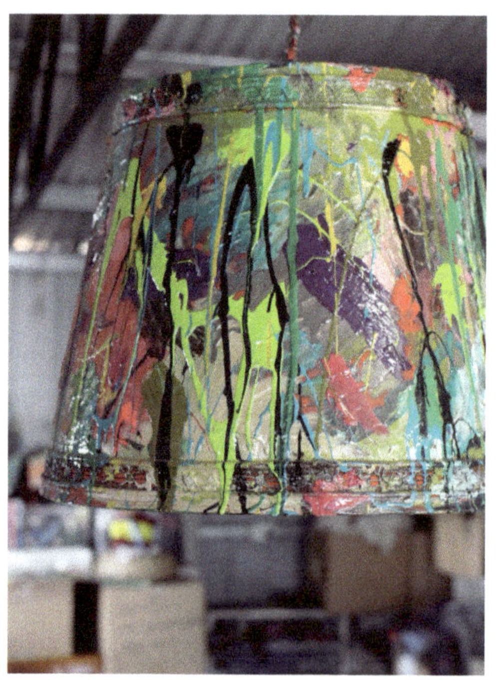

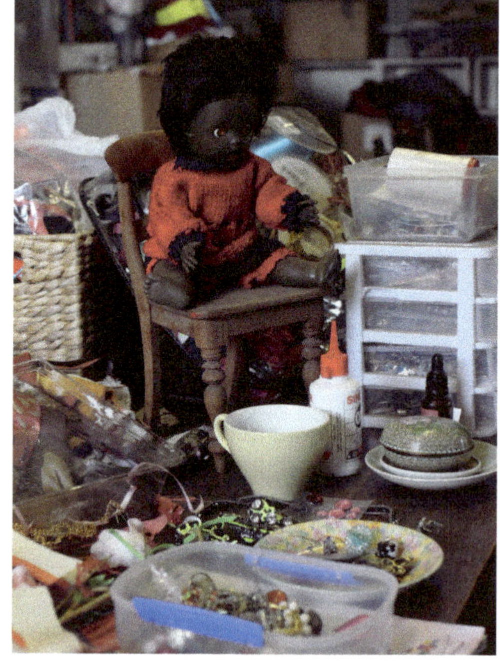

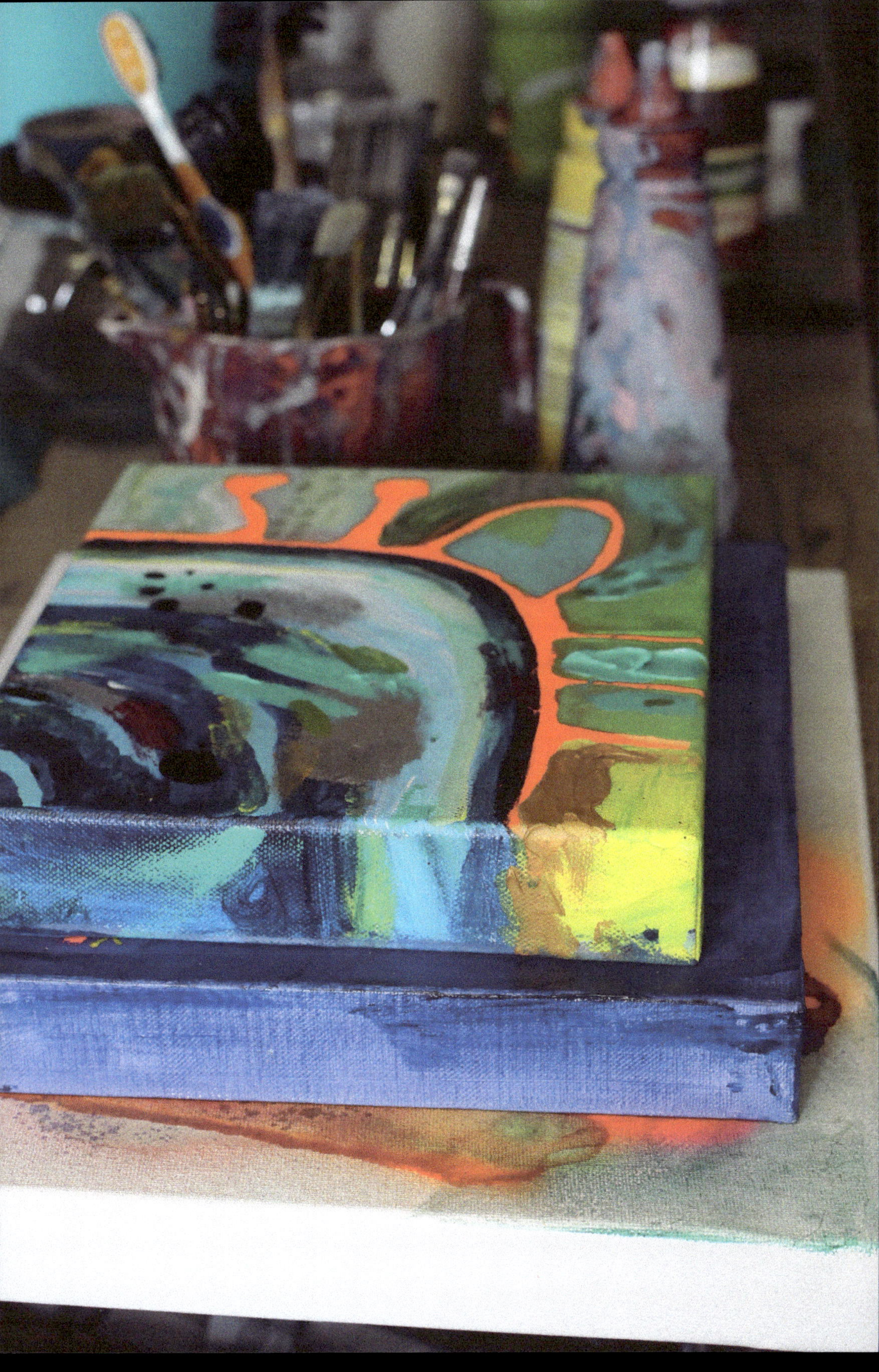

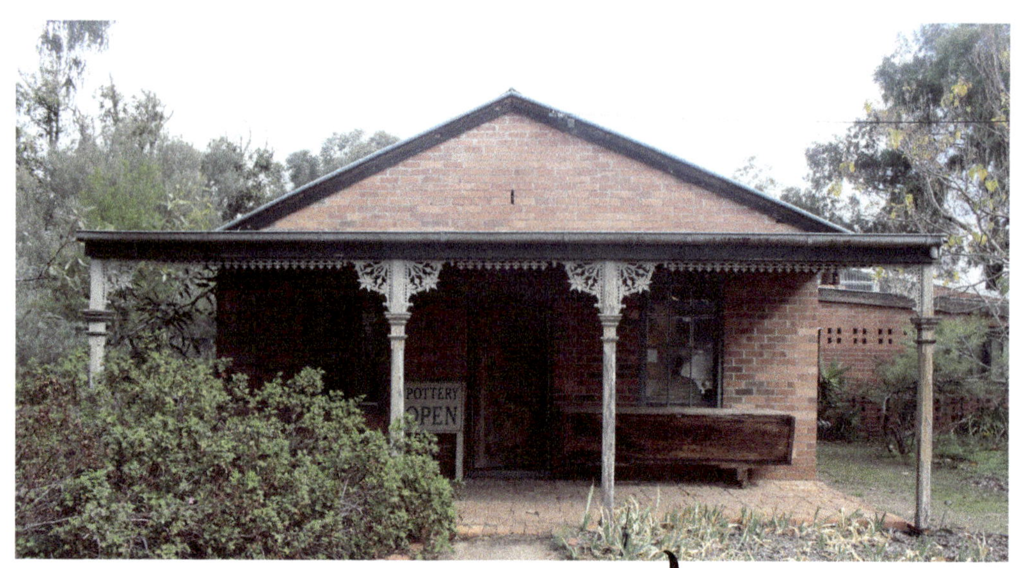

Garry Bish

On earthy pursuits

Past the peppercorns at Potter's Arms the world is changing. It's a weekday afternoon. A commercial radio station is momentarily drowned out by power tools and the shouts of men in high vis. A new house is being built in the former front yard of the historic neighbouring property.

The Bendigo suburb of Ascot is being plugged up with homogenous brick veneers, concrete driveways and coloured steel fences. "I call it the cane toad of fencing," Garry Bish says. "It's taking over."

New owners of the 1868 gothic-style mansion 'Ascot Park' next door have carved up their couple of acres for housing lots. The same won't be happening at Garry's place. "I'm a farmer's son. I like space around me," he says.

Garry purchased his property 'Kilburnie' in 1970. He was a 20-year-old aspiring potter studying a Diploma of Ceramics at the then Bendigo Institute of Technology. "It was cheap and it was close to town," he says of the 19th century red brick house. "It had grass growing up through the hand basin, and lots of bits of floor missing. To me it was perfect." And topping it all off was the fact this place was the original home of George Duncan Guthrie, founder of the famous Bendigo Pottery.

The Glaswegian Guthrie came to Bendigo for gold, and instead discovered deposits of fine white clay. In 1858 he established the historic pottery, which has remained in constant production and welcomes visitors daily. The pottery has a historically significant collection of ceramic wood-fired bottle kilns, which are listed on the Victorian Heritage Register.

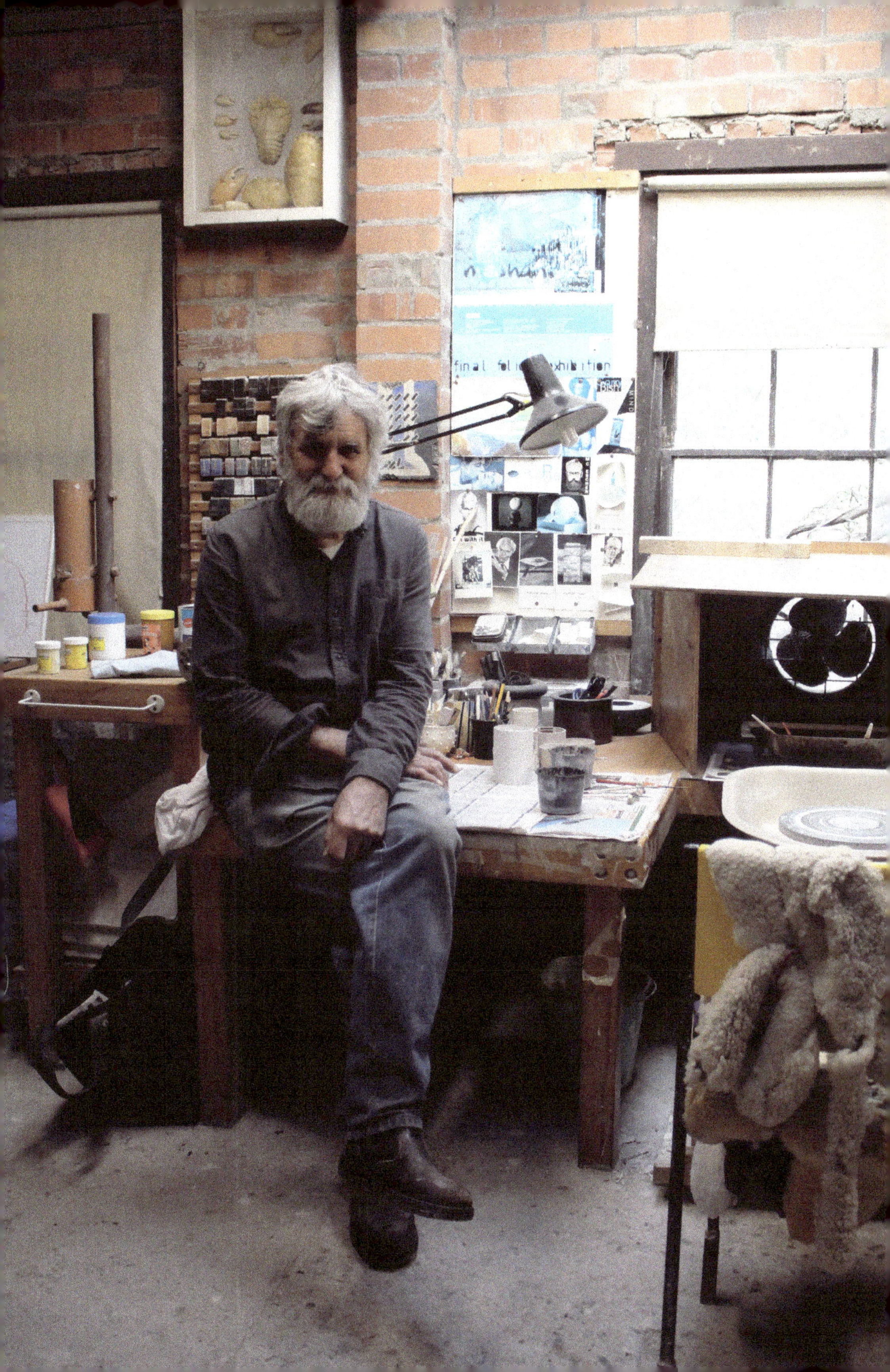

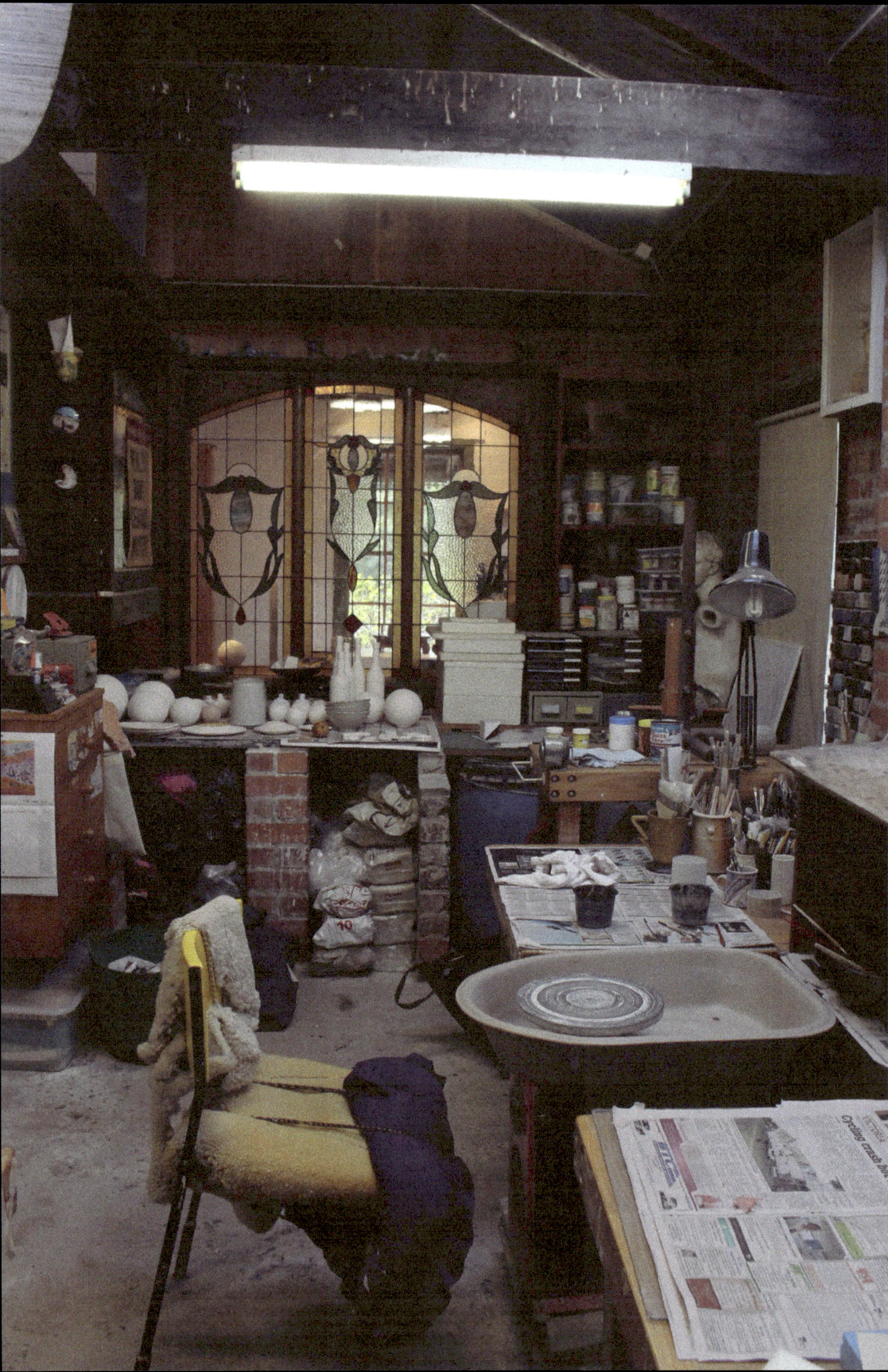
Cycling crash

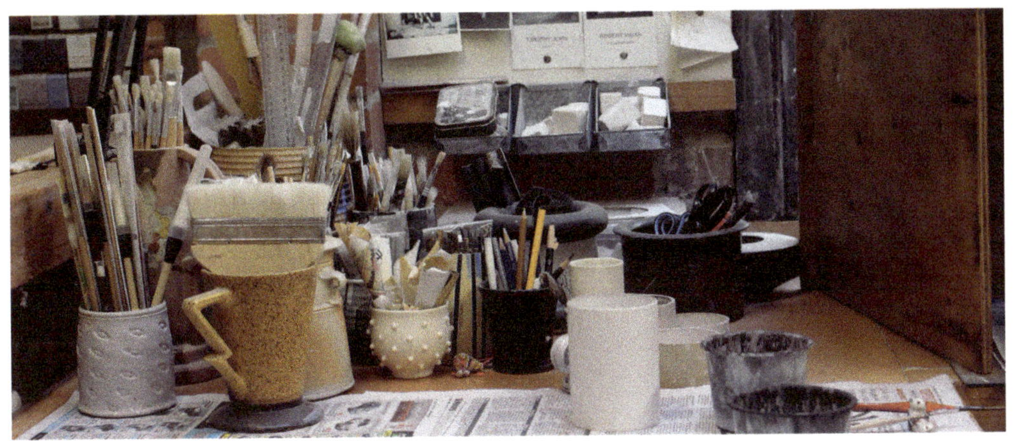

Almost 120 years after Guthrie built his home, along came Garry, with plans to establish his own pottery practice. He did so in the time-honoured tradition of rolling up his sleeves. “When I started nothing was produced for you. You actually had to source the materials and do all the experimenting and testing yourself.

“A fellow student and mate from the technical college was living here with me and we built our first kilns. The first glazes we did were ash glazes from the fireplace. They had a distinct character. And according to the wood you were burning you’d get a certain character, colour, specking, that sort of stuff. We had to do everything from the ground up, no pun intended.”

It was Garry’s resourceful nature that got him through those early years. “I lived pretty close to the earth, to be quite frank. I basically had to live it, and live pretty rugged. Because a, you don’t make the money and b, if you want the lifestyle, you’ve got to forgo some comforts.

“When I moved to the house I had no furniture. I used to eat breakfast off an old wooden crate that I’d found. But I’m not saying that it was hard, it was great. I’d do it again anytime.”

By 1972 Garry had built the Potter’s Arms studio and gallery beside the house. It’s all golden honey tones, chunky timber benchtops and exposed rafters laced with daddy long legs webs. The rafters came from a Bendigo demolition. As did an arched stained glass window, itself a work of art. “That came out of a place in Pall Mall,” Garry says. “They wrecked a lot of stuff in Bendigo back then. That was a good time for scrounging. You’d pay about $5 for that. I used to follow the demolition truck around.”

Once settled, Garry began forging a signature style to distinguish his work from the other local potters. “Mine was wheel thrown, functional decorative work,” he says. “I used to do a technique called glaze trailing, which is taking a coloured glaze in a squeezy sauce bottle and drawing the design. You know how you drew your maps of Australia on your pie? That sort of thing. That was exactly what it was like. They’d go into the kiln looking like some sort of over-the-top Italian wedding cake, then they’d kind of melt and form into one surface in the kiln.”

Garry writes of this early work in *An Angel by the Water*; a book of essays in honour of Garry’s ceramics lecturer Dennis O’Hoy.

"The works were well received in a climate that was rabid for ceramics, having a resonance with the prevailing romantic vision of 'alternative' lifestyle, the theme song of the 'make it, bake it' generation," he writes. "The pots drew breath from local clays and were rendered permanent in a newly-constructed Catenary-arch gas kiln. The tone of the showroom was set by mission brown paling walls, burnt Oregon timber tables, orange hessian and macramé." Yes, it was the '70s.

As the decades changed, so did Garry's work. He blames his short attention span. "It got to the point where it became absurd to stick to the one thing because I just wanted to explore stuff, and that's what I could do on my own. Then over the ensuing 40-something years that I've been working here, I've gone through so much stuff."

That 'stuff' has taken Garry from kitchen tables to the National Gallery of Victoria. His work was part of the wave of potters taking their place alongside painters in commercial galleries. He became interested in the "tools of mass-production" such as mould-making and slip-casting, and soon adapted these to his own distinct style. "I got really interested in optical illusions and ambiguous figures, and that's where a lot of the work comes from," he says.

Garry is renowned for his vessels of flat surfaces featuring pictorial depth. But still, it's only part of what happens here. "Even now I'm making commercial stuff. I think it's always been one of those keynote things about Bendigo potters. We have this reality where you can't just be an artist because you actually have to make some money.

"The other thing is, you don't want to be deathly serious all the time making 'high art'. You don't have to be profound with everything you make. I certainly don't. I want to have a bit of a laugh too."

There's cheek in his latest project. It's autumn of 2016 and he's started work on a solo show at the Bendigo Art Gallery scheduled for late 2017. He's adorning ceramic forms of goldfields-era bottles with his distinct architectural steps and patterns. It will be added to, bottle by bottle, until time comes to exhibit.

"This piece is based on what I see happening around me," he says, with a nod to next door. "It's called Sprawl. I'm doing it in the same way as what I see happening. I'm just grabbing another building permit, and making a few more. And I don't want to premeditate the whole thing, because I don't see any of that happening. It's all pretty random the way I see it."

Garry steps back into the construction noises bouncing around his garden. It's a dearly-loved space that has sustained Garry and his wife, Heather, and their three children, for the best part of 40 years. "Heather's an avid gardener. She's an earth person," Garry says. "She's like me, she likes her hands in the mud."

It's finally soft underfoot. Old bulbs will soon push through. This place is alive. You can see it in the rising roots of a giant Morton Bay Fig beside the house. Like the mansion next door, its scale is from another time. Garry's worried about that tree. He knows those roots stretch far and wide. Far beyond boundaries of coloured steel fences.

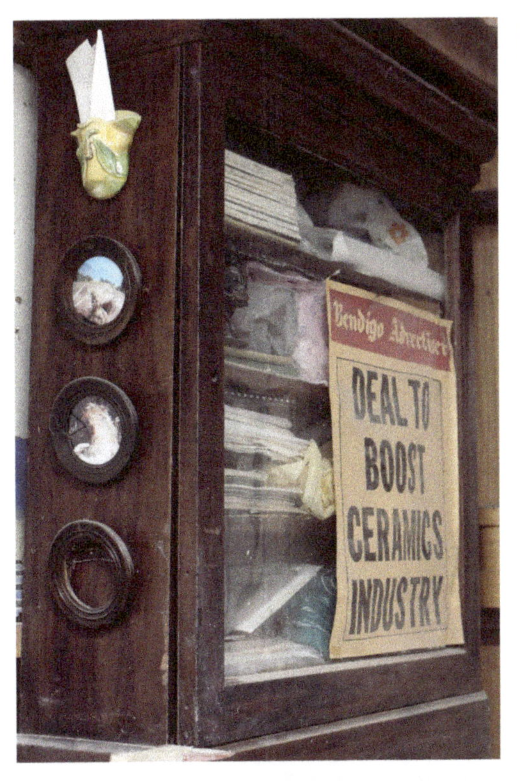
Bendigo Advertiser
DEAL TO BOOST CERAMICS INDUSTRY

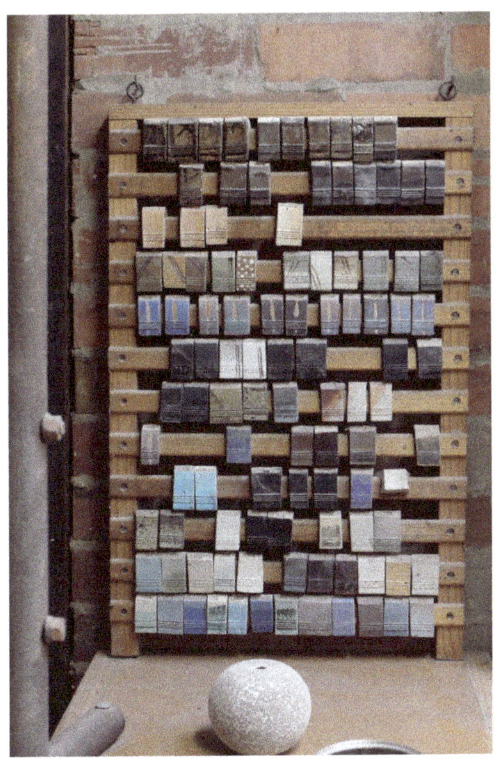

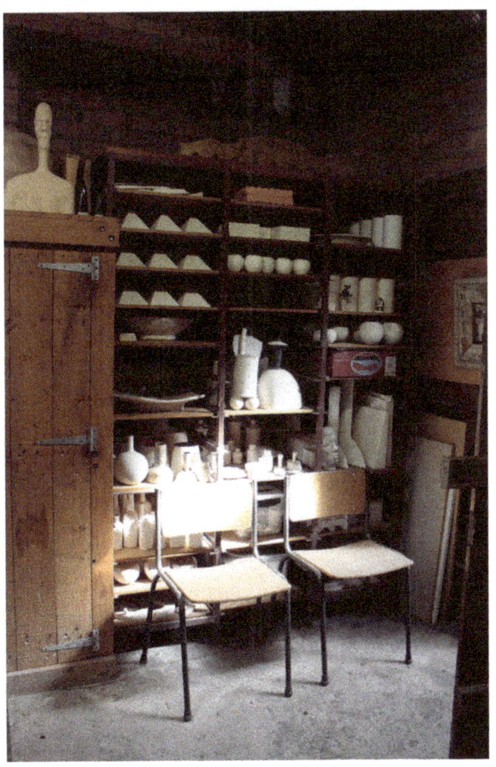

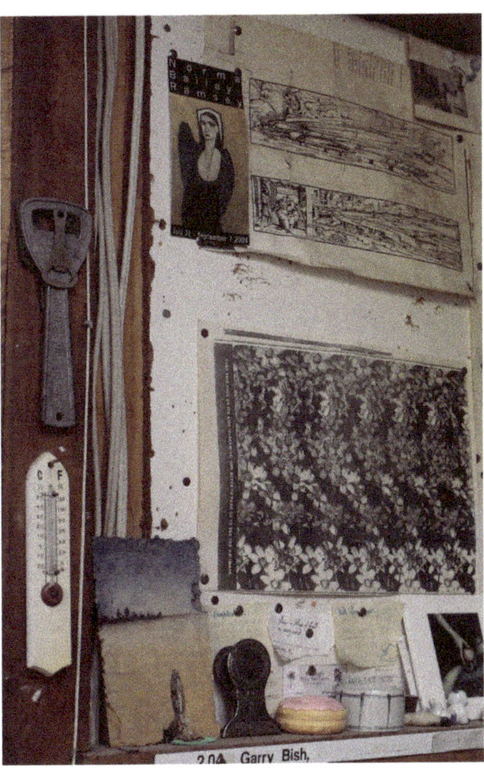
Norma
Bailey
Ramsay
C F
2.04 Garry Bish,

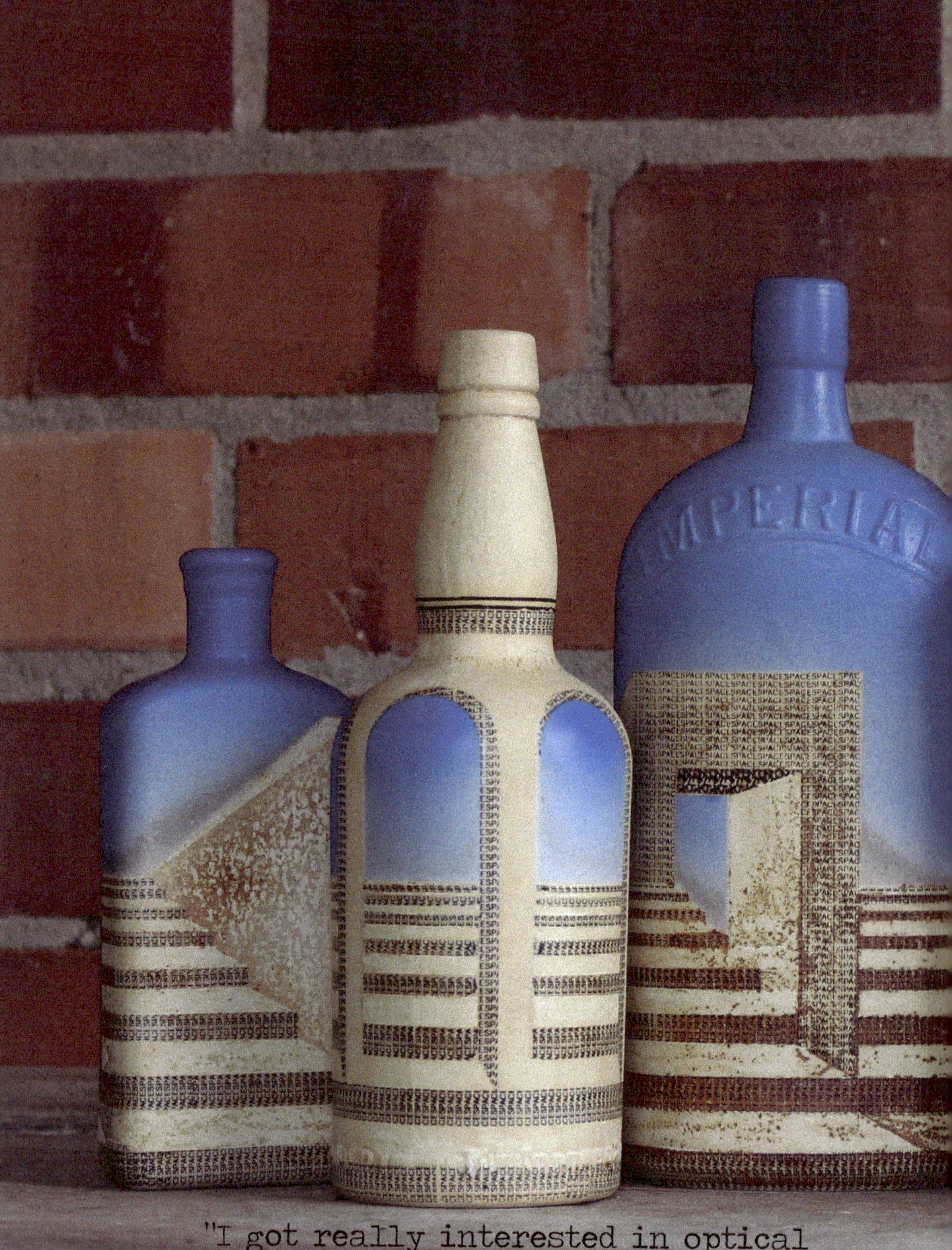

"I got really interested in optical illusions and ambiguous figures, and that's where a lot of the work comes from."

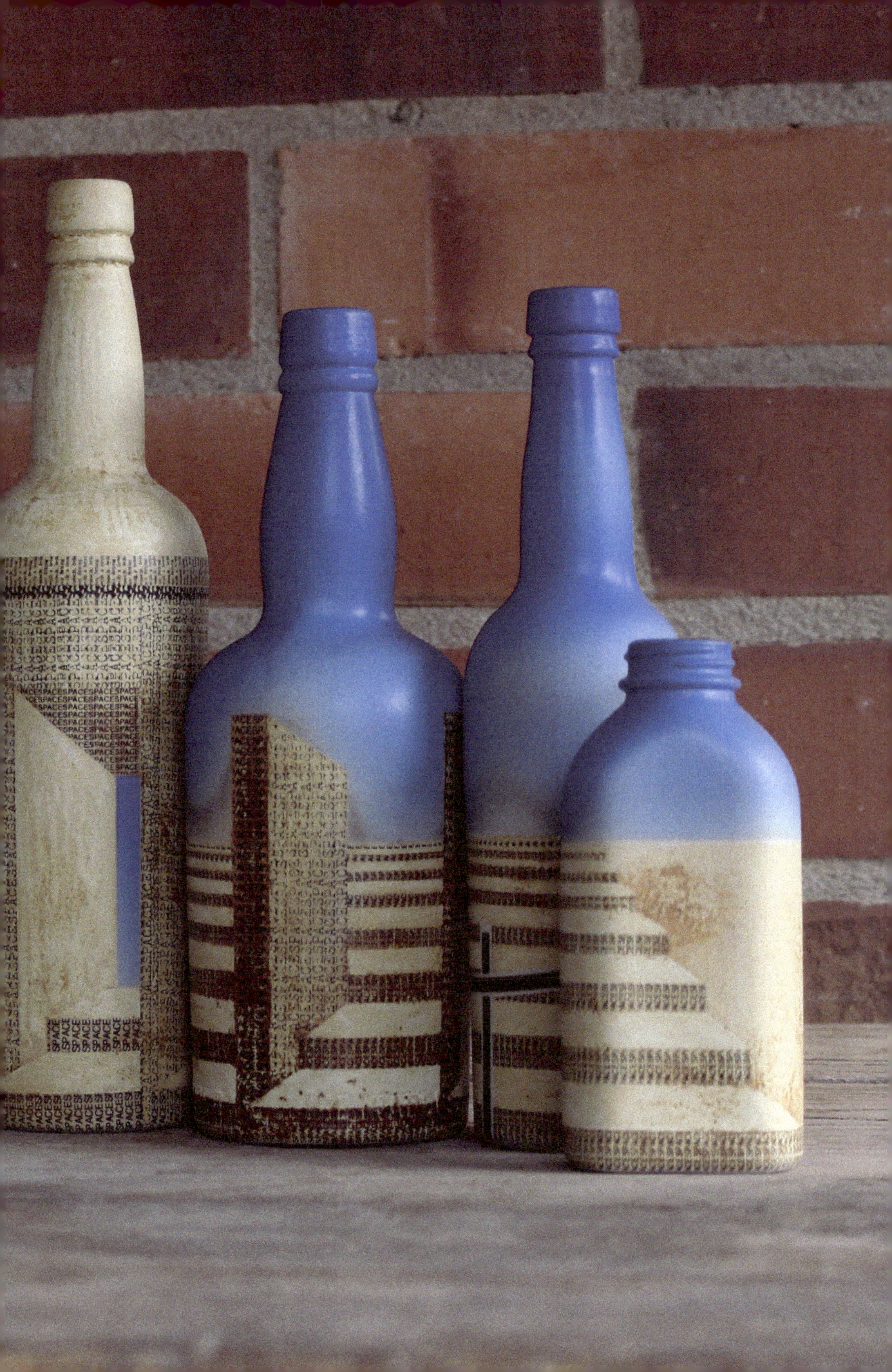

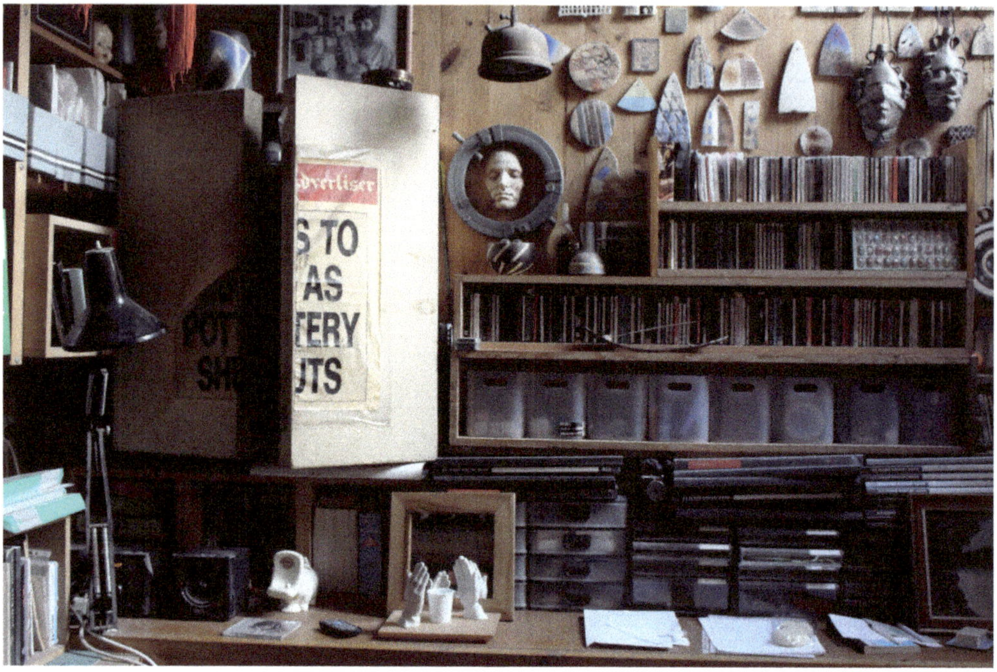

This place is alive. You can see it in the rising roots of a giant Morton Bay Fig.

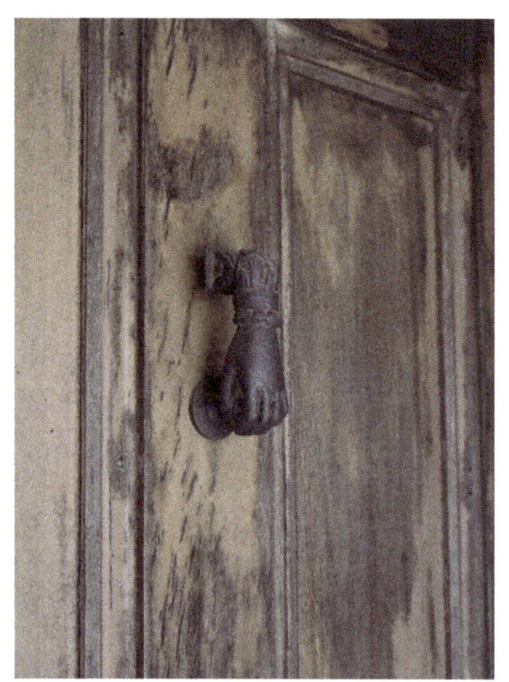

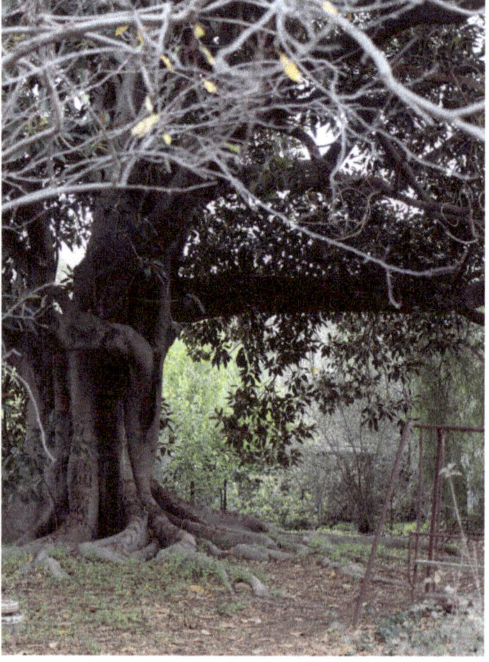

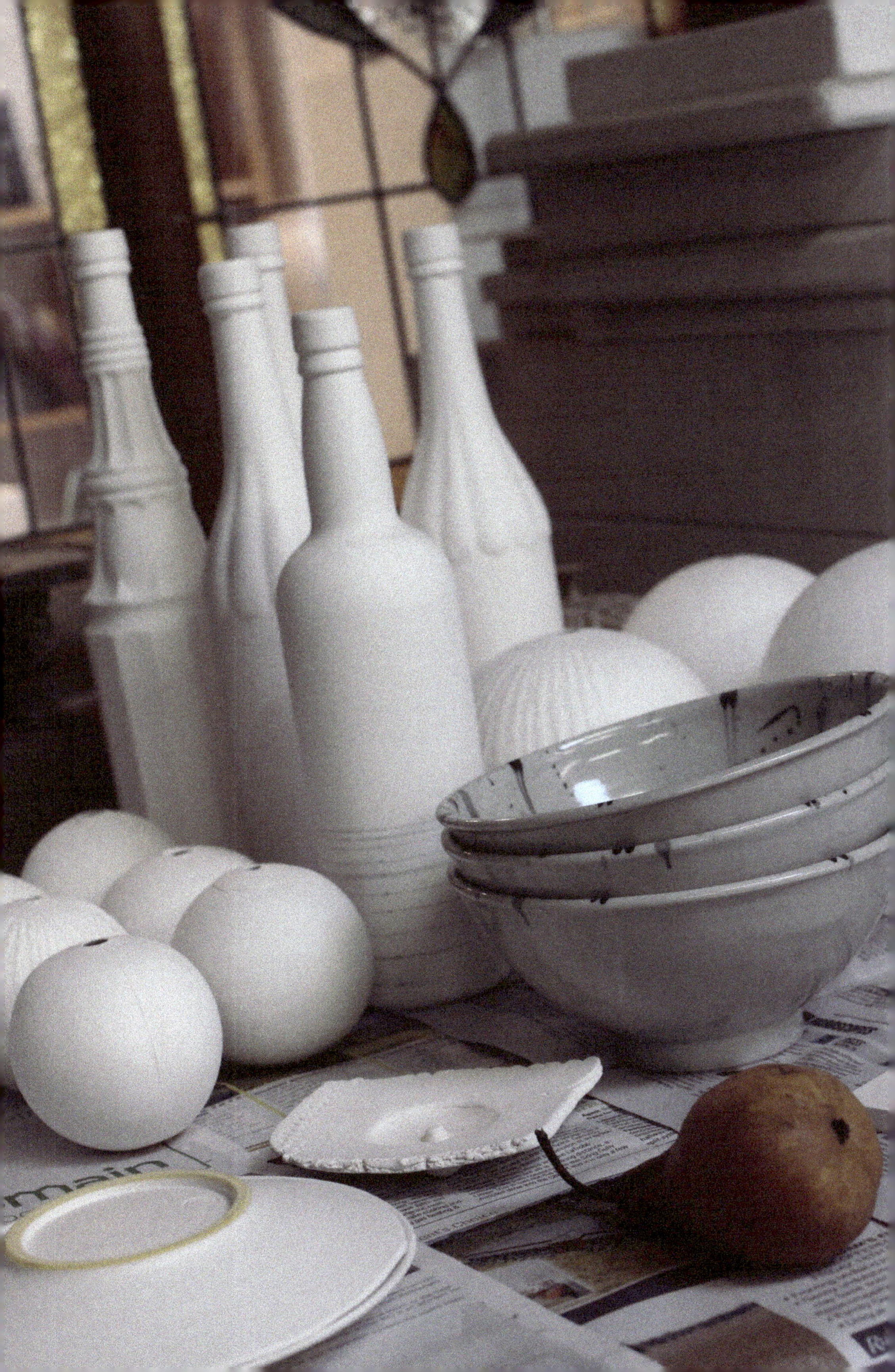

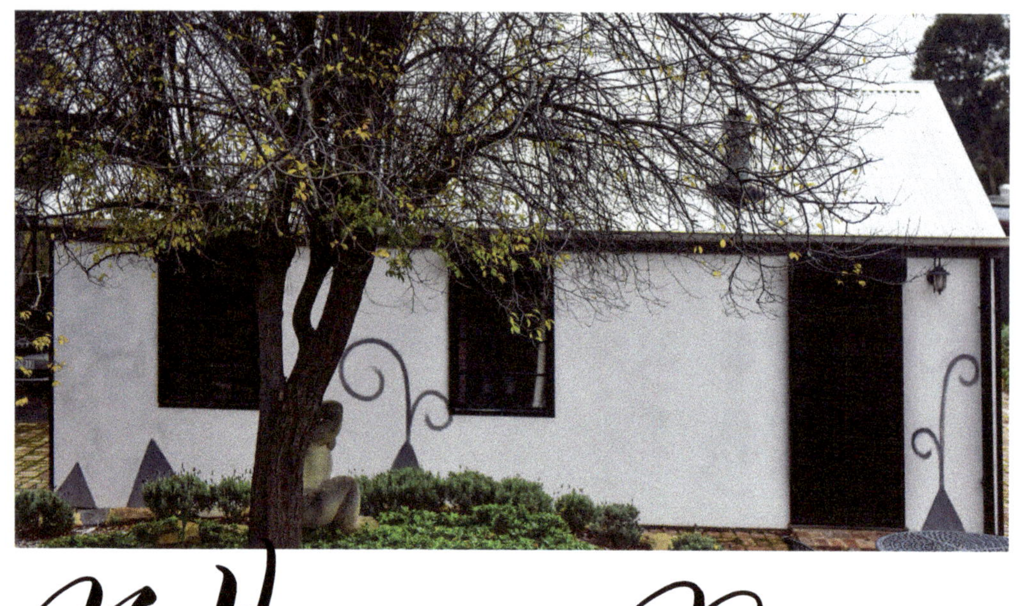

Katharina Rapp

Once upon a time

This artist's story is a fairy tale. Oh, it's all true. More Grimm in parts than Disney. A father gone before his child drew breath. Long winters icing over fragile hopes. An escape to fair Paris, music, laughter, colour, pictures. Oh, the pictures!

Look at them here. Wide-hipped women who care a whiff for convention. Dancers and gardeners. Wattle-draped and carefree. Cat women. Can't you tell their creator drinks of life?

"It's the joy of living," Katharina Rapp says. "It's innate. And it just wants to come out. I love to make people laugh. It's the same with my writing. It's OTT – more comedy than anything else. The world is unspeakably sad and if we wallow in that, we might wither away. I think the soul needs a little light relief."

It's Katharina who says her life has been like a European folk tale. She was born in South Germany, shortly after the Second World War. Her mother had shifted from East to West to be with her father. He died. Russia closed the border and Katharina's mother was separated from her family – including another child. She became one of a town-full of "red-eyed widows in mourning clothes. Life was harsh and people's spirits were broken".

Katharina's father had also been a painter. Fledgling but much respected. One painting was sold on his untimely death at 29. The money paid for the funeral and one year's frugal living. A few landscapes remain, and Katharina treasures them.

"They weren't the happiest of times," she says of her childhood. "There was

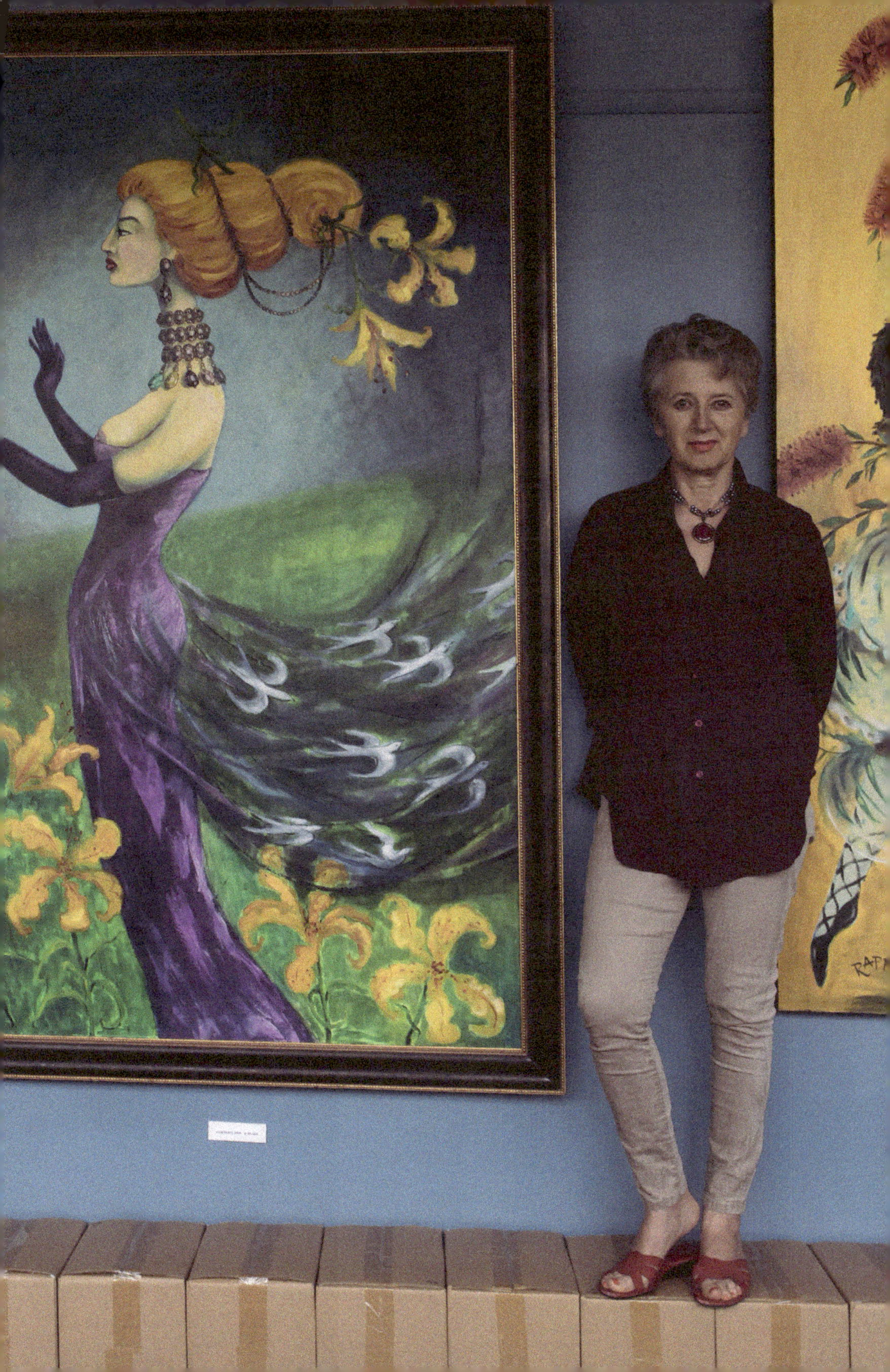

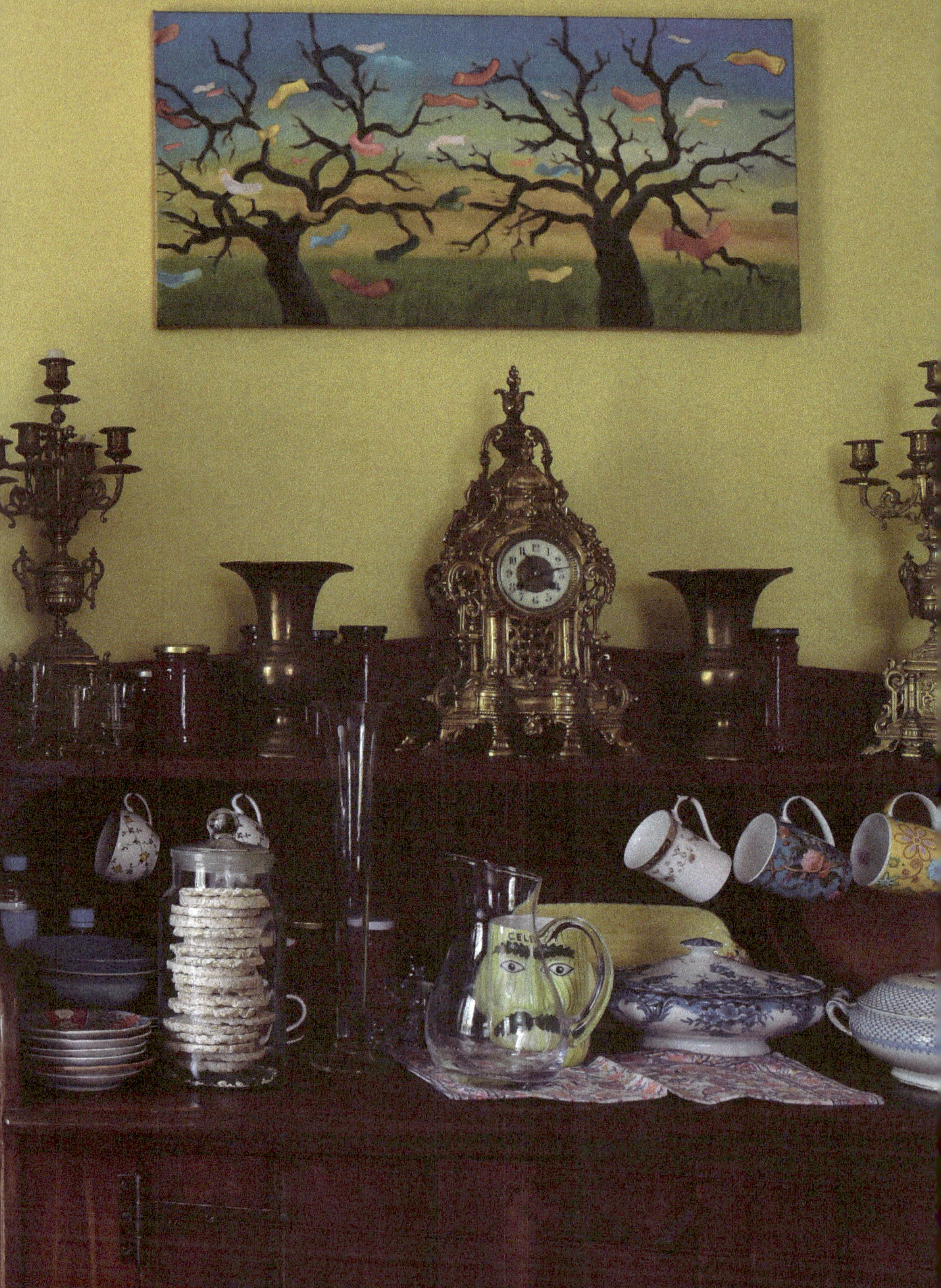

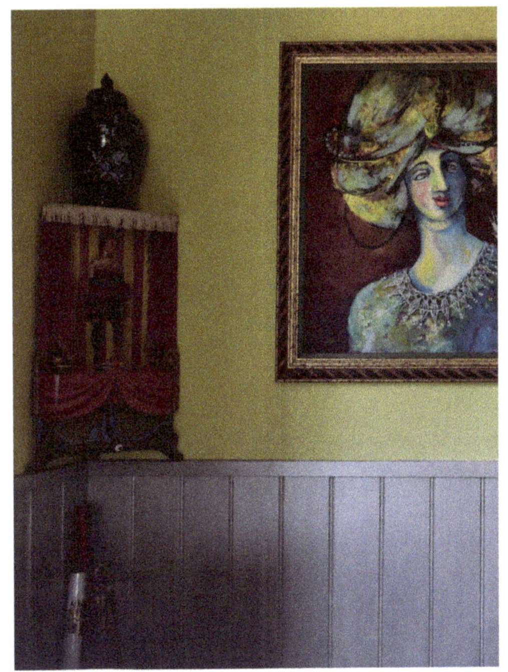

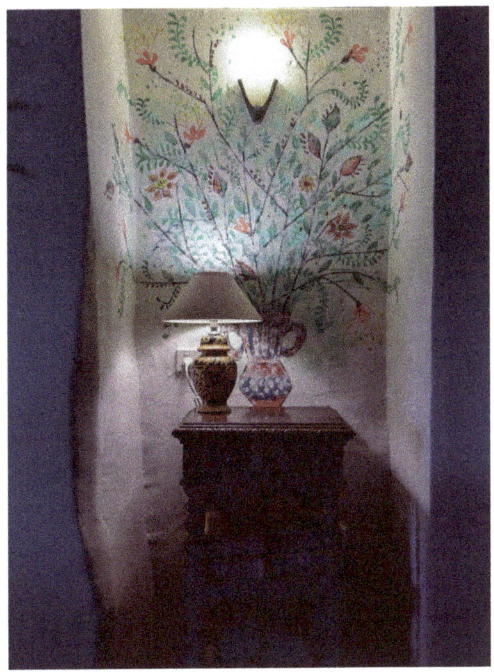

very little to eat. I couldn't do the things the other children could do – so I became an observer. I collected characters like other people collect trinkets."

Those characters are still with her now, in this gingerbread-esque cottage on the outskirts of Castlemaine. They inform her stories, both written and told. She is a storyteller because of them.

After her mother re-married, Katharina left her mountain village. "I travelled from Stuttgart to Paris by train with a sandwich, an apple and not enough money for a return ticket," she says. In the French capital she found work as an au pair, and studied at the Sorbonne.

Later she travelled to London, when the most glamorous thing a young woman could do was work as an air hostess. "But those plans didn't work out that way because I got myself a little bit pregnant in London," she laughs. Through her love of music Katharina had fallen for the general manager of the New Philharmonia Orchestra. They married and had three children.

So, how did she end up here? In this tiny cottage in the cradle of a mining landscape. A place reached by dirt road, with views of a classic central Victorian valley. "Why not here? I've lived in Paris, London, Geneva, Edinburgh, where else would I go?" she asks.

"I lived in Doveton Street (in Castlemaine) before here and from a professional point of view it was a lot better. It was a bigger house with lots of internal walls and small windows. I could fit close to 100 paintings in there. But I always just sat at my desk, working. I thought it was stupid heating a big house for one person in a corner. I thought I'd find myself a hidey hole, something low maintenance so I could also be free to travel to Italy and install myself at a pavement café with my laptop, looking frightfully intellectual."

Home was not nearly so charming when Katharina purchased it four years ago. "It was an eight-metre by eight-metre stone cube with an indoor swimming pool," she says. "This whole room was waterlogged and it had a dirt floor. Everything inside was brown Masonite with nicotine stains. People thought I had lost the plot."

But the artist saw something else. In her mind she saw a bright white cottage, an edible garden, a studio and gallery beside the house, a place of plants, colour, music and pot tea. It was a bold vision, considering the harsh reality. "The block was just a rubbishy paddock, with broken glass everywhere. For three years I picked up broken glass. It was a tip. But it had a stone house and I've always loved stone houses." When Katharina took ownership, mummified rats were found in the mud that held the local stones in place. Nothing deterred her.

Much of the work Katharina has done herself, and as such, the house is an extension of her creativity. "It actually looks like a Katharina Rapp painting," says photographer Brendan McCarthy, moving a bowl of oranges within the frame of the aubergine woman.

There's a silver cove ceiling, Turkish rugs on terracotta tiles and hand-painted curly tree frescos in the living room alcoves where others may have placed a television. "...no television," Katharina says. "I don't want to bring the violence of the world into my house."

Instead, she spends her evenings writing. Her days pottering and painting. The painting takes place in a studio beside the cottage. It's a re-purposed school portable, with good natural light and lots of wall space, painted a deep peacock blue. Those walls prop up the most wonderful paintings. They're stacked in happy commune, they're hanging cheek-to-cheek. Paintings of the most wonderful women, happily ever after.

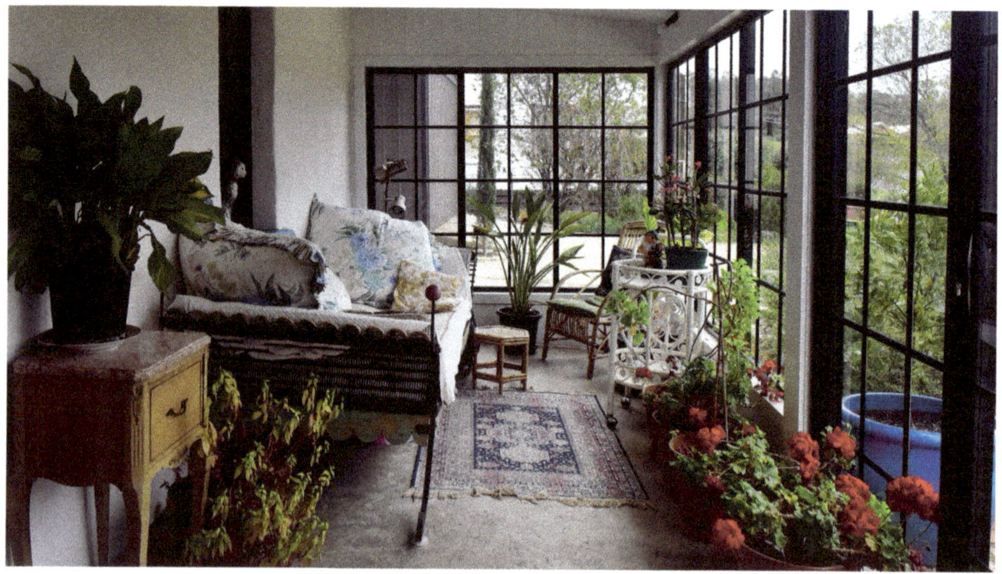

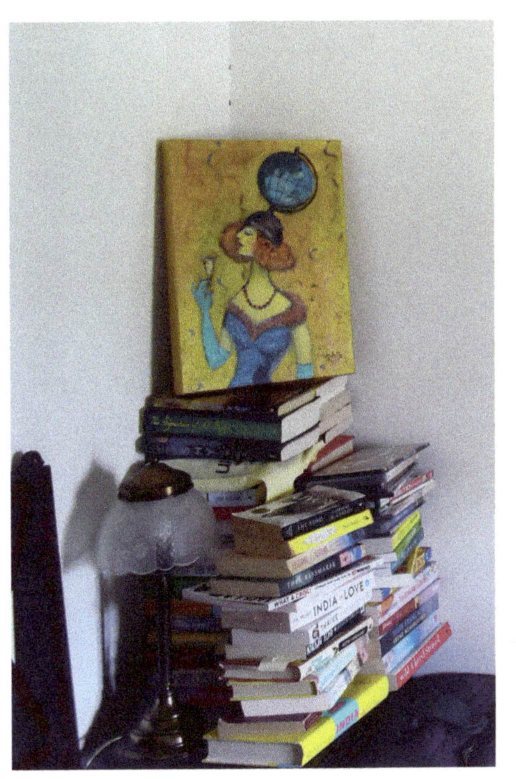
INDIA LOVE
INDIA

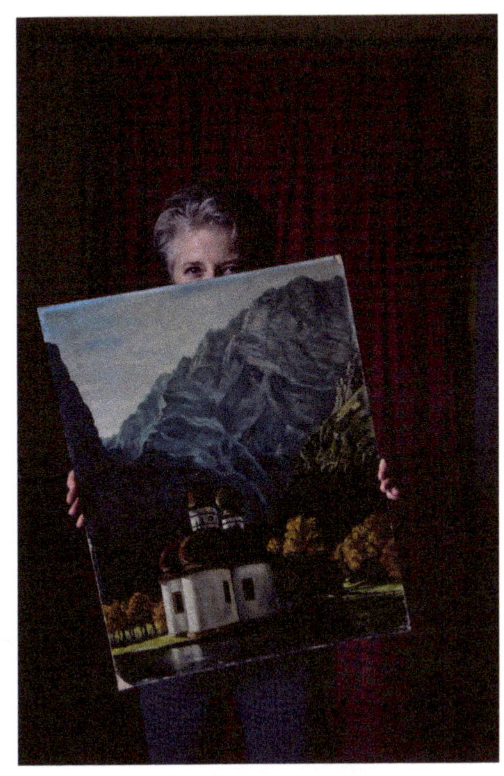

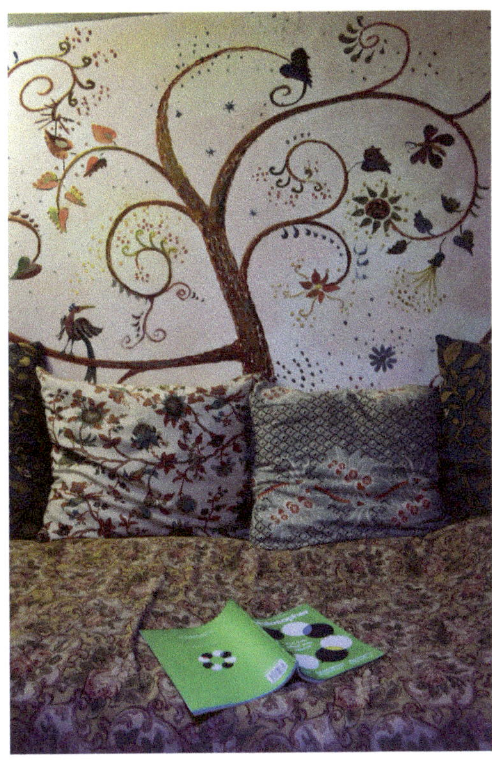

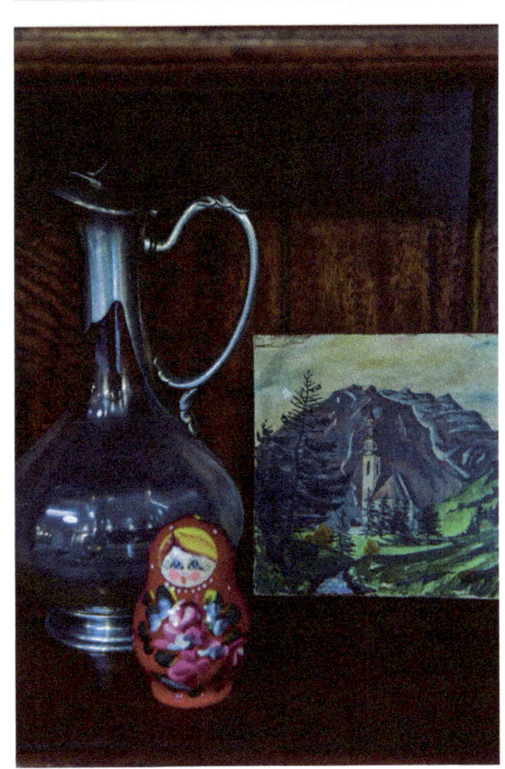

"It's the joy of living...
I love to make people laugh.
The world is unspeakably sad
and if we wallow in that, we might
wither away. I think the soul needs
a little light relief."

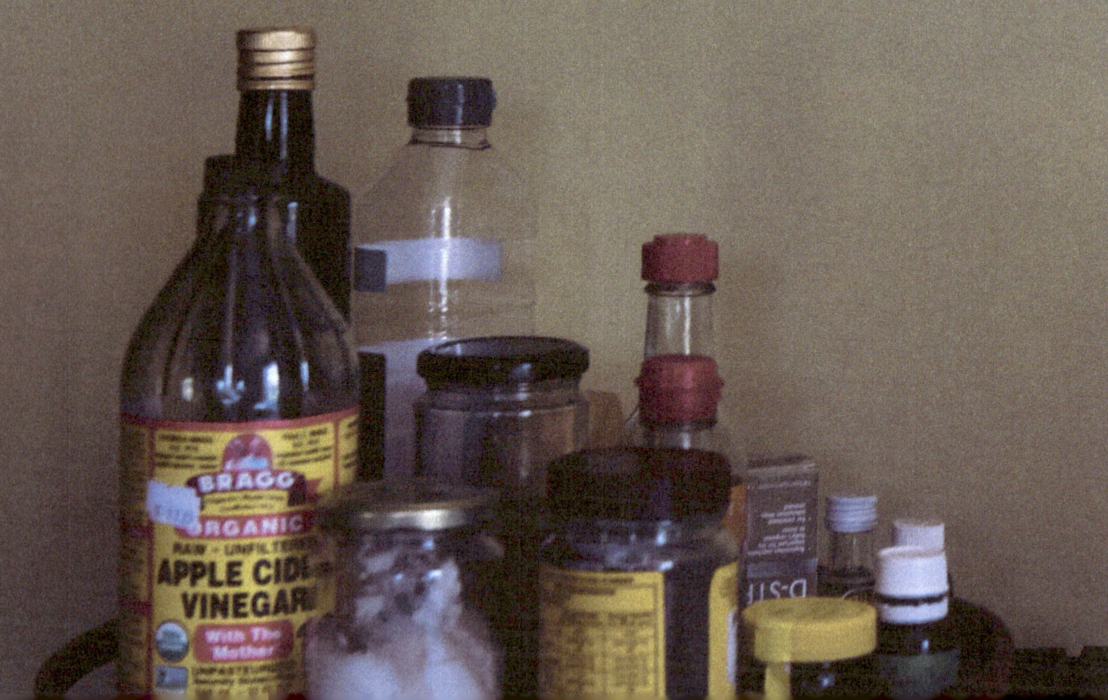

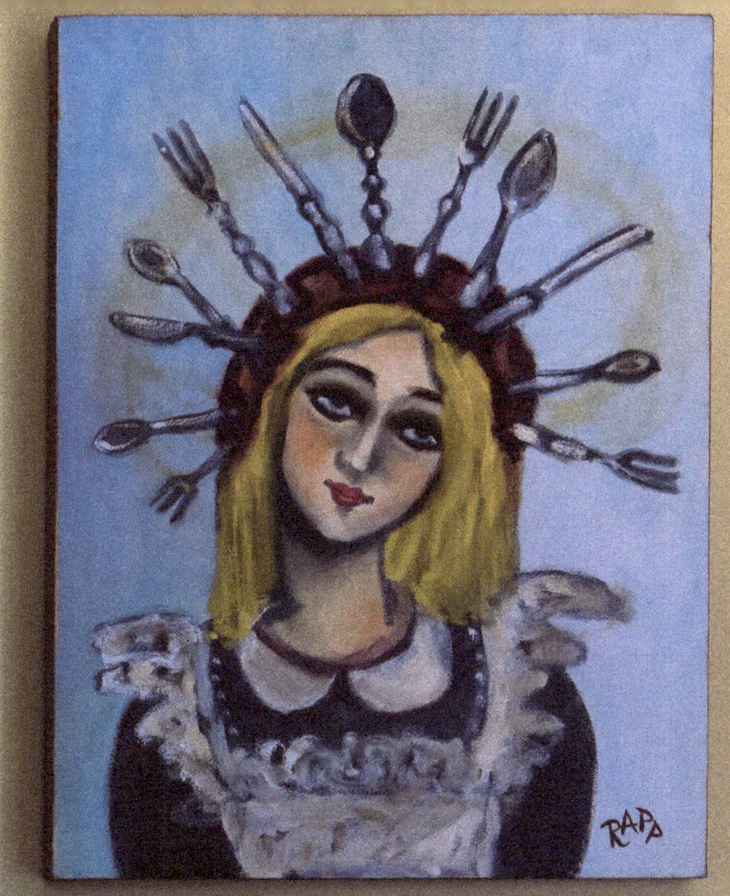
RAPP

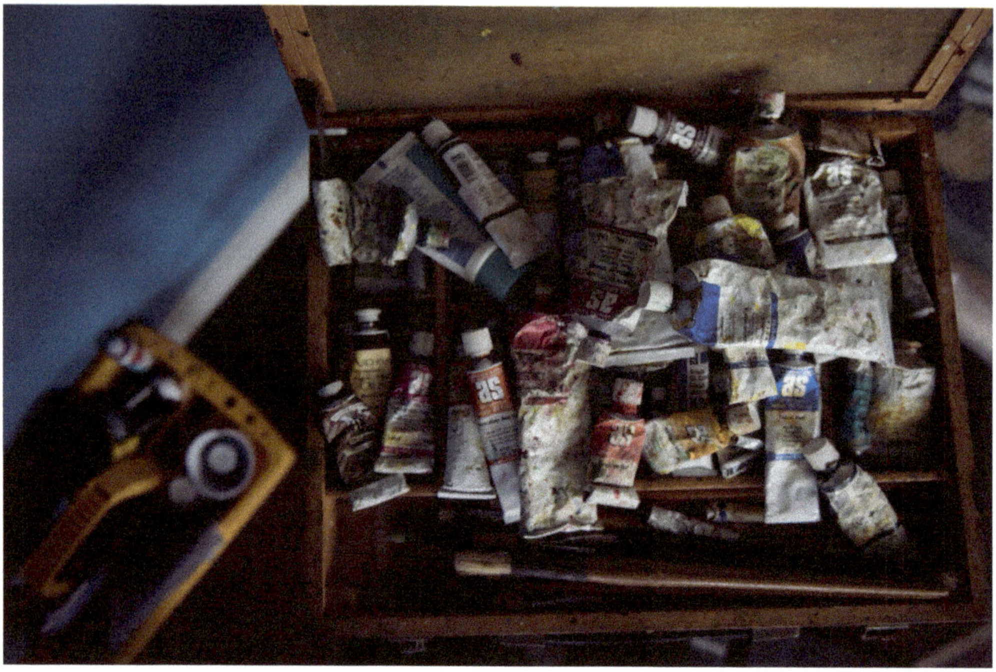

The painting takes place in a re-purposed school portable, its walls a deep peacock blue.

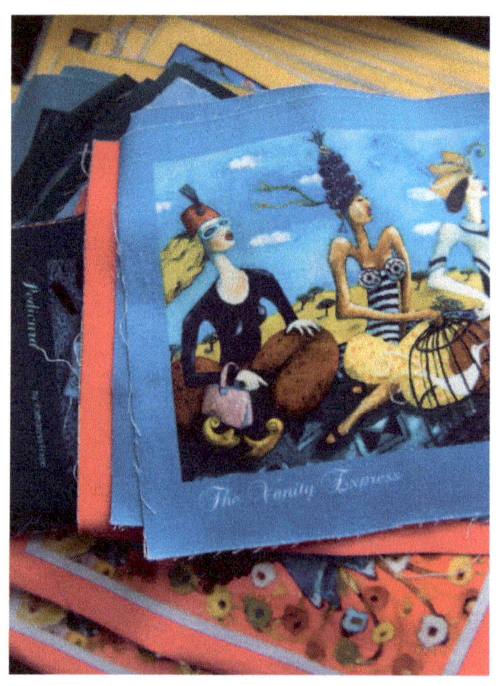

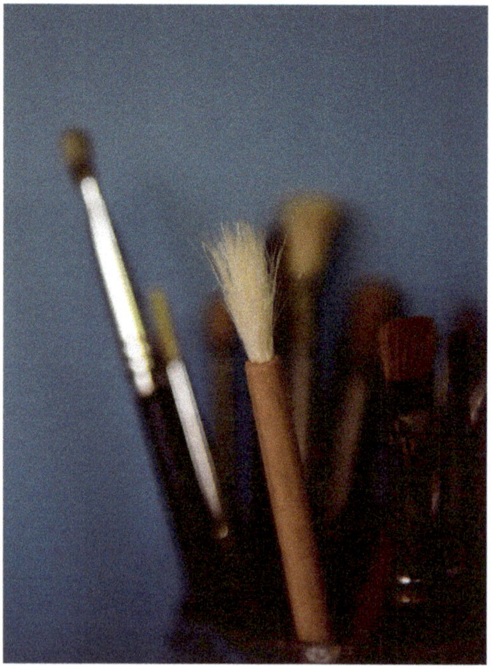

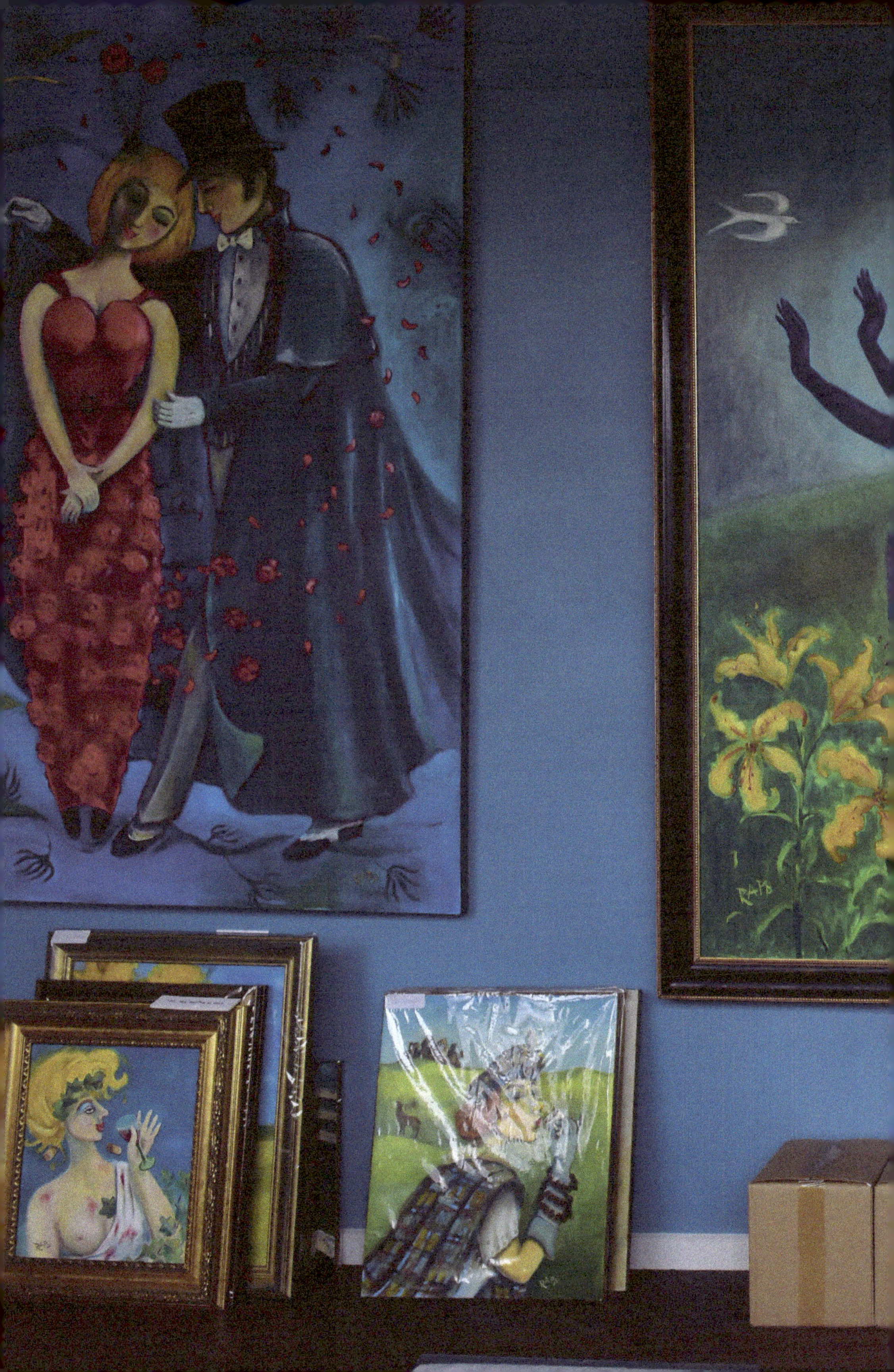

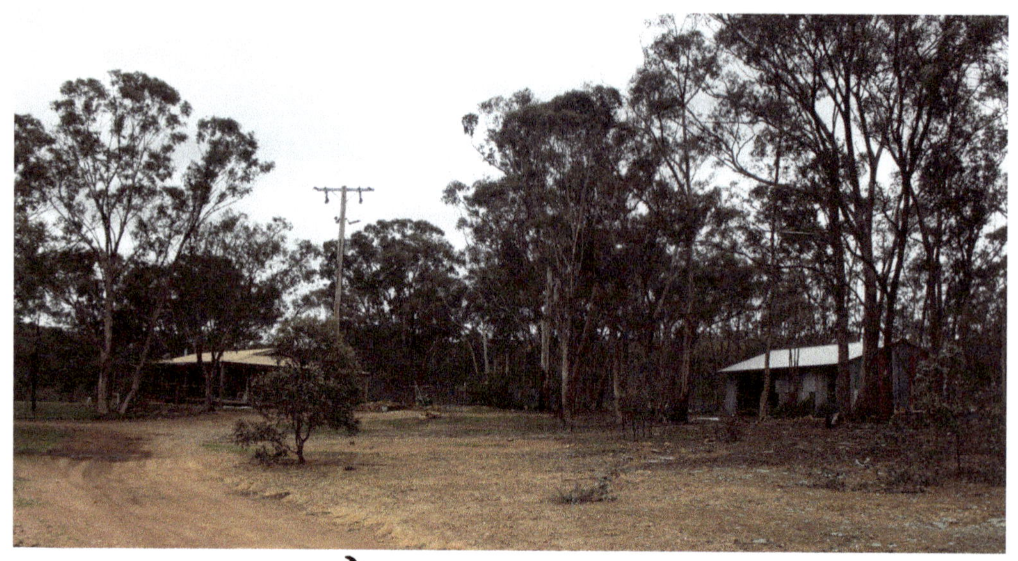

Sarah Boulton

The secret painter

On the roughened southern outskirts of arty Castlemaine is Campbells Creek. Mixing art and sport for just a moment, the township lays claim to the highest score in a senior Australian Rules football game. In 1990 Campbells Creek defeated Primrose, 634 to 18.

It's otherwise known for its old gold days. The historic main street still sports the 1857 Diggers Store, 1858 post office and 1855 Five Flags Hotel – named for the many nationalities that worked the goldfields here.

Behind this precinct and past the new subdivision sprawl, the road turns to dust. Here lies Sarah Boulton's place; part paddock, part box-ironbark bush, with a rough-sawn log house at its heart.

Sarah lives here with her partner, his border collie, and her 11 Staffordshire terrier dogs. They've got the run of 60 acres. "The property is fenced, so they can run down to the dam and we can walk in the bush," Sarah says. "I'm sort of the pack leader and they follow me and do as I say. Sometimes. It's hectic, but they do behave themselves. People say it's staffy heaven here."

The property is known as the 'Home of the Happy Staffy'. Sarah is a registered breeder, with a waiting list of people around the country hoping for one of her pups. She says locals mostly know her as the "staffy woman" or "the crazy dog lady". So when she exhibited her paintings during the 2016 Castlemaine Arts Open, she surprised more than a few of them.

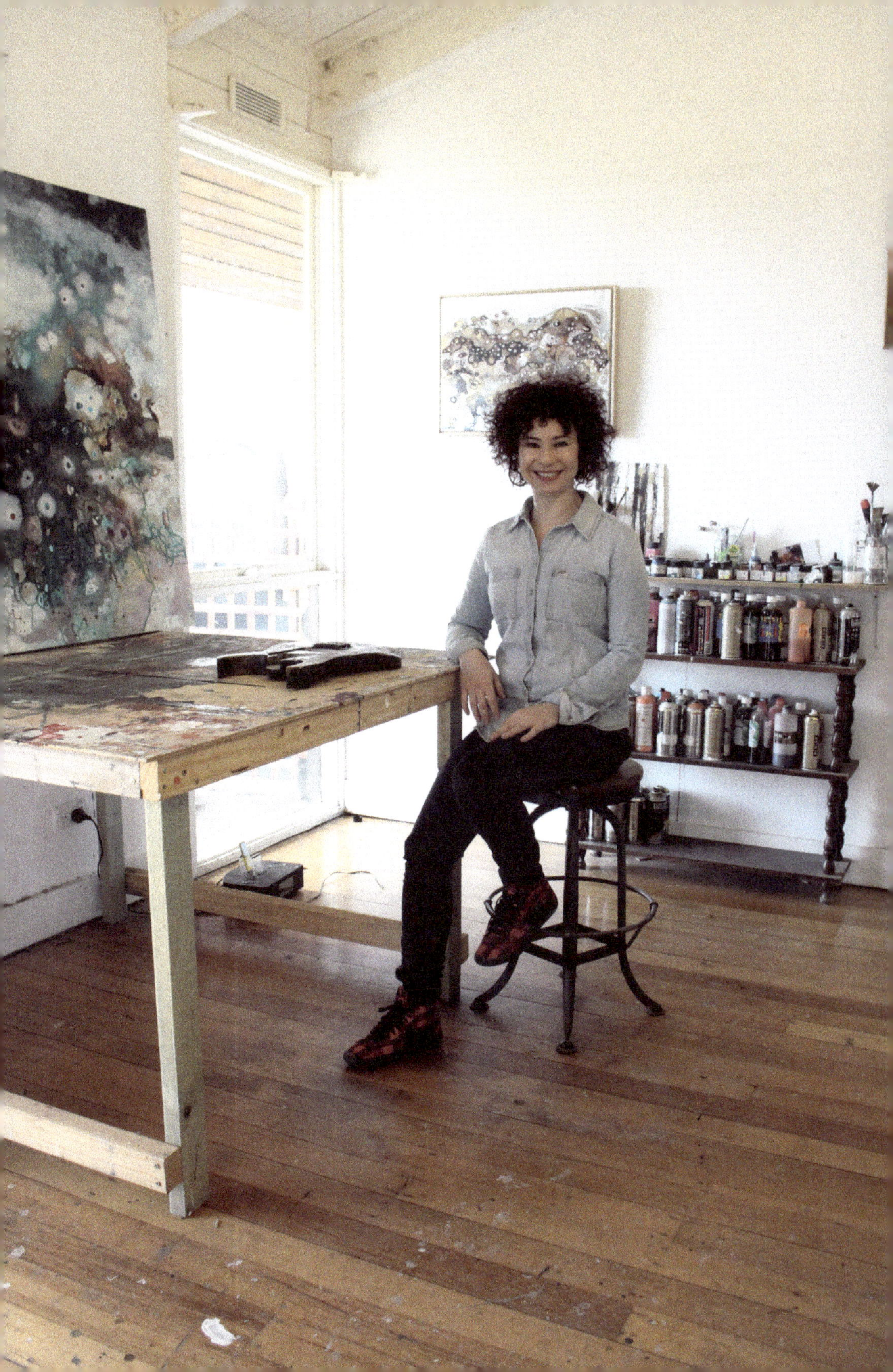

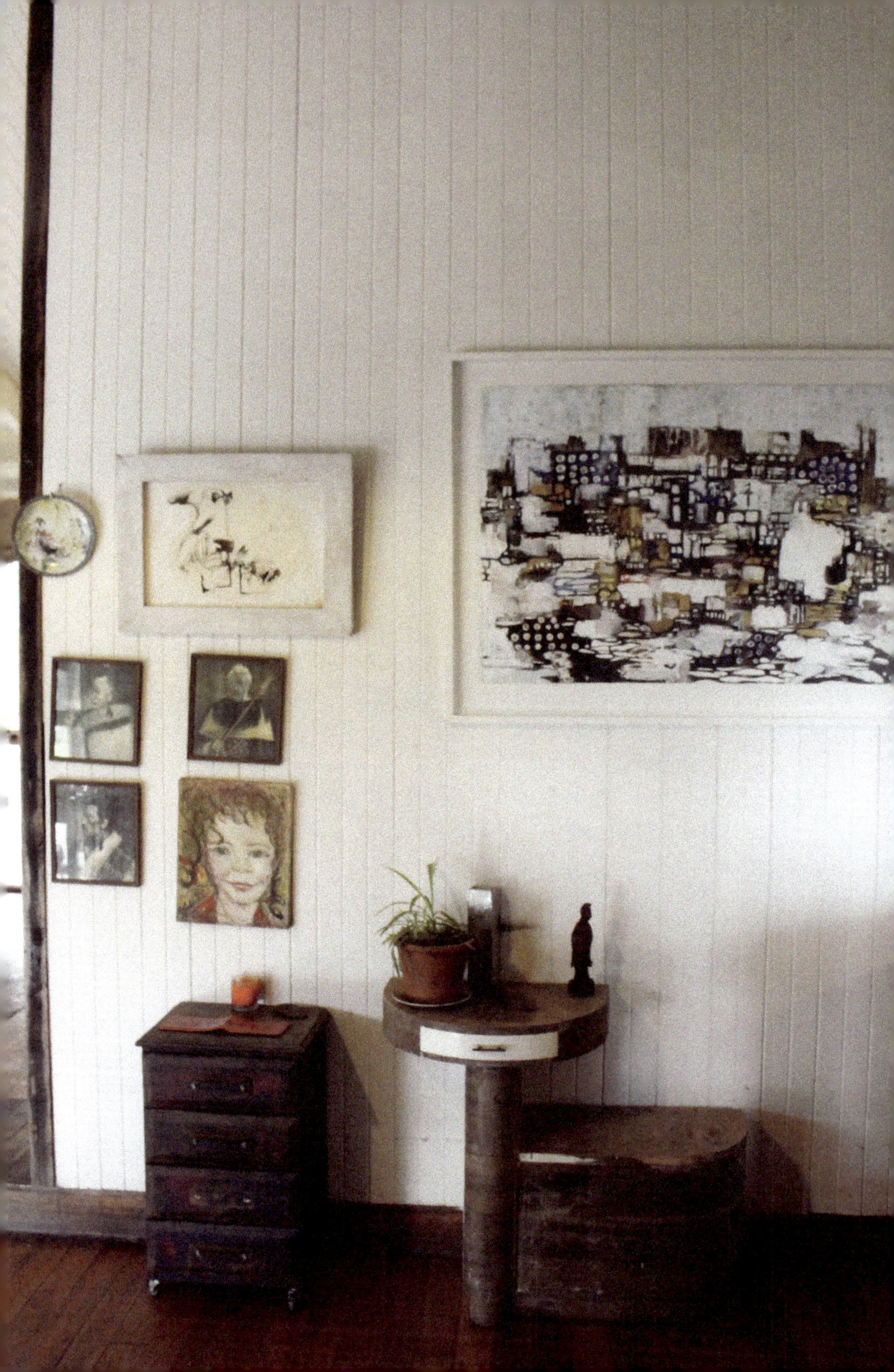

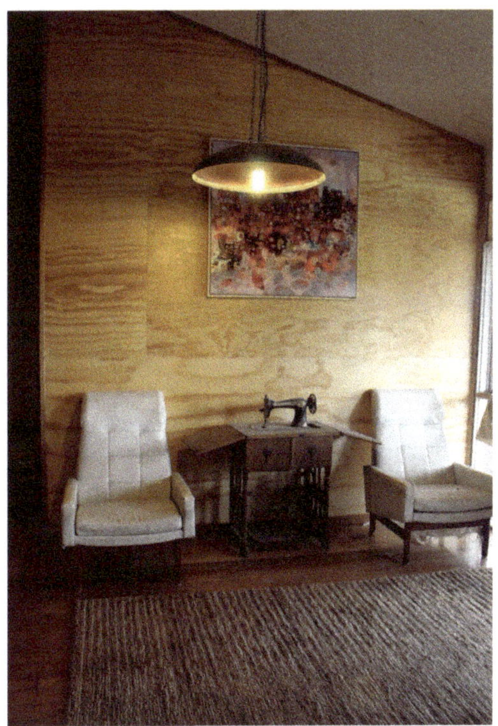

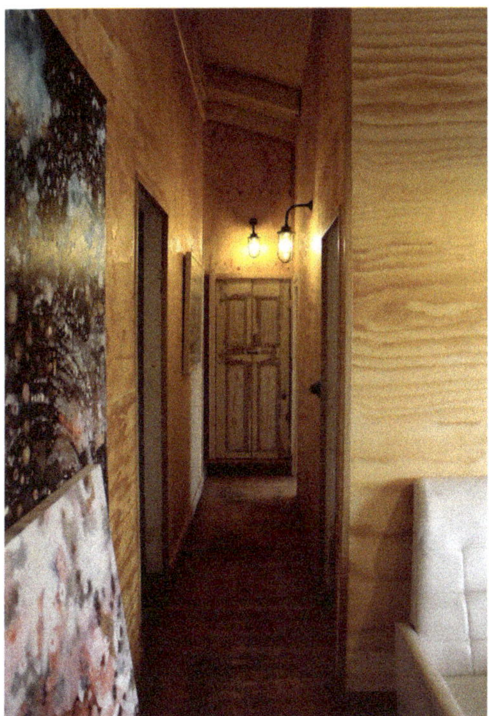

“People here don’t really know I paint,” she says. “When I had that show at the Old Castlemaine Gaol people who’d seen it were stopping me in the street asking if they were my works and saying they had no idea. Really, I just paint for myself, then whatever happens, happens.”

Sarah is a quiet achiever. After those works left Castlemaine they were exhibited in Singapore. She also shows her paintings in three contemporary Melbourne galleries; Tusk, South Yarra Art House and Manyung. She says when Melbourne people who’ve bought a pup come to pick it up, they often comment on the paintings in her home. They’re sure they’ve seen them in the city. The exquisite combination of paint and metallic ink is pretty damn memorable.

There is a reason Sarah likes to remain under the art radar. “I don’t like the bullshit of the art world to be honest,” she says. “All the little scenes. And people can be very judgemental. I do this because I enjoy it and that’s my only reason. It’s always nice to sell a piece because I can put that money back into the art. Buy some more inks. I love my inks.”

For Sarah, art is therapy. The dogs are her love, and she also works part-time as a vet nurse in Bendigo. “I need to do something else to make a living because you can’t do that just from art. And I don’t want to have to dedicate my life to it, it’s too stressful. I like to use the art for therapy when I’m feeling stressed.” It’s something that’s served her well throughout life.

Sarah grew up in the Melbourne bayside suburb of Sandringham. Influenced by her creative mum, her later high school years were largely spent in the art room, "when everyone else was in the park smoking bongs. My mum was a painter. She really wanted me to do art. Being Jewish, my dad wanted me to marry a doctor or a gynaecologist."

After school Sarah started studying painting at RMIT. Her works from that time are indicative of the effects the city pace had on her. "In Melbourne I had a very small space, and the work I was doing was very deep, almost too complex," she says. "There was too much going on in those pieces.

"I was feeling anxious being in the city so I had to get out of Melbourne. My partner-at-the-time's mum lived in Kyneton and I'd started going up there. This whole area is sort of arty, so I chose Castlemaine."

Sarah was only 19 when she bought this place, in 1998, yet she had a dire need to bed down. "I just felt like I wanted to hide away and do my thing," she says. "I was looking for a home where I could have a few dogs and a painting studio. This was the first place I looked at and it suited me. Although it was really rundown. There were car bodies and junk everywhere. It had shagpile carpets, but I just thought 'this is it'. It was really good to be able to come out here and have some space. I bought it when the prices were cheap and it was one of those good decisions you sometimes make without thinking too much about it."

Sarah's paintings soon began to reflect the change she made. "My painting has been more abstract and free since coming here. I have more fun with it."

She's had fun with the house, too. She describes it as a work in progress. One of the first things to go was that shagpile carpet, followed by the old kitchen. Sarah found a muso-cum-tradie to make her chunky industrial-style timber benches and rustic kitchen trough.

The timber floors have been buffed bare by the pads of countless inside dogs. The big sliding doors have views to the paddock on one side, the bush to the other. This is a farmhouse, made soft by the femininity of Sarah's paintings. It's also been given a dose of scandi-cool of late. Sarah's partner is lining walls in pale plywood, and replacing stock-standard doors with second-hand ones, paint-stripped and full of character.

The studio is at the opposite end of the house to the open living room. It's a simple space, with a great view, a high ceiling, an easel, a desk, chair and collection of inks and paints. Sarah works in here most days. "I never know what I'm going to do before I do it," she says. "I just put down a canvas or piece of paper and I let it happen.

"My style is very experimental and I'm always looking for new ways to use different materials. My work was always very 'urban landscape meets country' but now I want to be more free and abstract. People have told me abstracts won't sell, that people don't understand them, but I don't really care what sells. For me, it's more about the artist's mark."

That artist's mark has well and truly been made on this once rough-and-ready place. Sarah needed a home, and she made one here, for life.

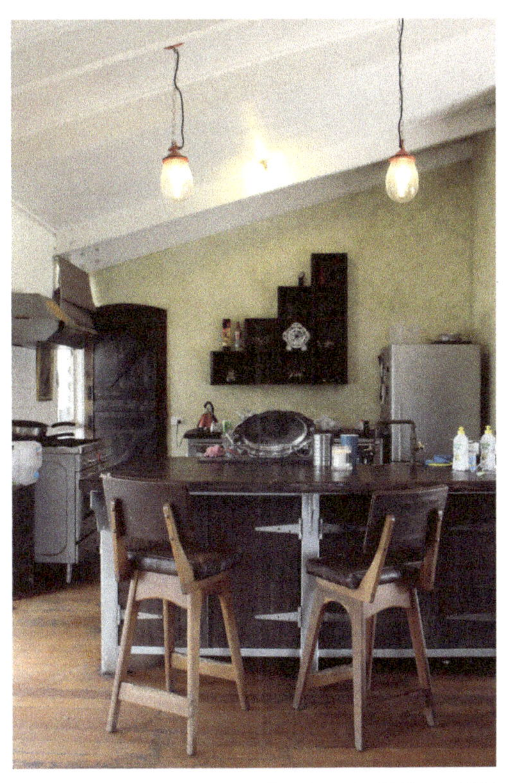
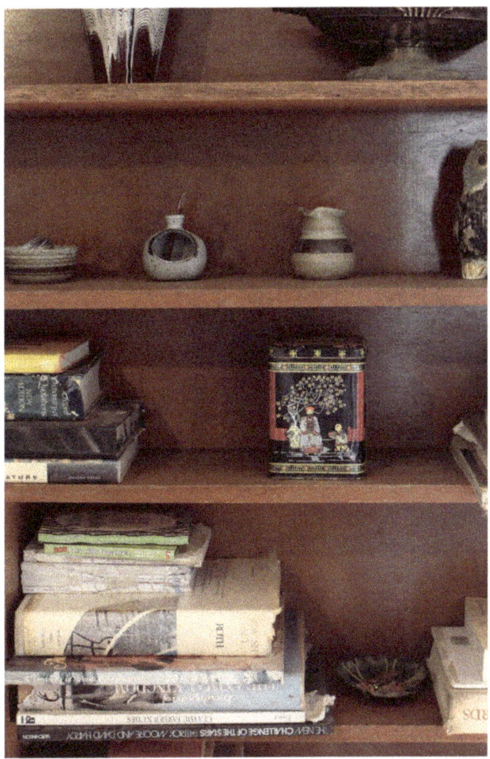
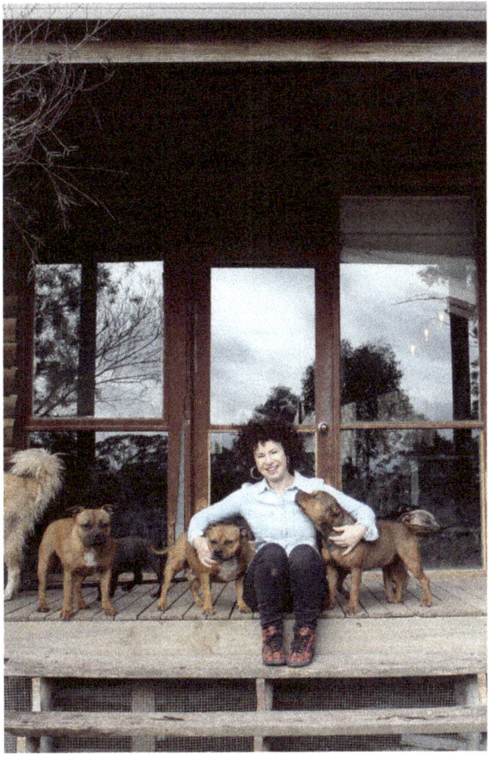
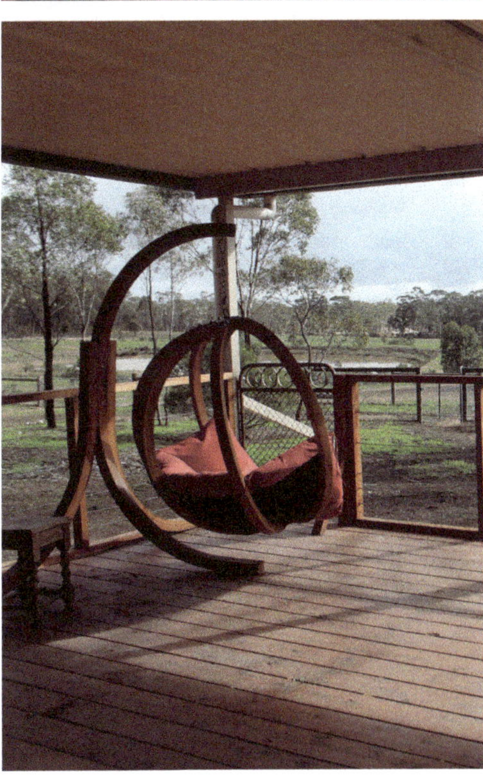

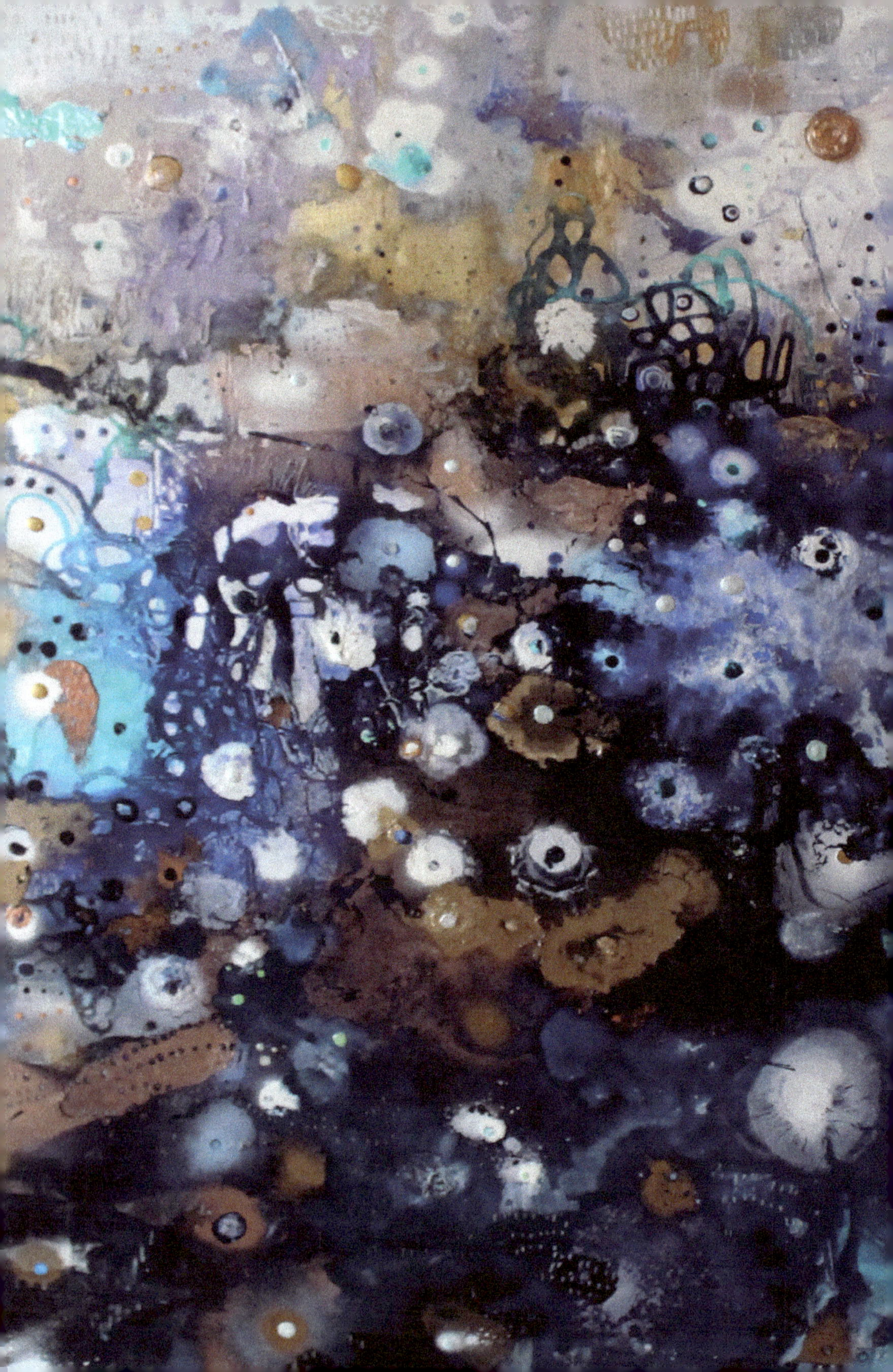

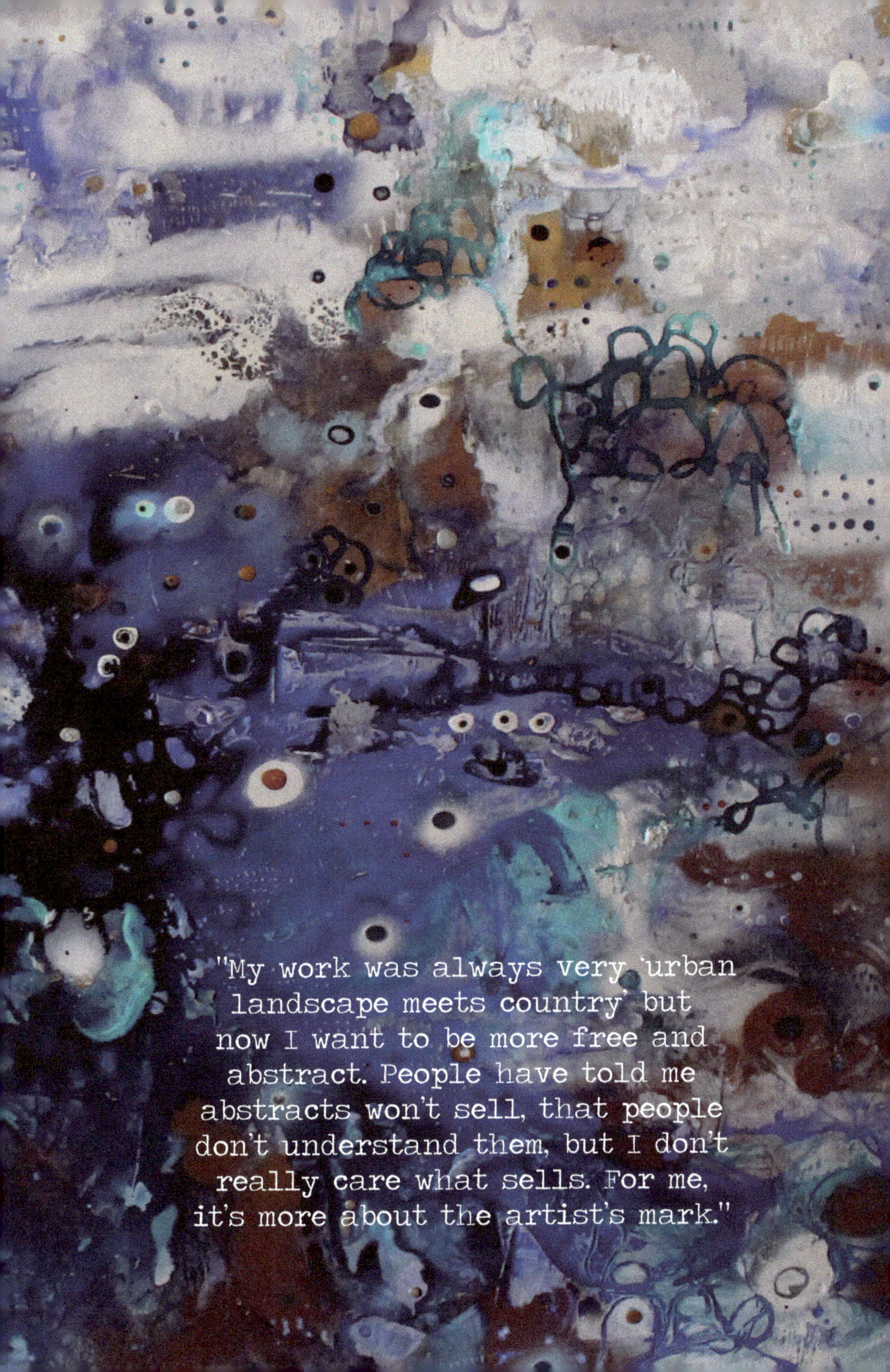

"My work was always very 'urban landscape meets country' but now I want to be more free and abstract. People have told me abstracts won't sell, that people don't understand them, but I don't really care what sells. For me, it's more about the artist's mark."

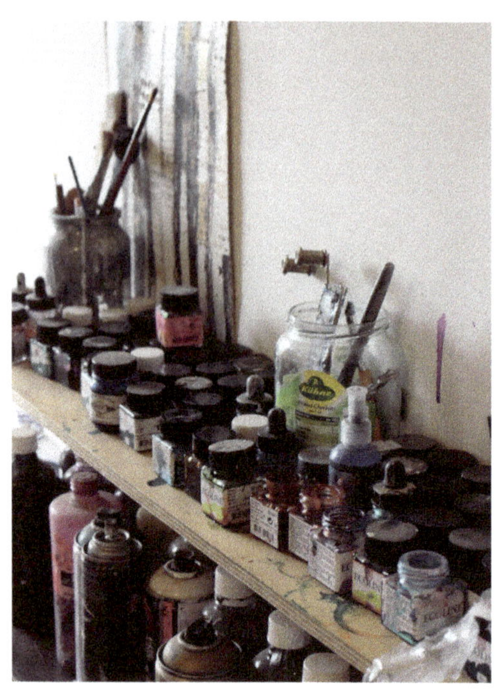

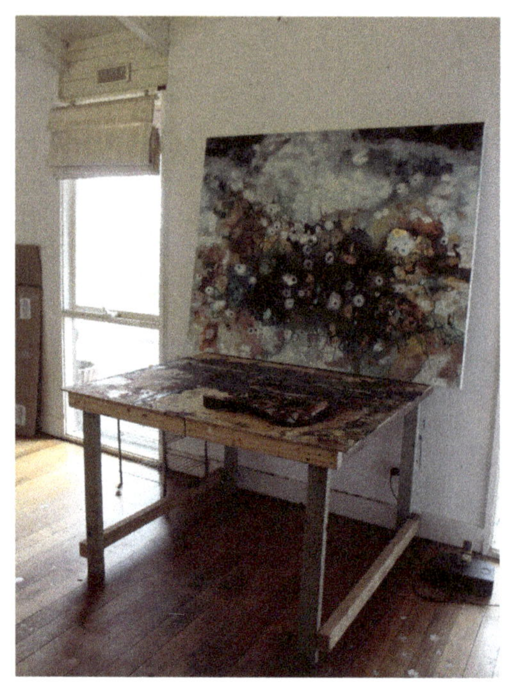

Sarah's partner is replacing standard doors with second hand ones, paint-stripped and full of character.

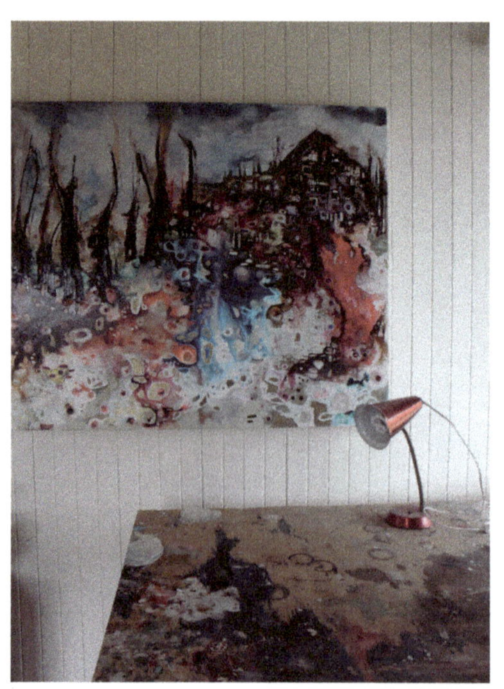

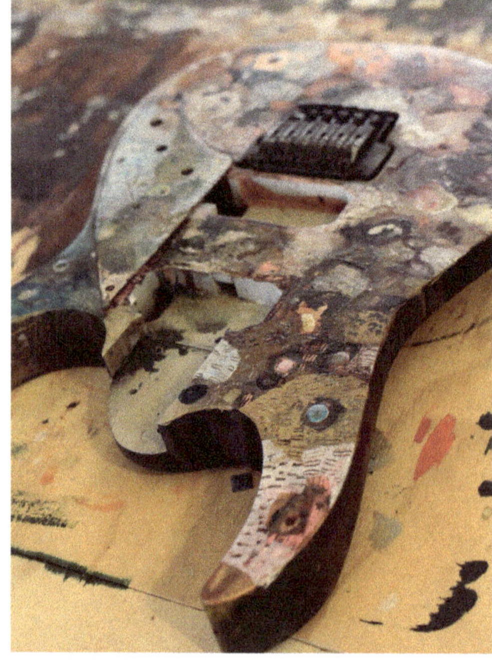

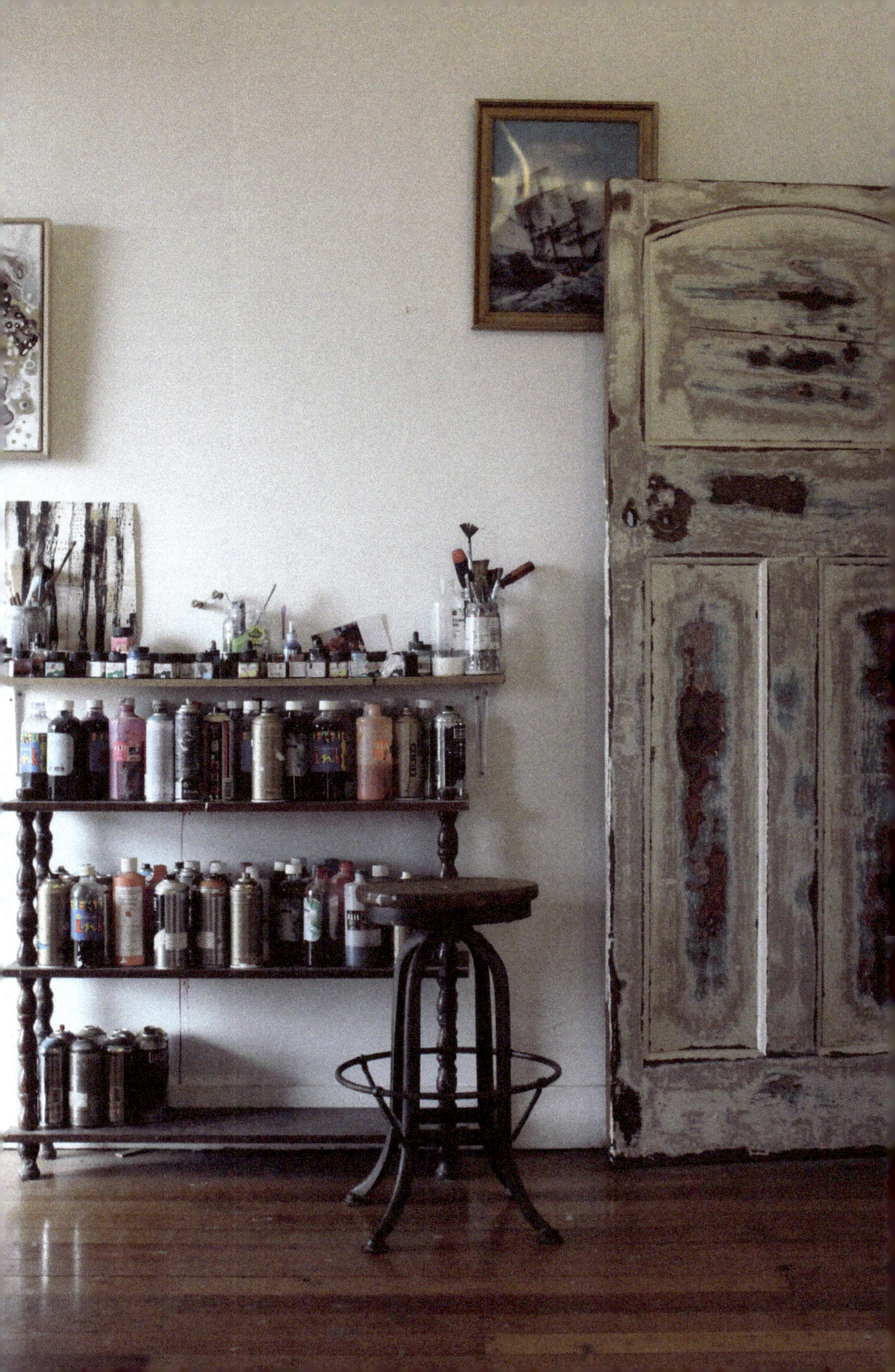

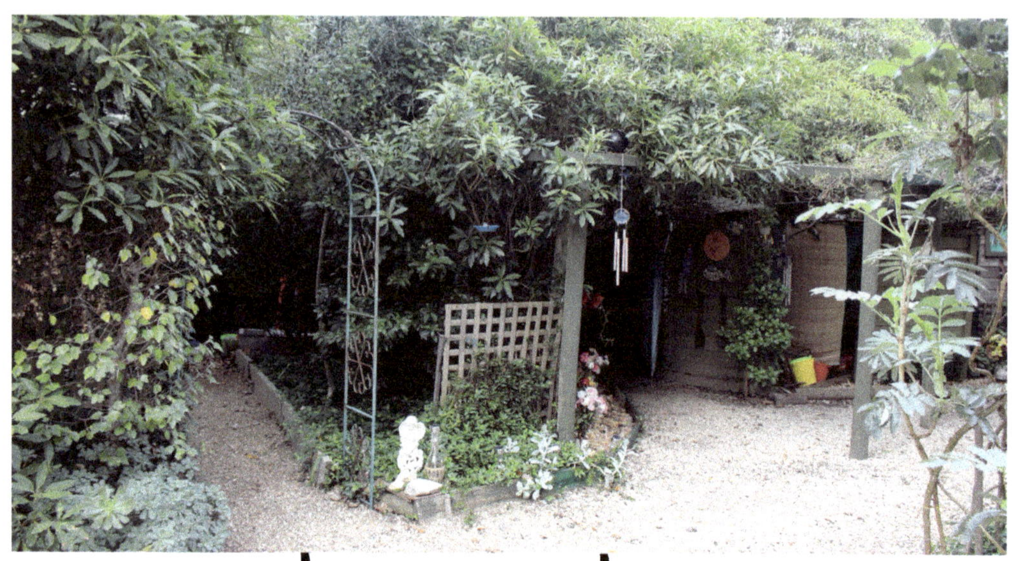

Stephen Phillis

Ships & small towns

Stephen Phillis makes one thing perfectly clear. "This is not the studio. It's the shed." It's where he paints, potters, listens to classical music. It's a precarious place – old carpet resting on a dirt floor, a ceiling so low you need to stoop in parts, the walls made solid by overlapping layers of pasted pictures.

The shed is in the backyard of Stephen's Maldon home of 23 years. Past the fish ponds and bird aviary and pet cemetery of beloved Chihuahuas. Danny Boy, Francie and Old Primrose are the current crew, on guard among strangers.

Stephen's latest work-in-progress sits on an easel just within the shed door, borrowing daylight. Other paintings are stacked up in here, plus a plastic tub of life drawings, far removed from the work Stephen sells to tourists and holiday home owners from central Victoria to Sorrento. "I've been a Castlemaine Life Drawing member for 20 years," he says.

Stephen is best known for his figurative/semi-abstract paintings of landscapes, beachscapes and country towns. He works with a lavish pallette and is not afraid to use it. It's a style that's developed over many decades of work.

Stephen was born in 1947. He studied at Newport Art College, South Wales, then immigrated to Australia just before his 18th birthday. "I saw a future here, from a drizzly old South Wales," he says. "I told my parents I was going to Australia and they sold up and came with me, because I was an only child."

In South Wales he'd worked on the docks. Hence the little balsa wood models

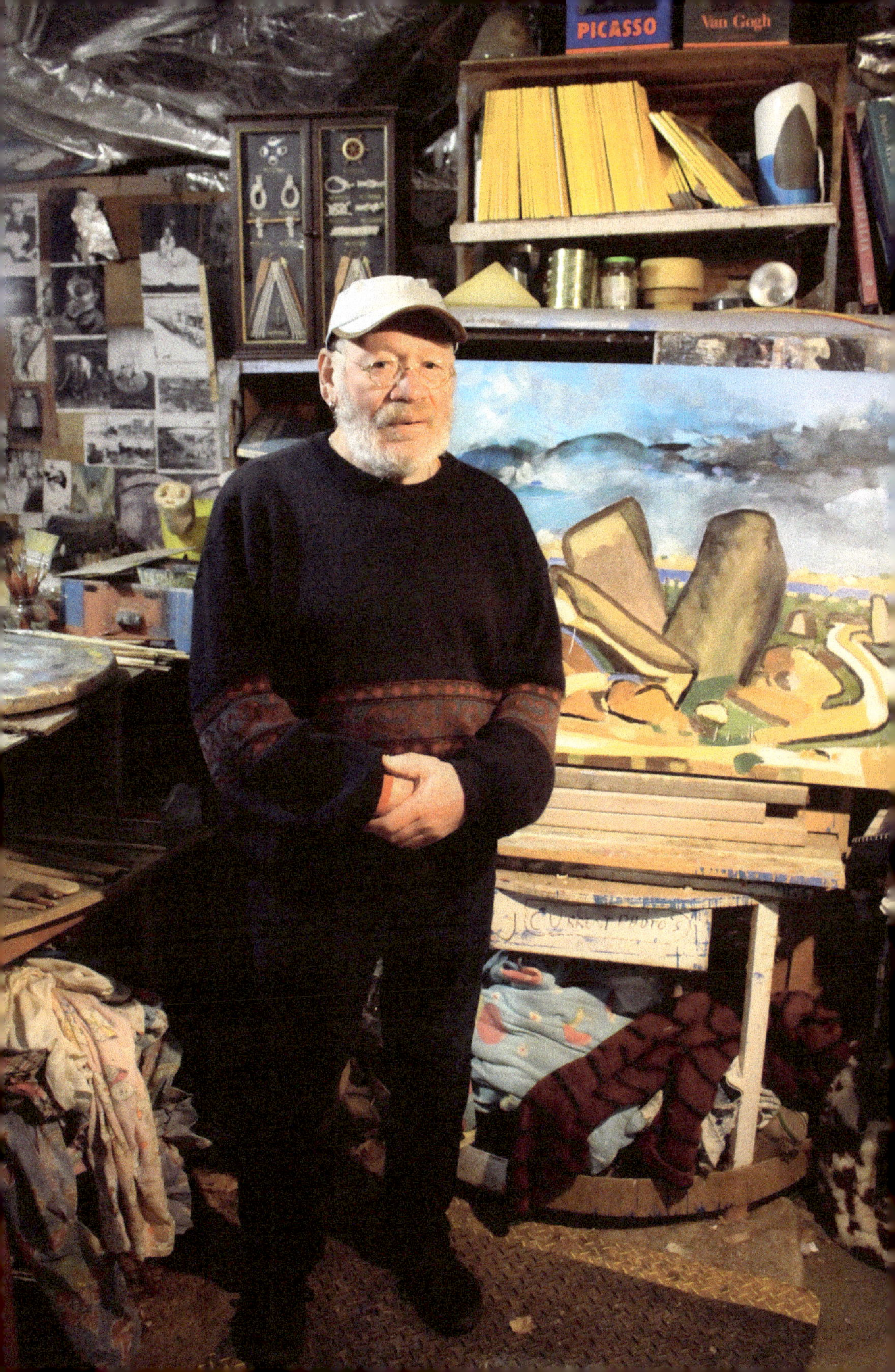
PICASSO
Van Gogh

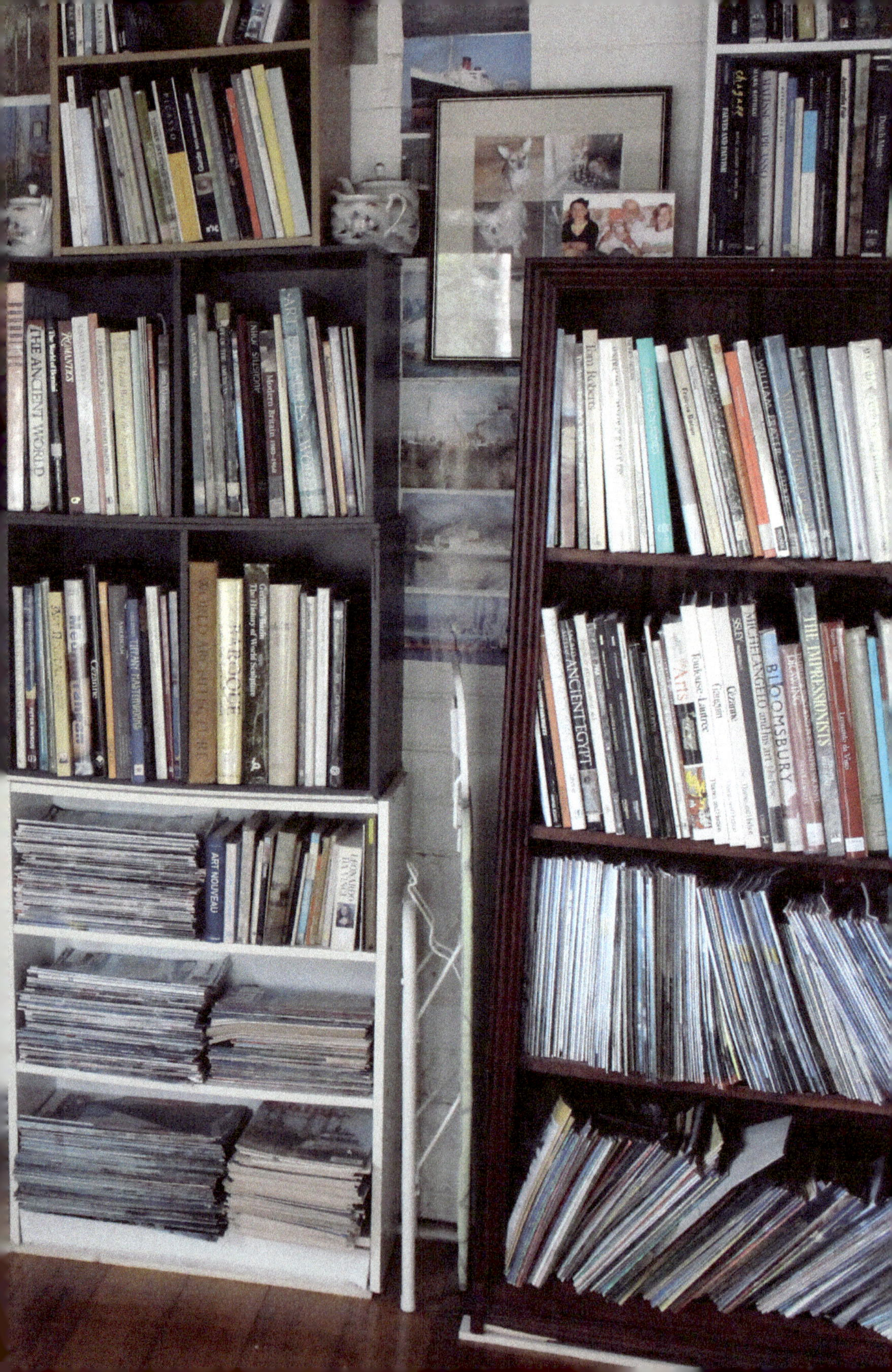
PICASSO
THE ANCIENT WORLD
Modern Britain
ART NOUVEAU
BAROQUE
The History of World Sculpture
Cézanne
Tom Roberts
ANCIENT EGYPT
Toulouse-Lautrec
Gauguin
MICHELANGELO and his art
BLOOMSBURY
THE IMPRESSIONISTS
Leonardo da Vinci

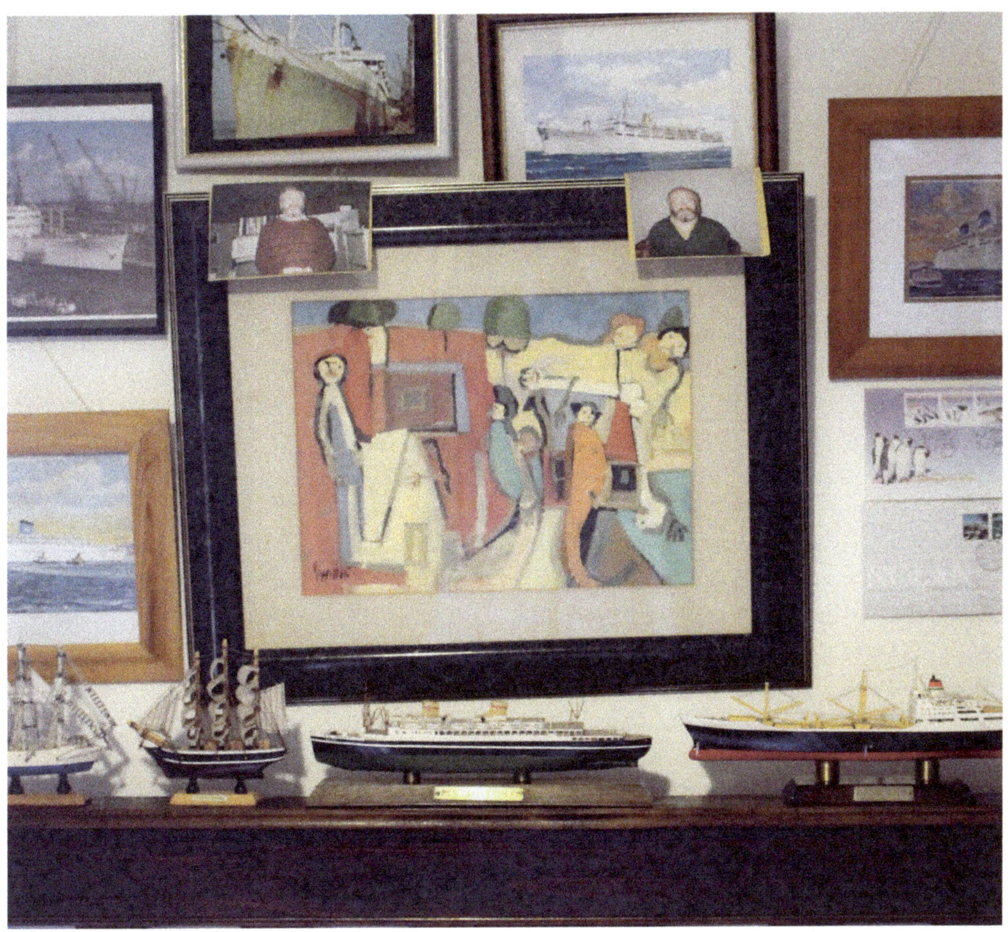

and postcards of ships dotted throughout his home and shed. "I was in charge of the tally clerks who used to count everything... All the goods would be frozen by lunchtime." Such was the ferocity of the ice wind coming off the ocean.

This affection for the sea has never left him. "I've been around the world three times. On passenger ships, not cruises," he says. "I've been through the Suez Canal, the Panama Canal, around the bottom of Cape Hope in South Africa..."

Stephen travelled to Australia on the *Castel Felice* then settled in Narre Warren North. He began painting with oils; old towns, historic buildings and views of the Dandenong Ranges, using fine brush strokes in warm sepia tones. They proved popular. In 1970 he won the City of Cardiff Art Prize.

Stephen says he used to front up to galleries, full of chutzpa, with paintings under his arm. Most warmly received his work, including Tom Roberts' grandson, who owned the Kew Gallery.

Stephen's had 40 solo shows, and counting. "Quite a lot of galleries ask me for work now," he says. His work is represented in the Castlemaine Regional Gallery, Sale Regional Gallery, Philippines National Gallery, Water Board of North Wales, P&O Shipping Company Collection, Frau Munz Collection in Stuttgart, Germany, and in many private collections in Australia and the UK. Those who'd like to purchase one of Stephen's paintings need only visit Malmsbury's Tin Shed Arts, which keeps a steady supply of local landscapes.

"I've probably sold about 2000 paintings in my life, so that's not bad," Stephen says. The demand for his work helped raise his family of four sons – the commission a supplement to his day job as a pump salesman and estimator.

"I'm always a cheapie. That's why I've sold so many. I'm a bit of a socialist you see. The way I look at it, I make affordable art. Art that anyone can enjoy. I just believe that everybody should be a bit equal. I mean, everybody's born naked and everybody goes the same way."

It was his socialist ideals that led him to Maldon, in a roundabout way. "I wasn't a communist, but I had a friend in the communist party, in the 1960s. He used to come around to see me. He was the one who introduced me to Maldon. He brought me up here in 1966 and I've been painting the Maldon landscape ever since. In those days most Melbourne people didn't know where Maldon was."

Stephen likens life here to living in the 1860s. The year he discovered Maldon was the year the National Trust classified it as 'Australia's first notable town'. As such, the whole place is under a heritage overlay. The main thoroughfare, Reef Street, is one of the country's best-preserved 19th century streetscapes. This entire place is a mining relic. And it make a great muse.

Stephen's 1950s red brick house shows there has been some development in Maldon. And closer to home, the back porch has recently been enclosed as a sun room. It leads to a lean-to lined with art posters; Monet, Rembrandt, Picasso, Van Gough and co. Stephen's wife loves the classics.

Here, he also keeps part of his 400-strong art book collection. "Every conceivable artist I can think of, I've got a book on them," he says. Quite a number also feature his own work. Such as *Australian Artists of Today, Artists and Galleries of Australia*, and *Selected Contemporary Artists of Australia*. The pages on Stephen in this book eloquently dissect his style: "By no means is he afraid to brush on as many cadences as he can wilfully assimilate into his jewell-like surface. Phillis' expressionistic side is actively to the fore, his pictures having a clipped collage attitude, like a pastiche of private images stitched together as a fictional quilt."

Talking about private images; back in Stephen's shed, the walls are dripping with them. The odd naked lady, the odd family photo, the odd grandfather who captivated countless. "My grandfather, he was a hypnotist. A professional one," Stephen says. He has newspaper clippings promoting 'Charles Roberts, The Great International Hypnotist'. Charles' stage show promised to cure addiction and depression, headaches, stammering, smoking and drinking. But legend has it, he could do much more than that.

"He could look at you, and just like that you'd be hypnotised and you wouldn't know it," Stephen says. "He was in Germany when World War Two started. He talked to the officials and hypnotised them to sign the papers to let him out. Or so the story goes." He was a creative one, that's for sure.

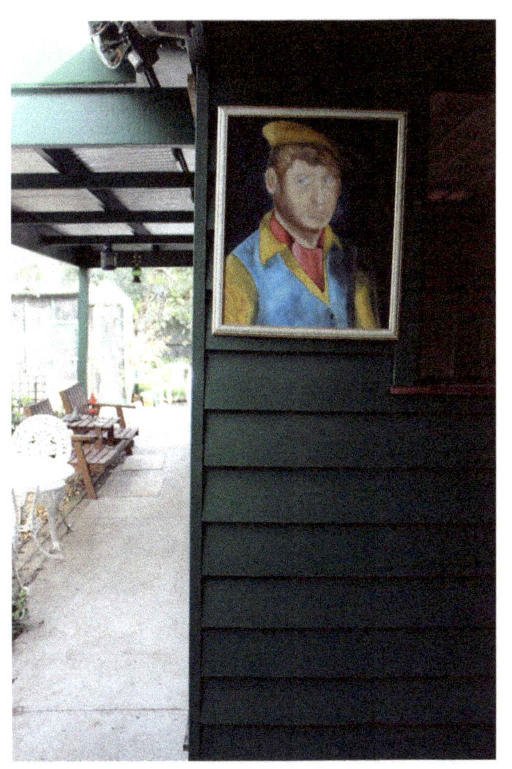

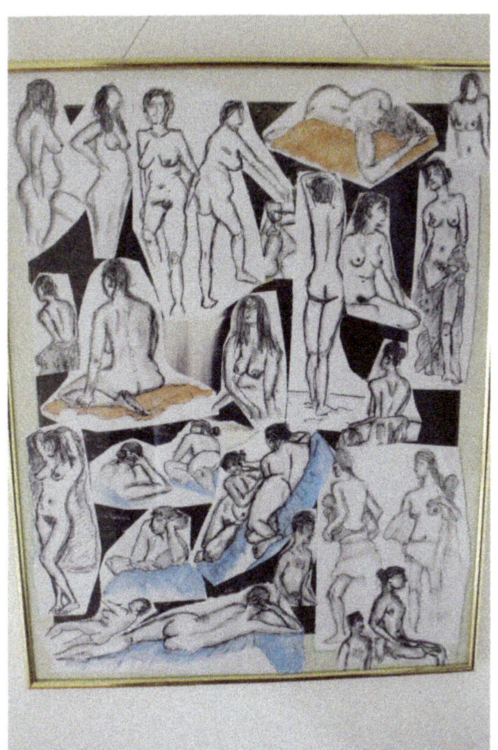

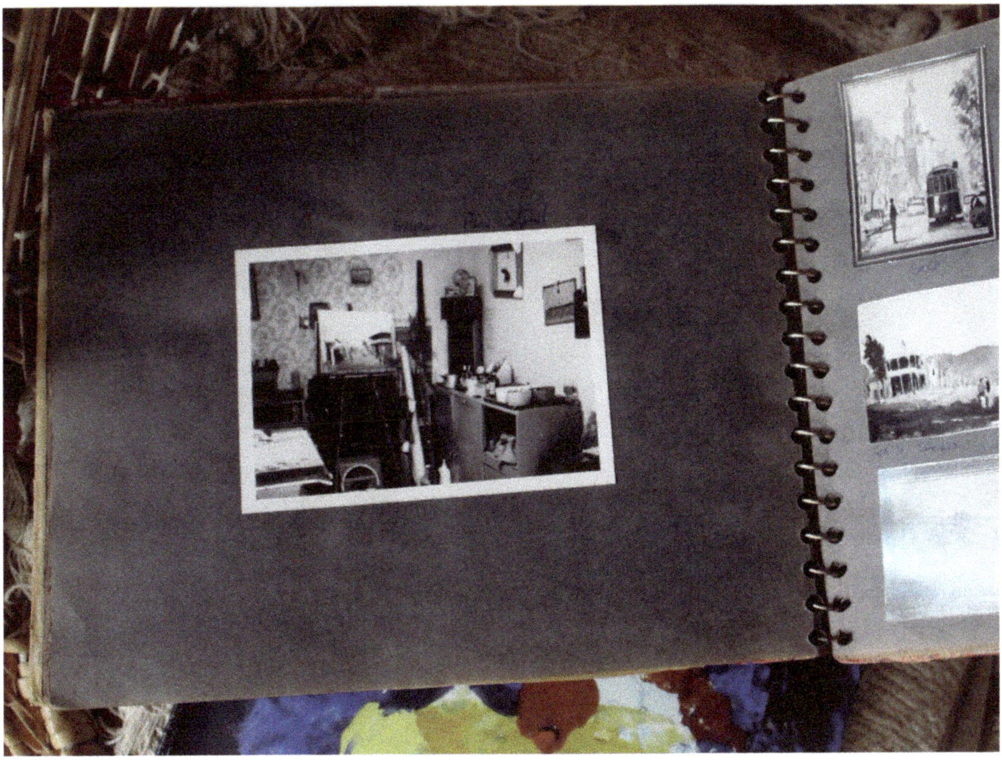

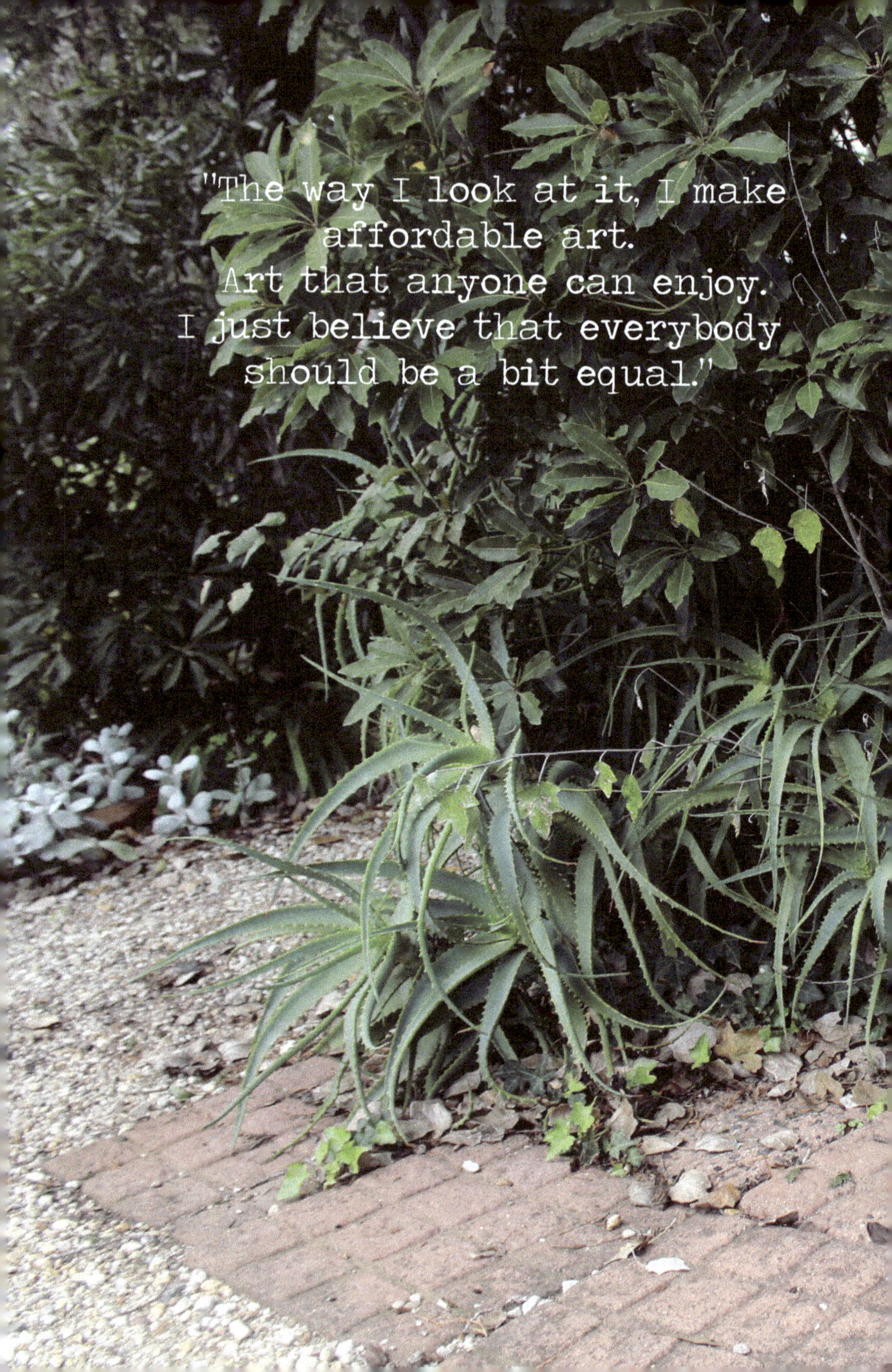
"The way I look at it, I make
affordable art.
Art that anyone can enjoy.
I just believe that everybody
should be a bit equal."

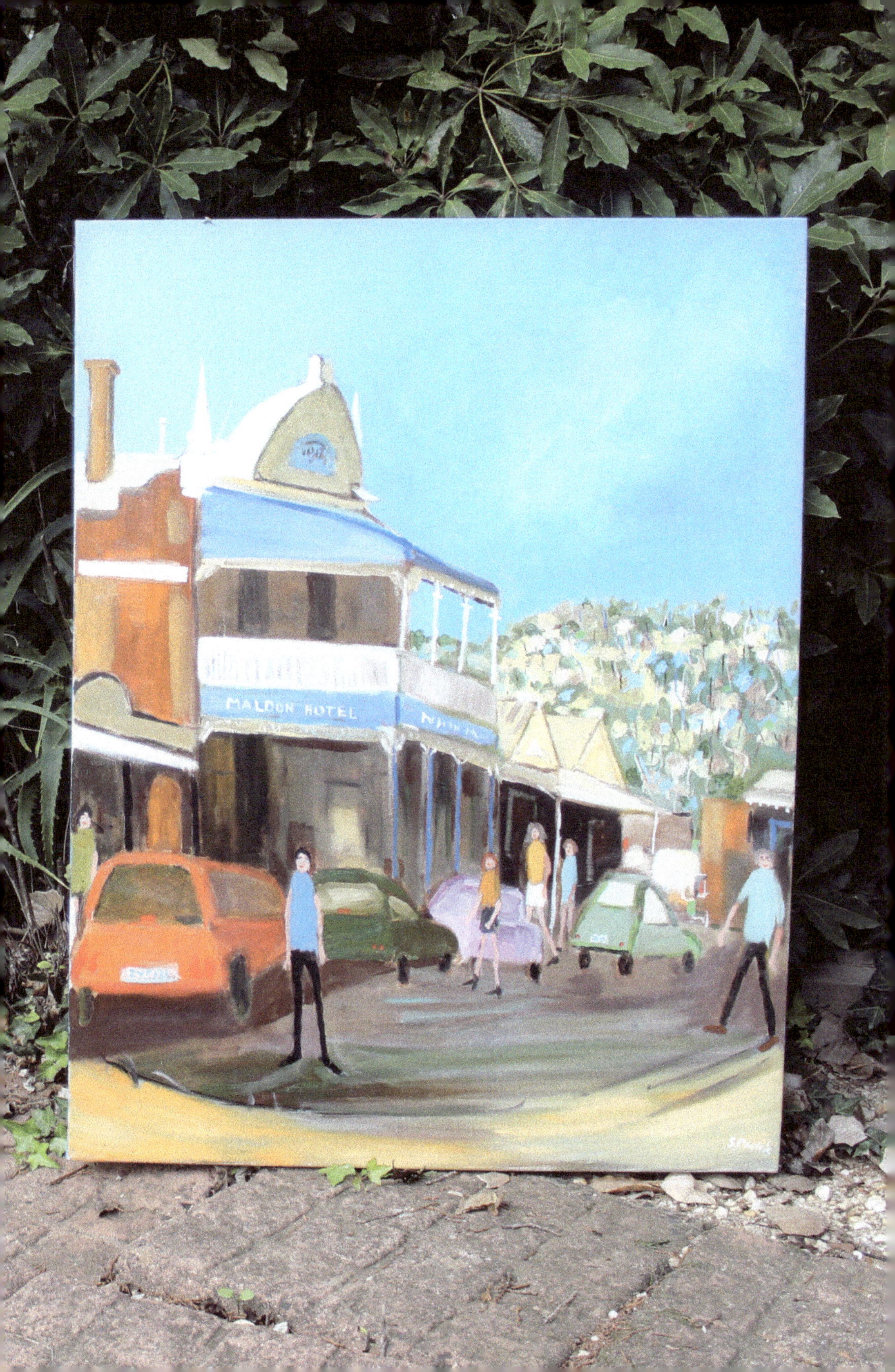
MALDON HOTEL

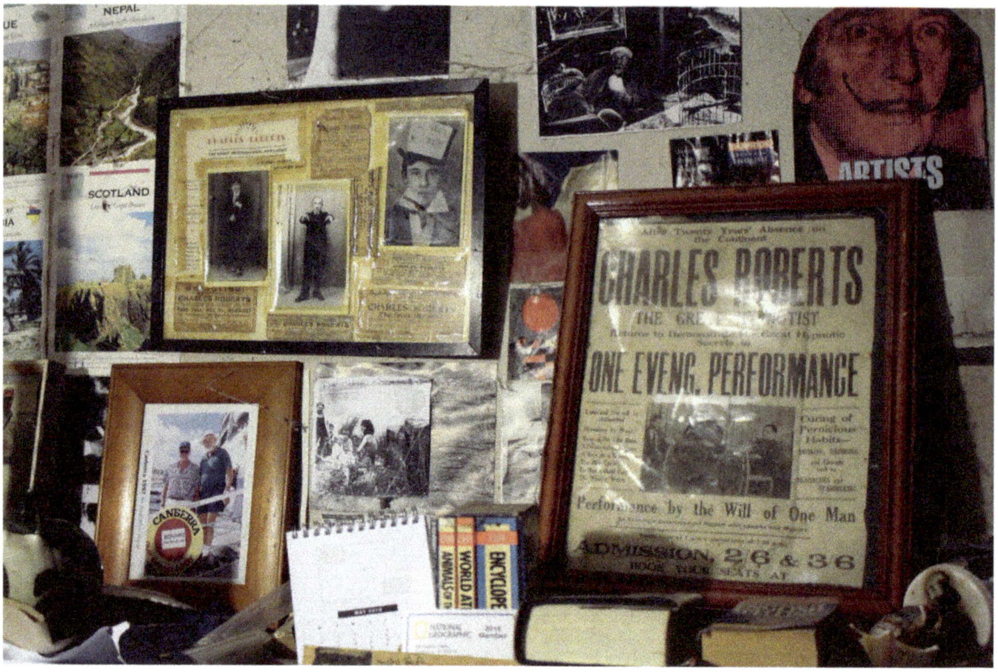

Charles' stage show promised to cure addiction and depression. But he could do much more than that.

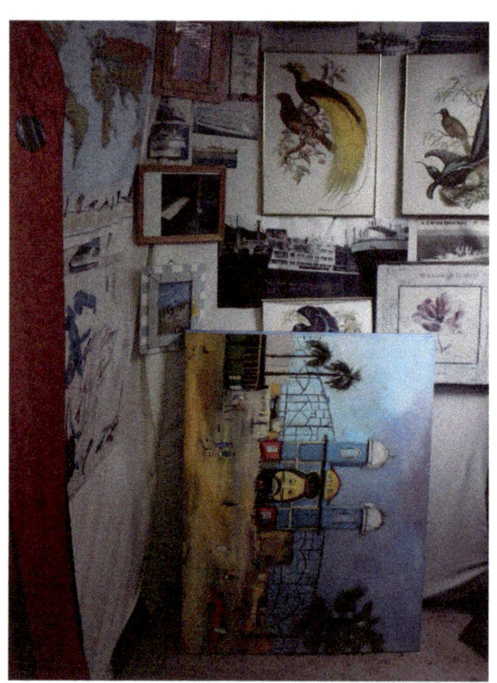

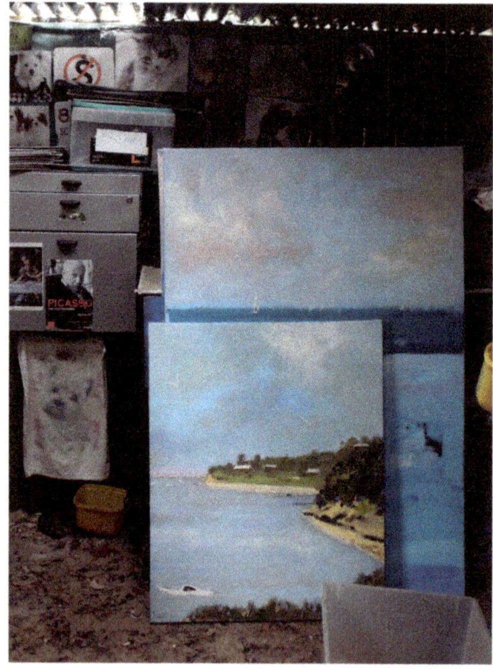

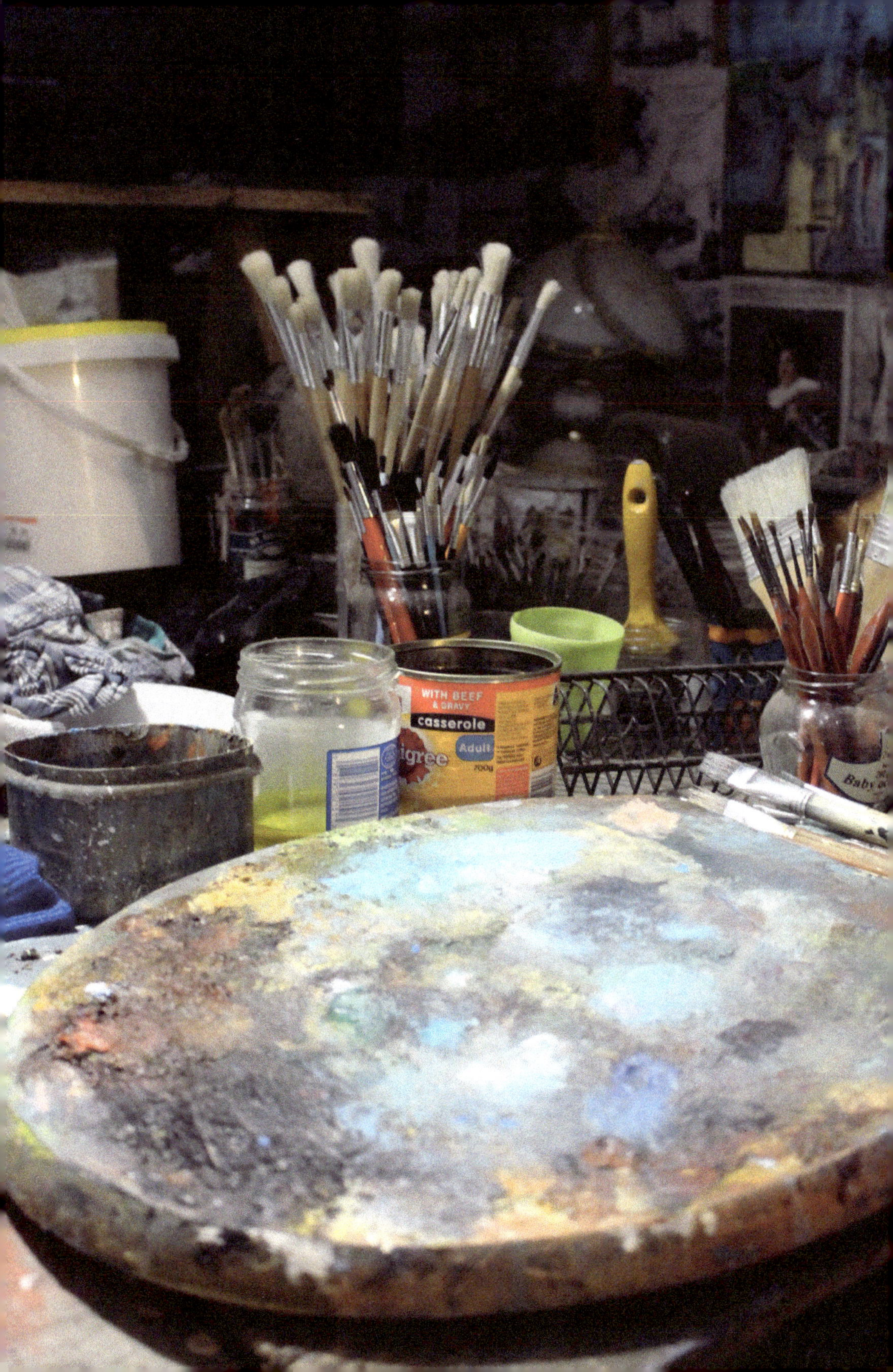
WITH BEEF
& GRAVY
casserole
Adult
700g

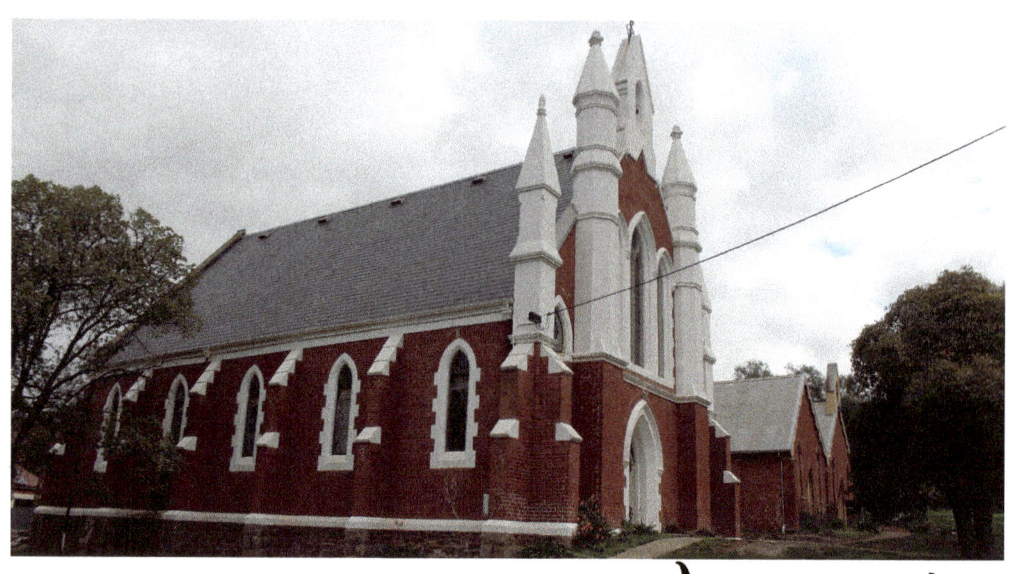

Kareen Anchen & Jeff Gardner

A creative revival

Kareen Anchen is standing in the dust motes of Maldon's old Uniting Church. Afternoon sun is warming the floorboards from high arched windows. Warming old bones. This building is about to come to life again. "You've come right at the genesis of our story here," she says.

"We bought this property two years ago but we couldn't do anything until we'd sold our house. We've just sold and are waiting for settlement, so now it's all systems go."

Kareen and her partner, Jeff Gardner, moved to the area 15 years ago to set up their arts practice in a former MG car museum at Porcupine Flat. They'd been looking for a shed within a two-hour radius of Melbourne to house Jeff's printing presses, and to call home.

"We came to Maldon looking at great sheds. We just needed a space to make art and somewhere to sleep. It was the typical artists' thing," Kareen says, describing the place they eventually bought and renovated as their dream home. "We didn't ever think we'd move." But historic churches have a way of converting the heart.

There was a lot of interest when Maldon's oldest church went on the market in 2014. The church had gone the way of many in Australian country towns. An aging,

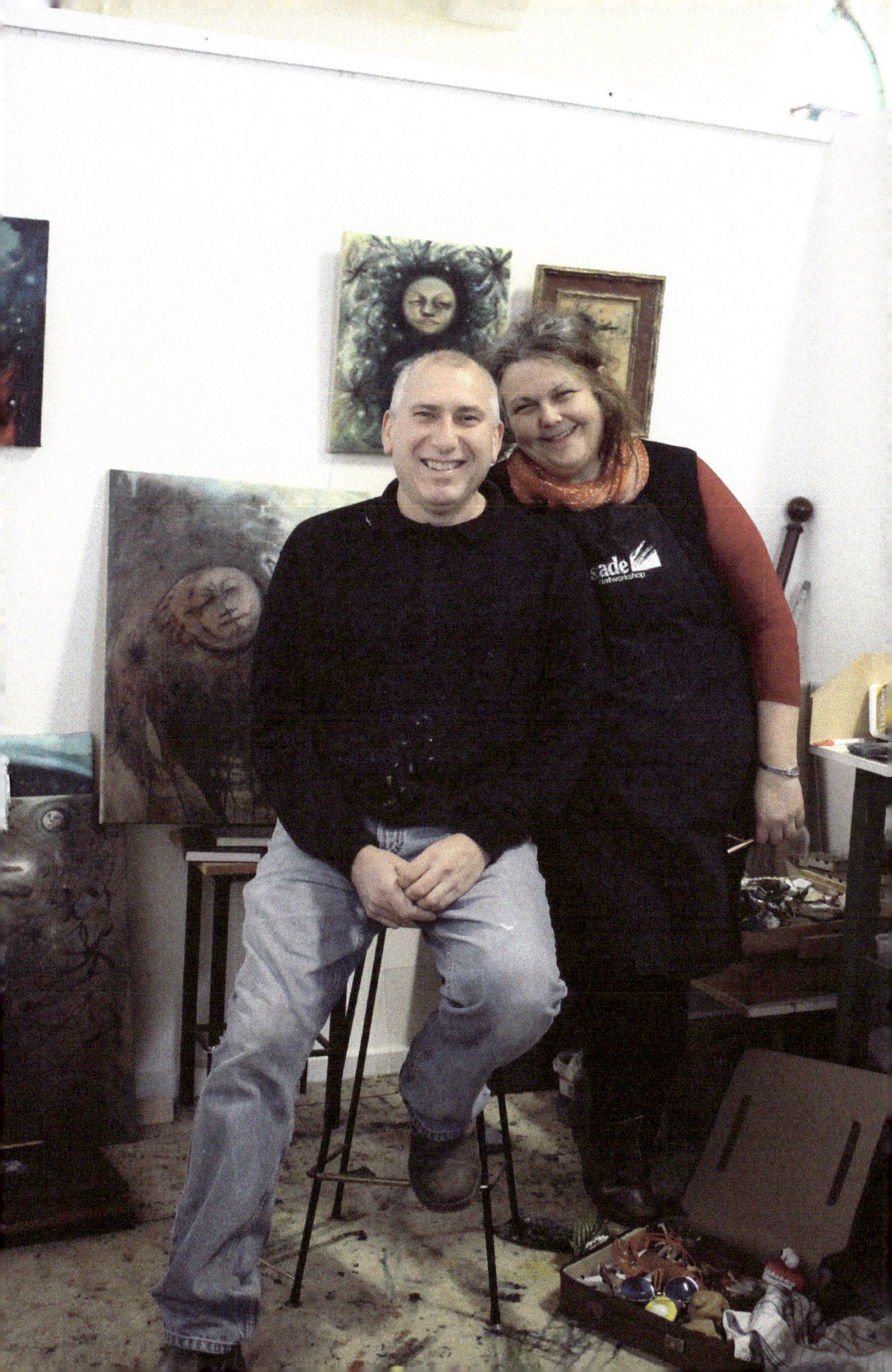

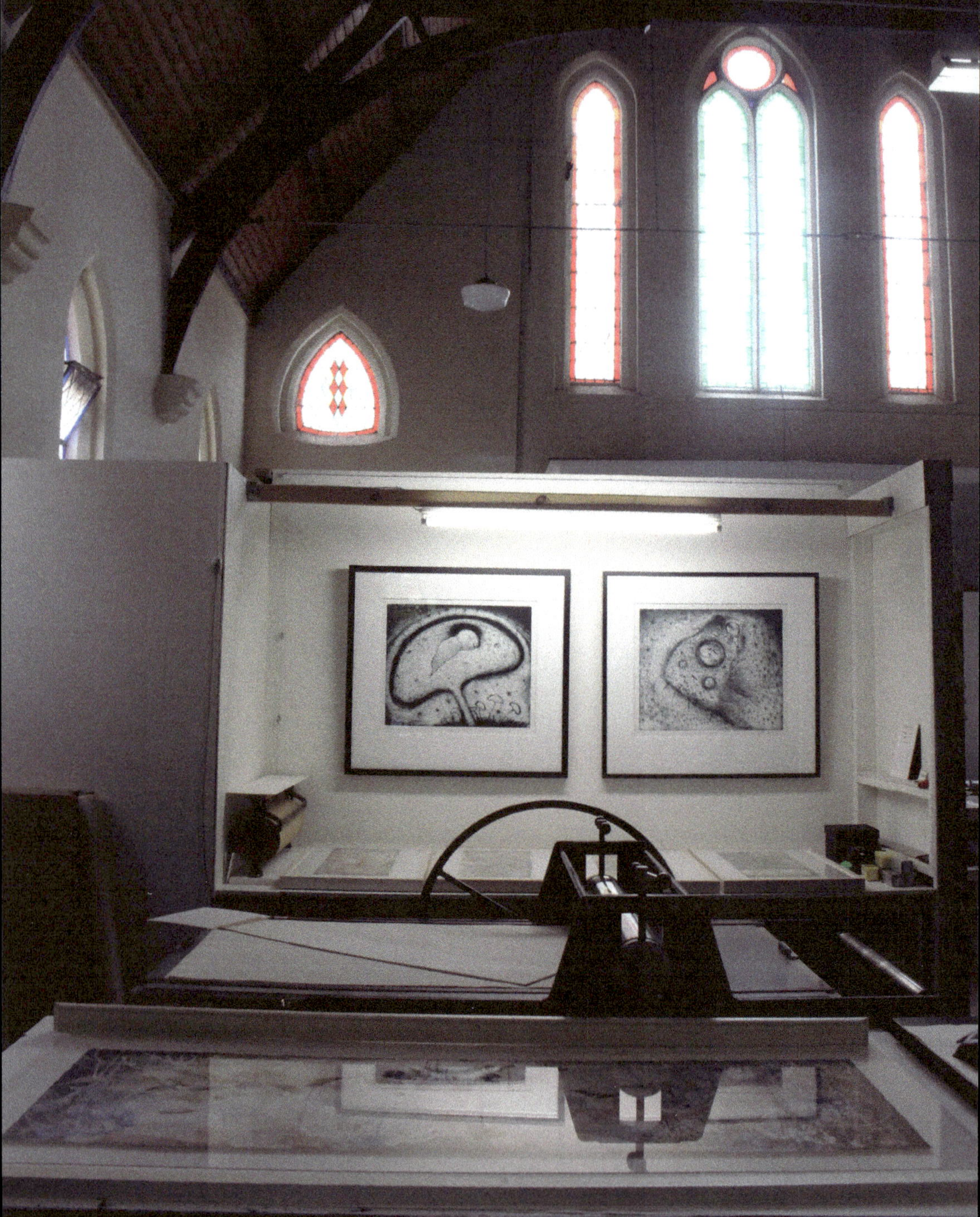

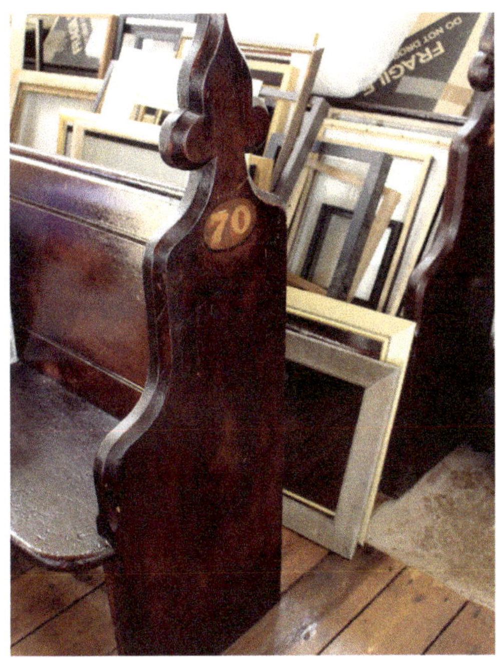

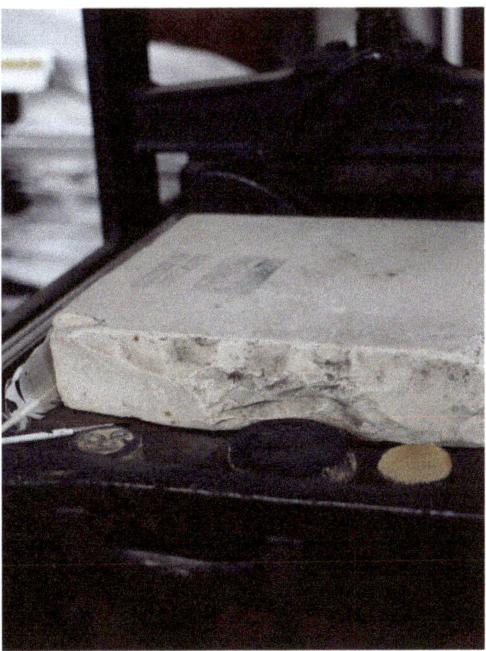

dwindling congregation worshiping in a historic building in need of upkeep.

This property actually consists of three churches. There's the imposing 1863 gothic revival church, the quirky 1853 soft red brick Sunday school beside, and the oak tree behind. The "pull-up-a-stump church", with a 30-metre branch span. Late autumn and it looks like it's barely lost a leaf, yet the soft fall below is at least a foot thick. It's a beauty.

"This is believed to be one of the oldest oak trees on the goldfields," Kareen says. Sermons were said around its young trunk in the early 1850s before the bricks and mortar church – later to become the Sunday school – was built.

"This is the building I fell in love with actually," Kareen says of the Sunday school that will soon be their home. "It's as cute as a button, it's just gorgeous. It probably needs a bit more structural engineering but we're not worrying about that. It's been here since 1853." She says coming from a tradie family, and with Jeff's carpentry skills, they're not afraid of the work to come. In fact, it's enlivening them. It's giving them a deeper sense of commune with this place.

"The day we became locals was the day we won the church bid," Kareen says. "There was only two of us bidding, but about one hundred people came for a sticky beak and when we won it everyone broke out into clapping."

The *Castlemaine Mail* newspaper editor was there to cover the event. "After we'd signed the documents we came out and he took a photo of us holding hands at the front of the church. He said it looked like we'd just got married." This is, after all, also a love story.

Kareen and Jeff met in the late 1990s at an exhibition in Melbourne. "I was coordinating an exhibition of post-Goughists," she says. (That's a group of arts college alumni which got a free education, courtesy of then-Prime Minister,

Gough Whitlam.) The group has held an annual exhibition on the 11th of the 11th since the early 1980s. "We'd moved in the same circles, and had both been to art school in Melbourne in the early '80s, but we'd been travelling different paths up until then. We're very lucky to have found each other, and it's because of art."

Together, their creative lives have flourished. Jeff and Kareen's work has become synonymous with goldfields printmakers. This region is said to have the highest concentration of printmakers per capita. "I think it's because we're close to Melbourne and Melbourne really is the capital of the arts," Kareen says. "Most people who want to keep practising need space and you can't often get that in the city. You can go to the coast and pay twice as much to live or you can go inland to central Victoria. Then, like attracts like."

Kareen has become a champion of their kind. Four years ago she opened the Cascade Print Room in Maldon's historic main street. The gallery and gift shop supports many of the region's printmakers, and a few from further afield, such as Dean Bowen and Michael Leunig. The shop also promotes Jeff's framing work.

Jeff is a prolific painter, illustrator, poet and printmaker, who juggles daily practice with commercial framing. As this story is recorded, he's framing Melbourne artist Judy Holding's latest exhibition, bound for Beaver Galleries in Canberra.

"We get to see it all before anyone else, which is exciting and quite a privilege," Kareen says. "It's a collaboration. You need to think about their exhibition. The works comes in as pieces of paper and goes out as a large exhibition. It goes out an as object."

Jeff now works in the belly of the church. One corner for framing, another for display, one for archives and the fourth for the presses. There's a lithograph press and a letter press and a beautiful cabinet of Gills Sans type. It's all used here. "We love the idea of high tech meets low tech."

Once the couple is settled, this space will be part gallery, part studio, part workshop. The community will still be more than welcome here. "Most of the church pews we sold to locals, but we've kept three to leave in here as a reflection space for people to come to," Kareen says. "This church still means a lot to people in the community. We have people calling in all the time saying they were married here or christened here. This was the heart and soul for quite a lot of people."

Now, the same can be said for Kareen and Jeff. They're about to set up camp in the Sunday school, and start converting it into a home. "Since we've had this property we've discovered that we really love Maldon," Kareen says. "You won't find a place as lovely as this anywhere." As the chimneys of the town's miner's cottages begin to fragrant the air with soft grey smoke, it's easy to agree with her.

"I'm getting a new sense of life here," she says. "I'm getting excited about making art again. I didn't think we'd move out of our last place. I'd moved 45 times in my life before we came to live there 15 years ago. Jeff had moved twice – he had a bohemian year in Fitzroy.

"I think you have to believe you can change and you have to have faith in what you're doing."

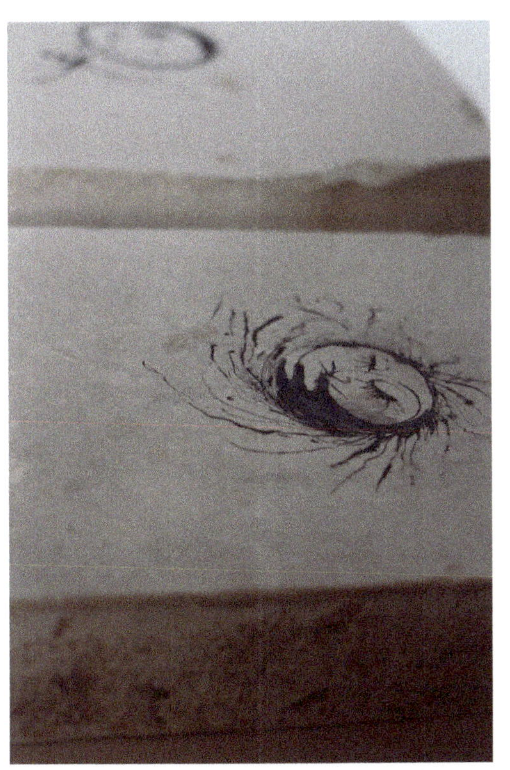
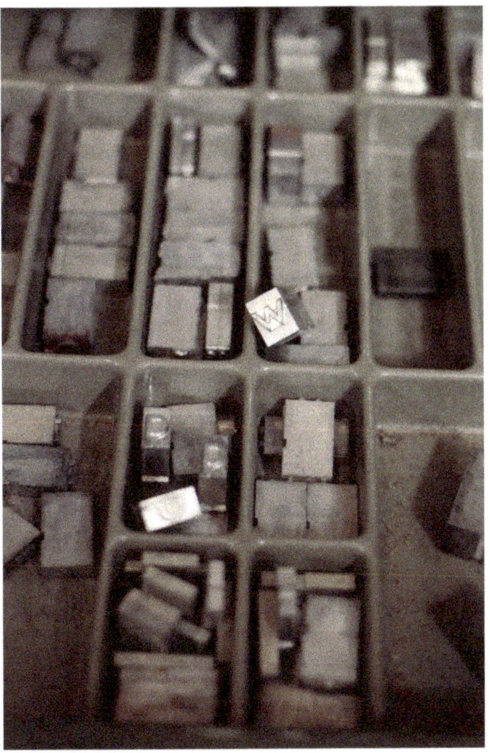

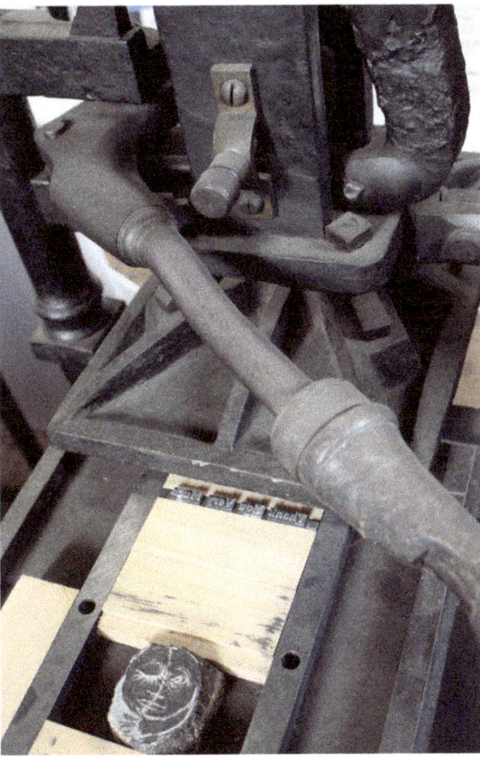

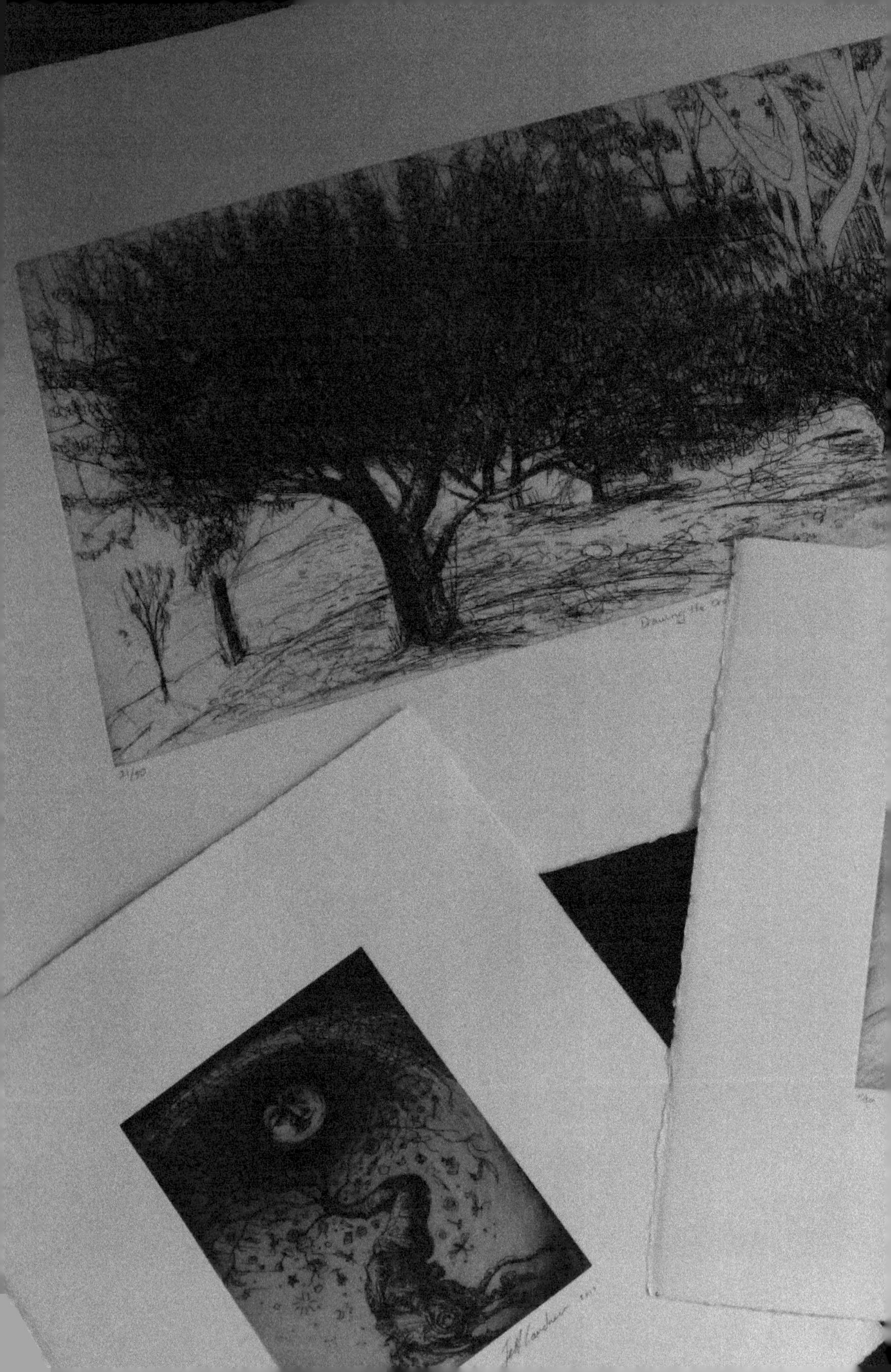

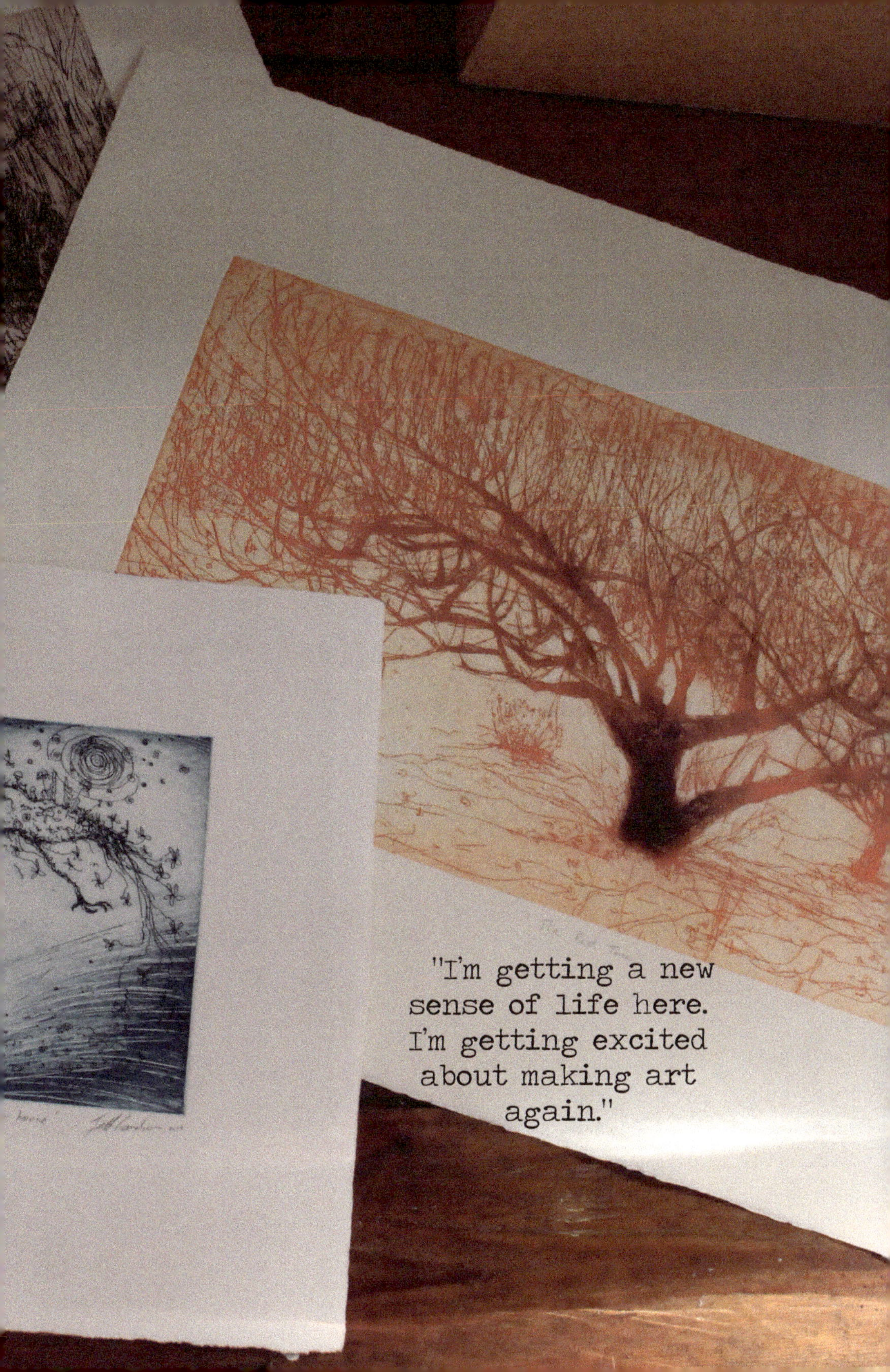

"I'm getting a new sense of life here. I'm getting excited about making art again."

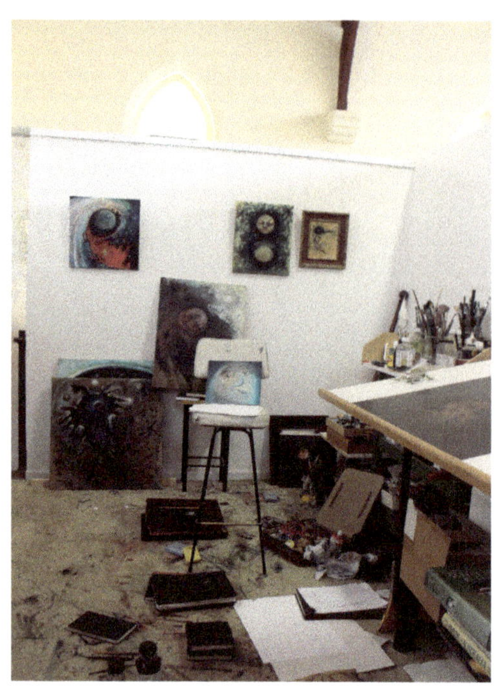

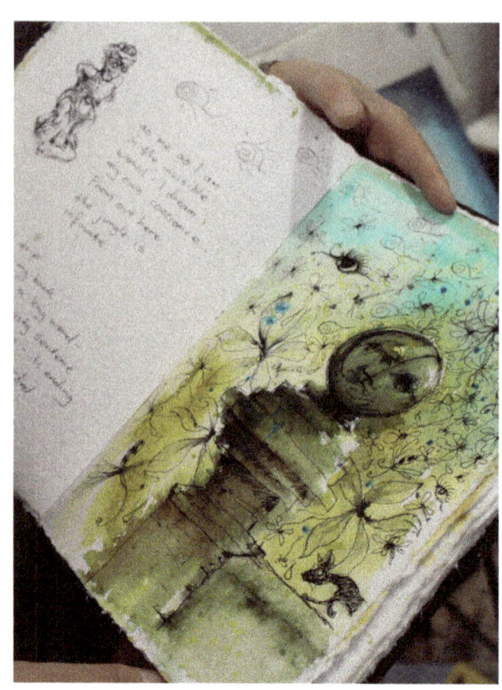

Late autumn and the tree has barely lost a leaf.
It's a beauty.

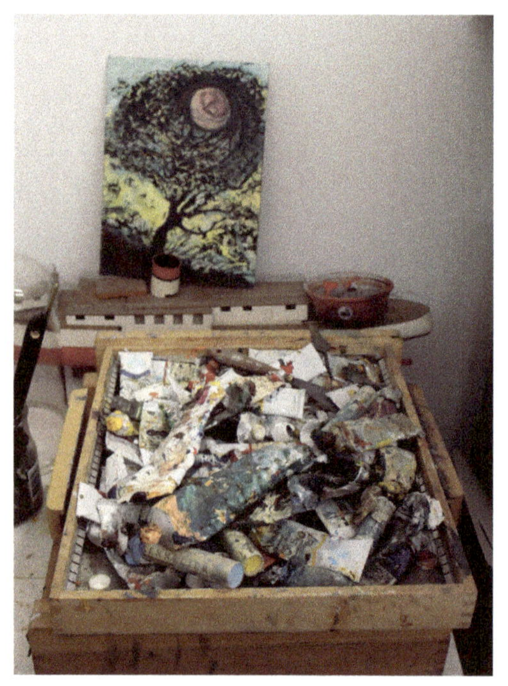

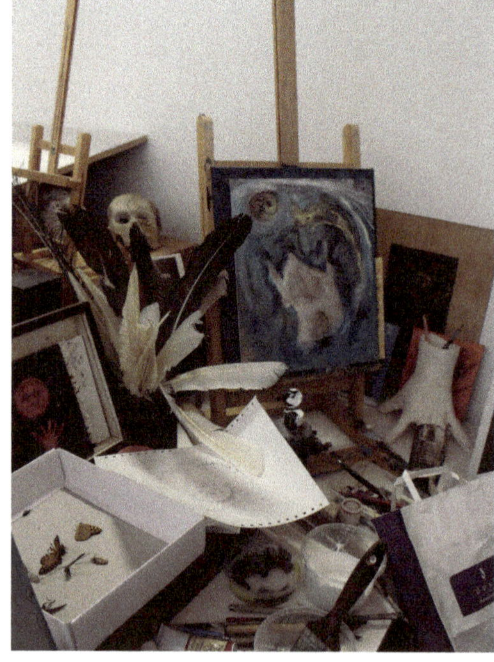

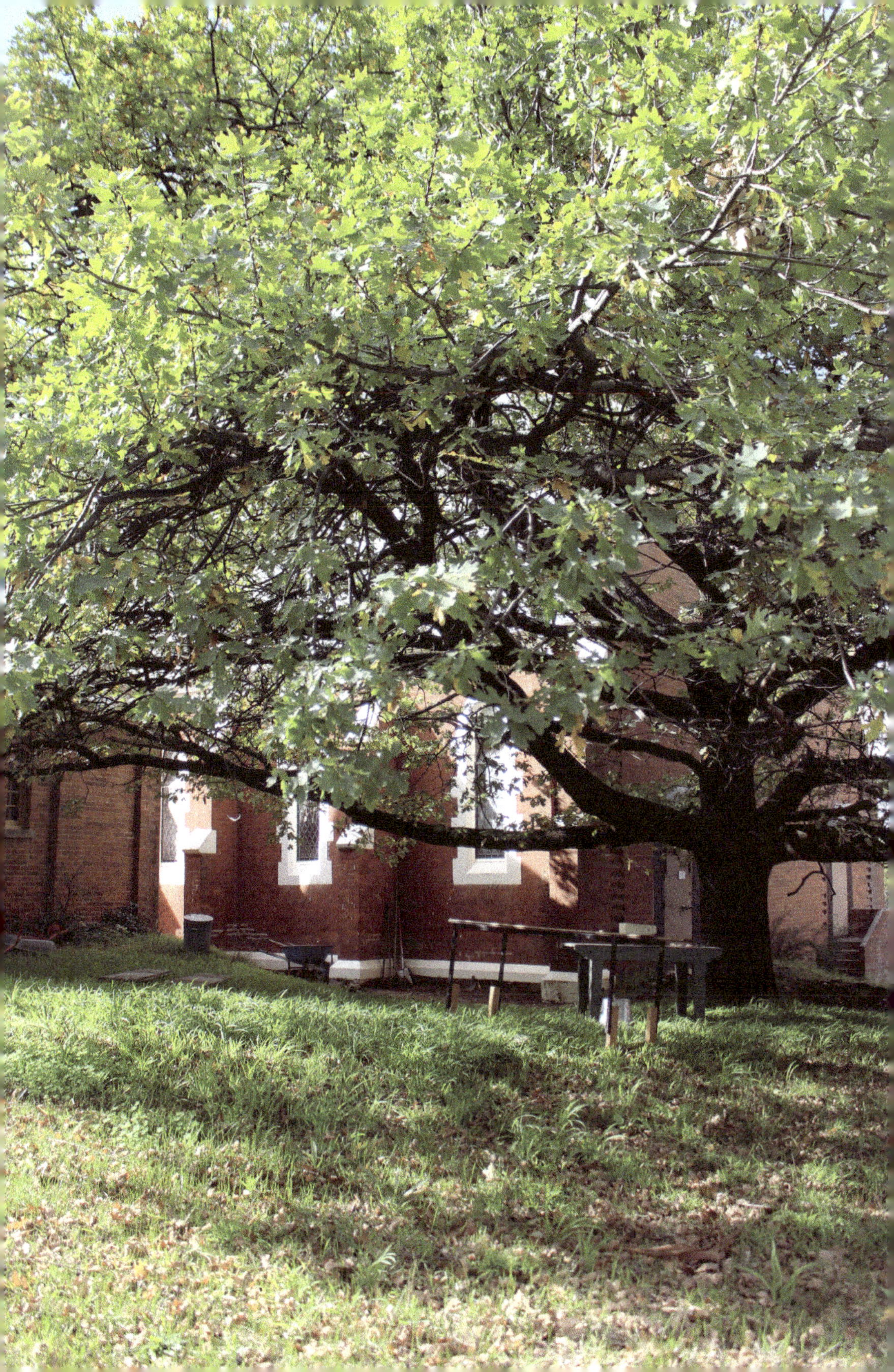

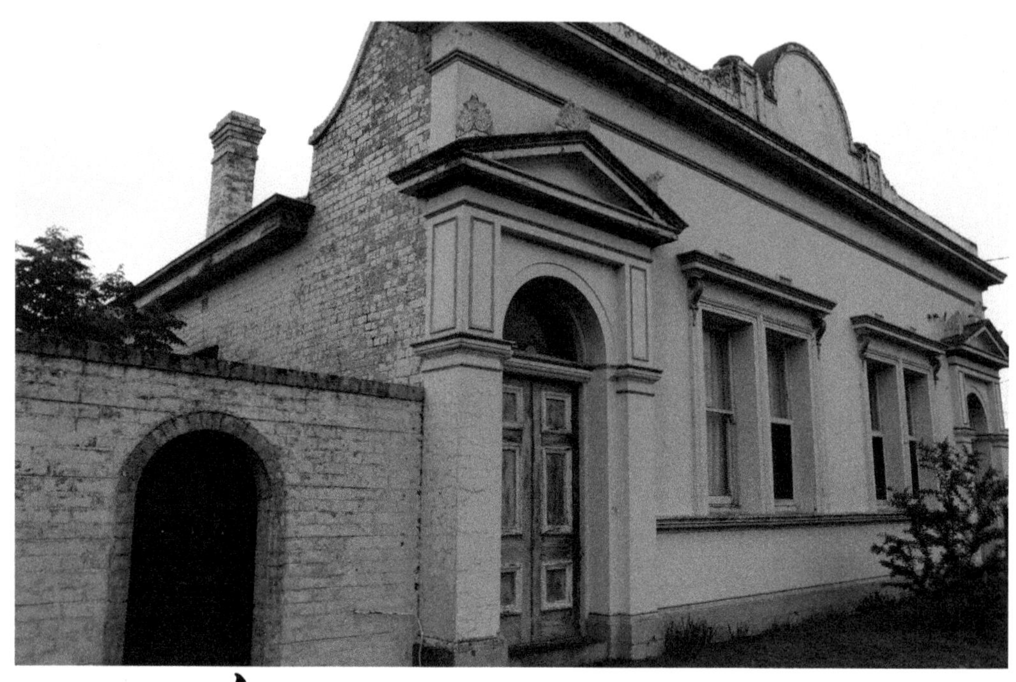

Helen Reimers

Banking on home

Helen Reimers apologises for having de-cluttered. Life's usual props have been packed away. Dealt with, cried over, kissed goodbye, for the time being. It's an important step in preparing to leave a much-loved home, this clean sweep of personal belongings.

A contract has been signed for the sale of Bridgewater's old bank building. Helen bought the place seven years ago. "Long enough to plant a garden. Long enough for it to feel like home," she says. "It's going to be hard to leave, but it's a practicality thing. It got to the stage where I had to choose between our life and this house." Helen chooses life.

It's this quest for experience and authenticity that led the artist and her daughter, Alex, to Bridgewater; a tiny town by the beautiful Loddon River. Helen wasn't looking to buy a property. This one just happened to grab hold of her. "My parents live about 15 minutes further on so I used to drive past all the time and I always loved this place. Then one day I saw the 'for sale' sign." It was a done deal.

This 1878 bank is one of famed architect William Vahland's work. "It's one of his less fancy banks, but there's just something beautiful about it," Helen says.

Vahland arrived on the goldfields from Hanover, northern Germany, in 1854

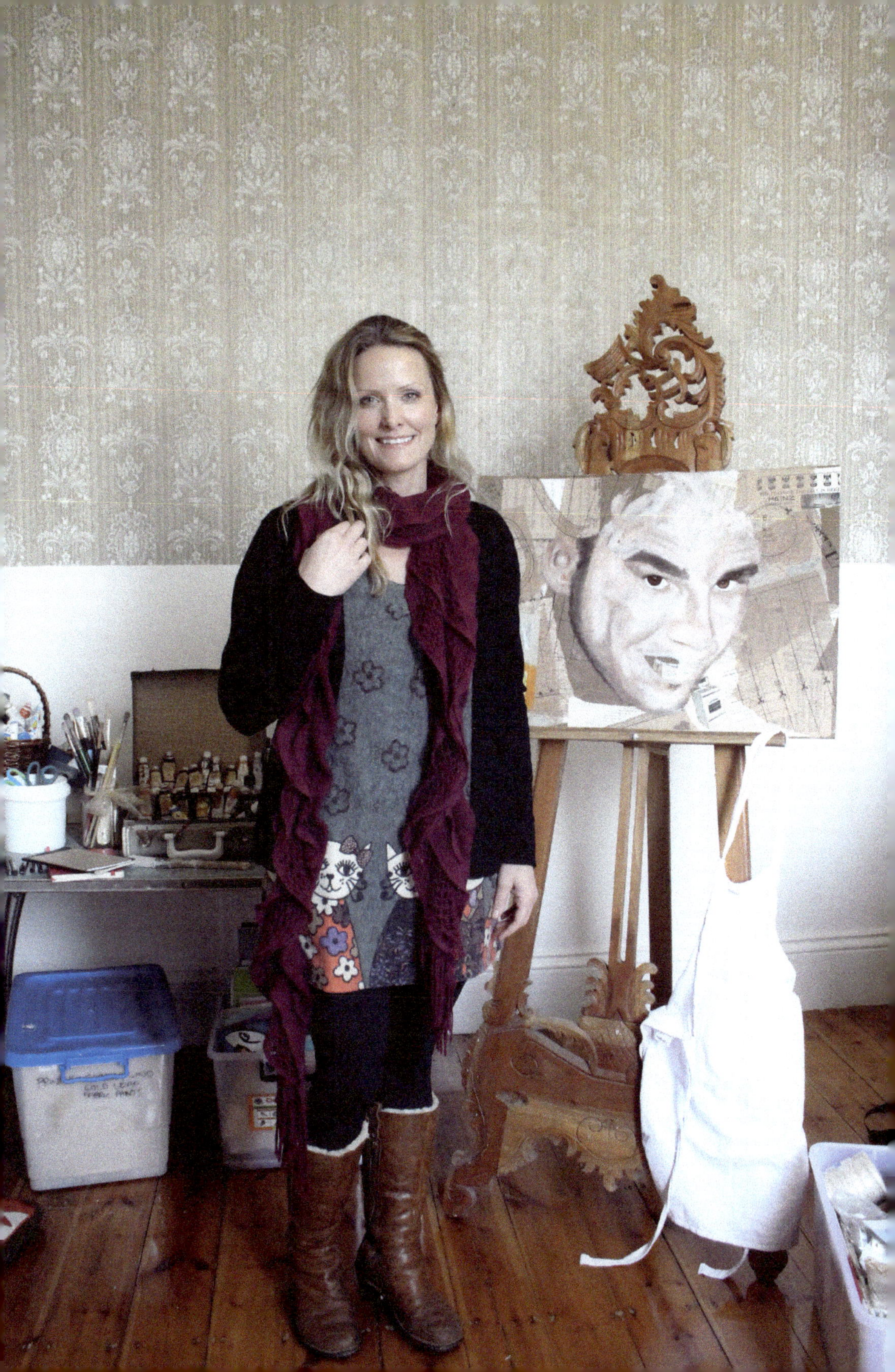

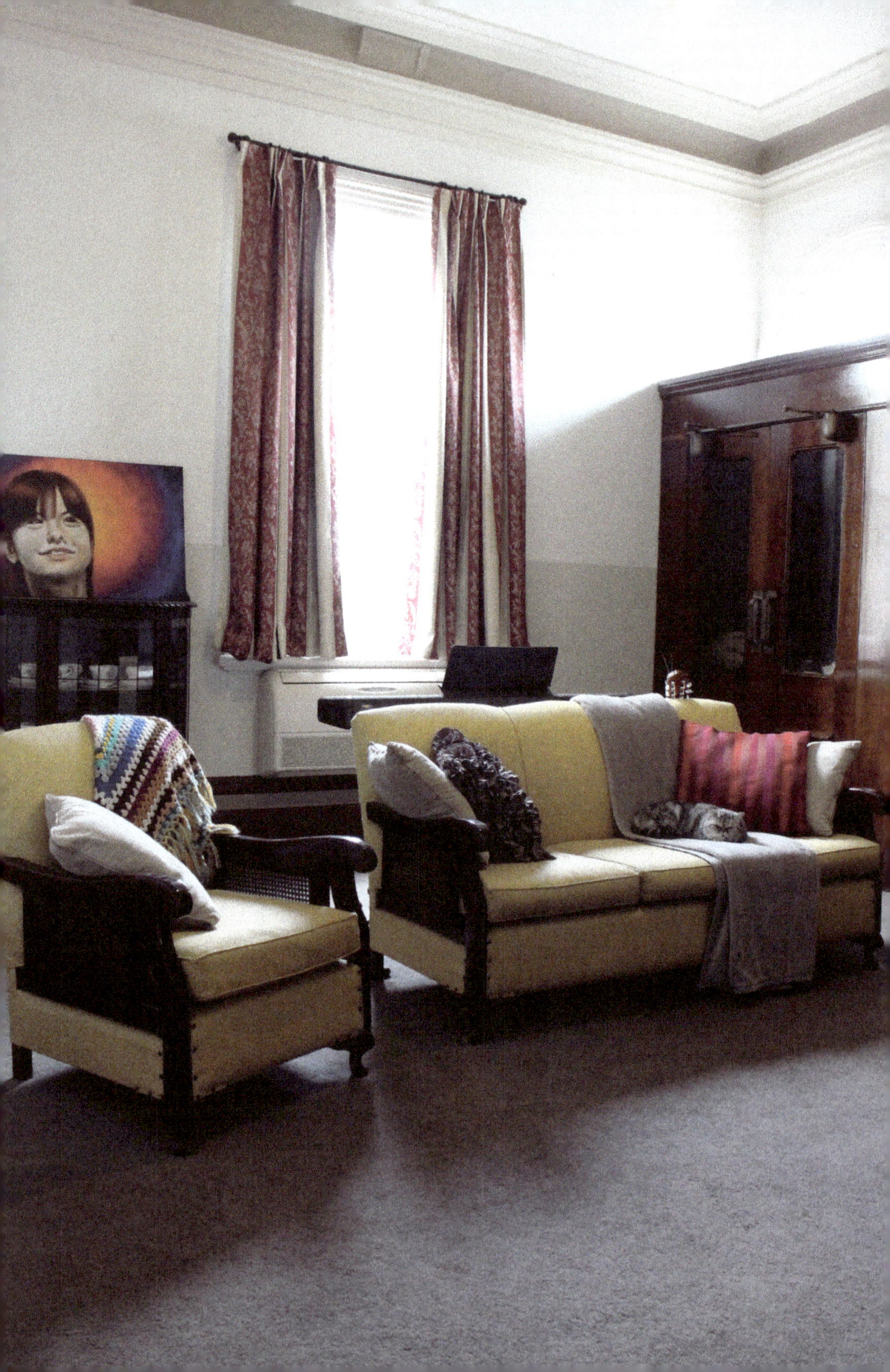

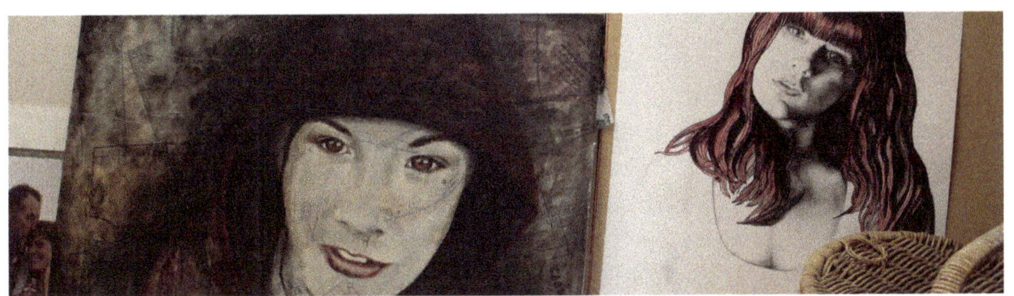

at 27 years of age. He proved to be no miner, but found a need for his carpentry skills, and later, architecture. His career spanned 50 years and almost 200 buildings, from the simple to the sublime. He designed some of the goldfields' most prized theatres, churches, galleries, hotels and homes.

His Bridgewater bank operated as such until the 1970s. Today, its dignified, faded façade is still one of the most impressive buildings in the town's main street. That and the double-story art deco pub overlooking the river. This is a historic town untouched by the real estate whims of city folk.

"You've got the river users, which are generally not necessarily locals," Helen says. "They're a transient community who come over summer for the water sports. They bring a different vibe to town. Otherwise it's a fairly slow-paced farming community. A nice community.

"When we moved here I felt like we'd found a little bit of paradise. When I had holidays and would think we should go somewhere I'd realise, hang on, we're already somewhere."

She says living in the bank grounded her. "I love the uniqueness of it. The high ceilings, the archways. It's so grand, but it's not pretentious. It's such a solid house. It feels so grounded. Safe. There's a quality of craftsmanship that's gone into building it. You can feel it. I feel it. Even the flood didn't do any lasting damage."

Less than 12 months after Helen and Alex moved here, the decade-long drought broke. Rain set in for January, the Loddon burst its banks and Helen's place went a metre under. The whole town did.

"I have really fond memories of the flood, which sounds ridiculous I know. The amount of people who came out to help was amazing. People kept turning up. There was real community spirit and I think it enhanced my feeling of home here."

Helen would come home to find fellow locals had poked packets of dog food through her fence, or left bags of groceries on the kitchen bench.

The bank was good, but she was wet. Helen and Alex ended up moving out for four months to let the old girl dry out. It was therapeutic in a way, Helen says. "Being a chronic hoarder I definitely had a lot of stuff I didn't need. The flood literally flushed out a lot of things I didn't need to be hanging onto. I love making things and it's hard to throw things out. I love buying old stuff and reclaiming it as my own, but it's a bit of a curse as well."

Helen says the bank's 14-foot ceilings gave her space to think, and dream. As such, it changed her life in many ways. The visual artist and photographer had been teaching art at the Bendigo TAFE. "I quit teaching and set up my own business a couple of years after we got here." Mostly commission work for design and photography. "I'm loosening that up again now and predominantly concentrating on fine art. Portraits."

Her portraits make people stop and look and see more in a person that the superficial. "I like to try and get those layers in there," Helen says. "I love people. I really do. Even the challenging ones."

None are more loved than daughter Alex, who has been Helen's muse in life, as well as art. The bank is peppered with portraits of her. "The house starts to look like a shrine to her," Helen laughs. "She's just so expressive, and I love her. I can quite easily look at a photo reference of Alex for hours and not get sick of it. She has these dancing eyes...

"But she's much more than a pretty face. She's an incredible human being who deals with challenges that most of us couldn't even imagine. She's someone who says, 'what can I do? I'm going to do that and enjoy it'."

Alex has cerebral palsy. She's in a wheelchair and communicates via an iPad. She's also a highly-creative person; a gifted poet who is studying creative writing in Bendigo. Many local writers have championed her talent. "People are drawn to her," Helen says. "I've watched that happen since she was young. She's like a magnet."

Neighbours have told Helen how much she and Alex will be missed when they move soon. But they won't be strangers. That road from Bendigo to her parent's place at Kingower, passing through Bridgewater, will always be the stretch that wears tyres. She says her parents' winery has been a bolthole for her family for generations. Like Vahland, her ancestors also came to the area from Germany during the mid-1800s gold rush. They didn't do too badly either.

Several famous nuggets were found at Kingower. The Blanche Barkley, discovered in 1857, is still the world's third largest nugget. In 1980 the Hand of Faith was found just 12 inches below the ground, weighing 27.21 kilograms. When the Reimers were mining here, the field was known as the potato diggings, for the spud-sized nuggets it regularly yielded. Helen's great-grandfather used his finds to purchase the family property, and to establish a knitting mill in Melbourne. Later family members planted vines.

"I had this amazing upbringing, going between Bendigo and Kingower," Helen says. "My connection to the bush there is really strong." She loves the stories her Uncle Alvin tells, of peddling his mum's Sunday roast to old neighbours living alone. To the four surrounding properties, separated by the classic box-ironbark forest of old gold country. After lunch the neighbours would pick up instruments and play. Their music would find each other through the distance. "The bush was so still back then," Helen says. "I just imagine the sound of this collaborative concert happening from somewhere you couldn't see. I love that."

Helen may have started packing already, but her favourite paintings are still on the bank walls. Her art supplies are still in the front room with the flocked wallpaper. She'll be making art here, right until the final goodbye.

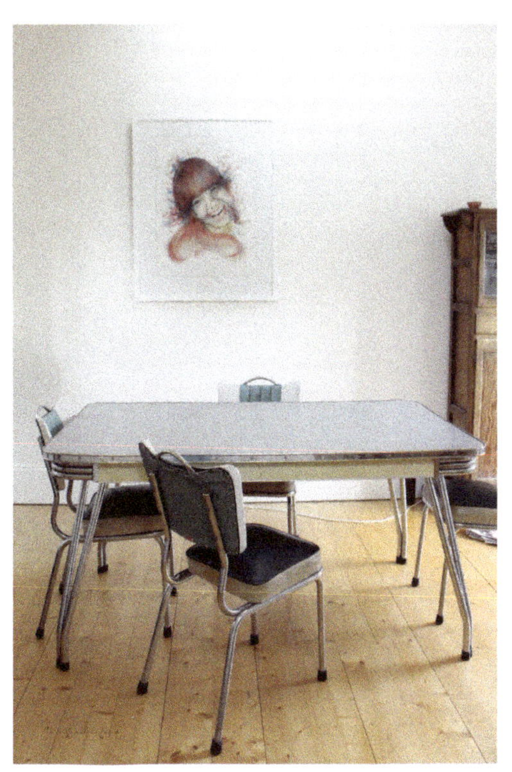
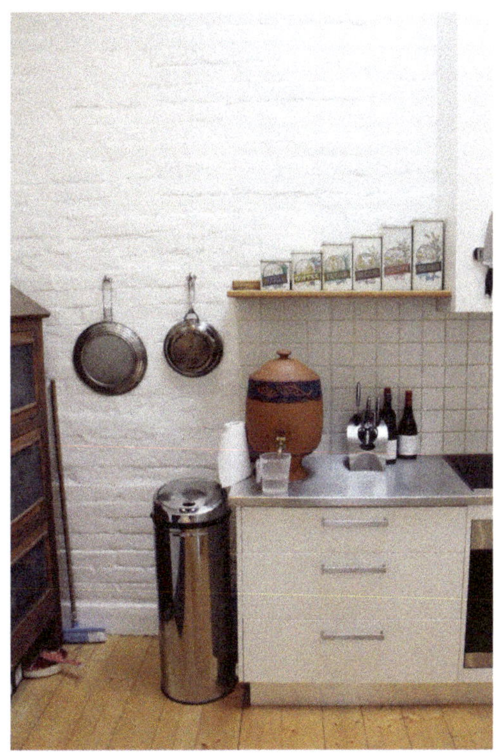
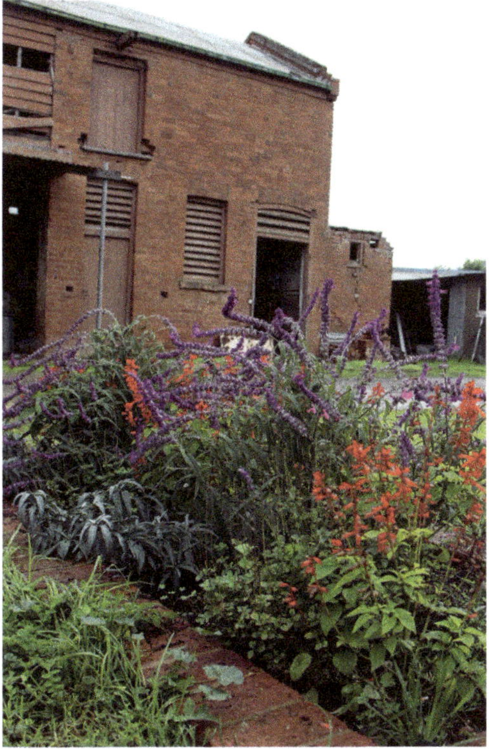
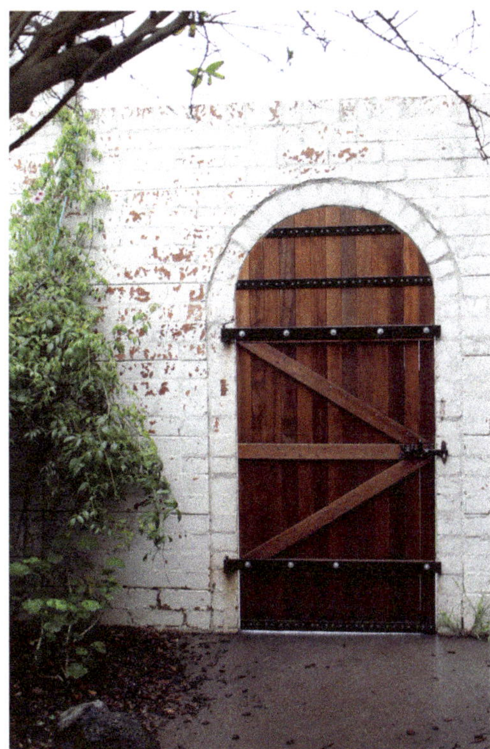

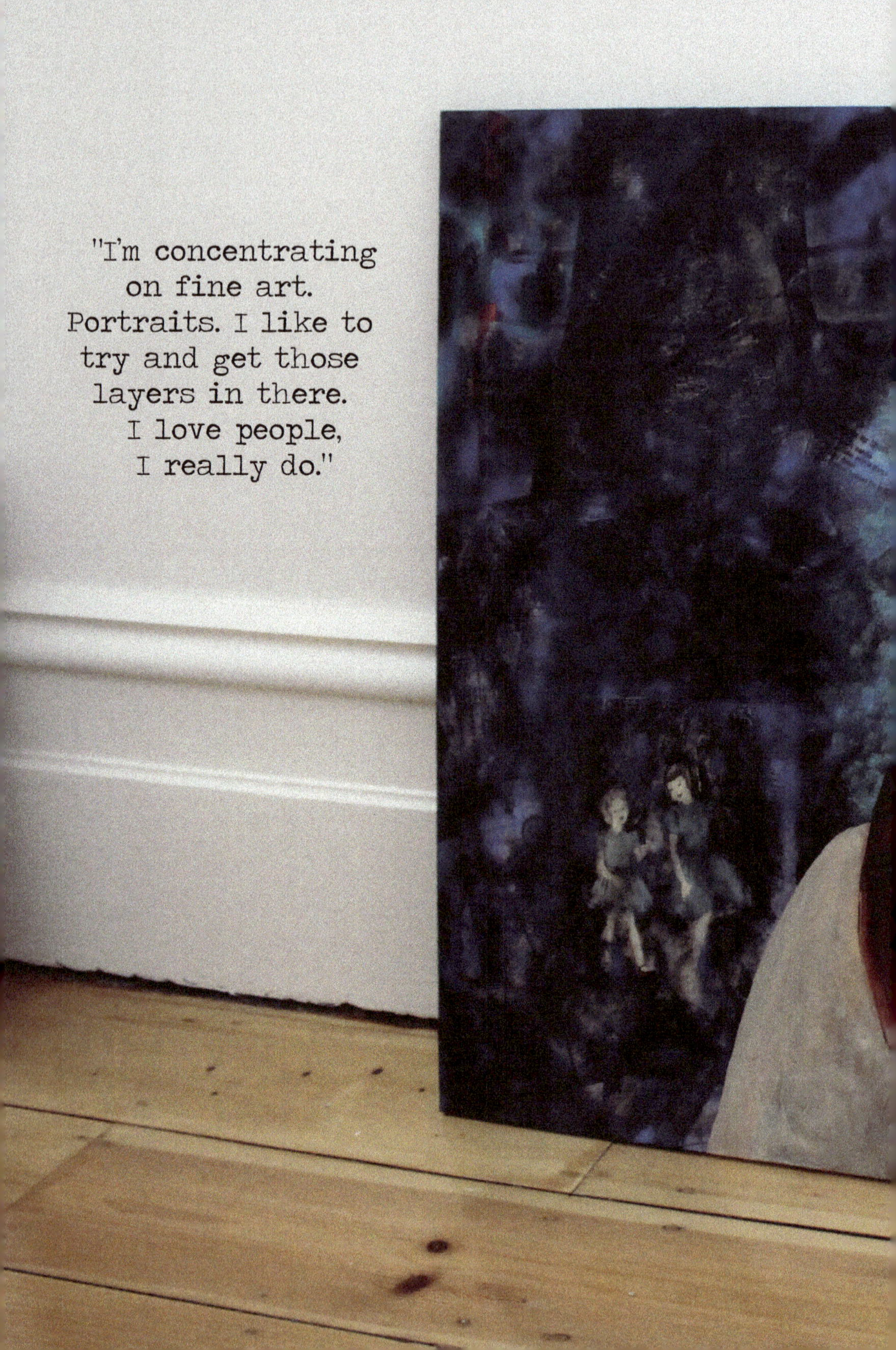

"I'm concentrating on fine art. Portraits. I like to try and get those layers in there. I love people, I really do."

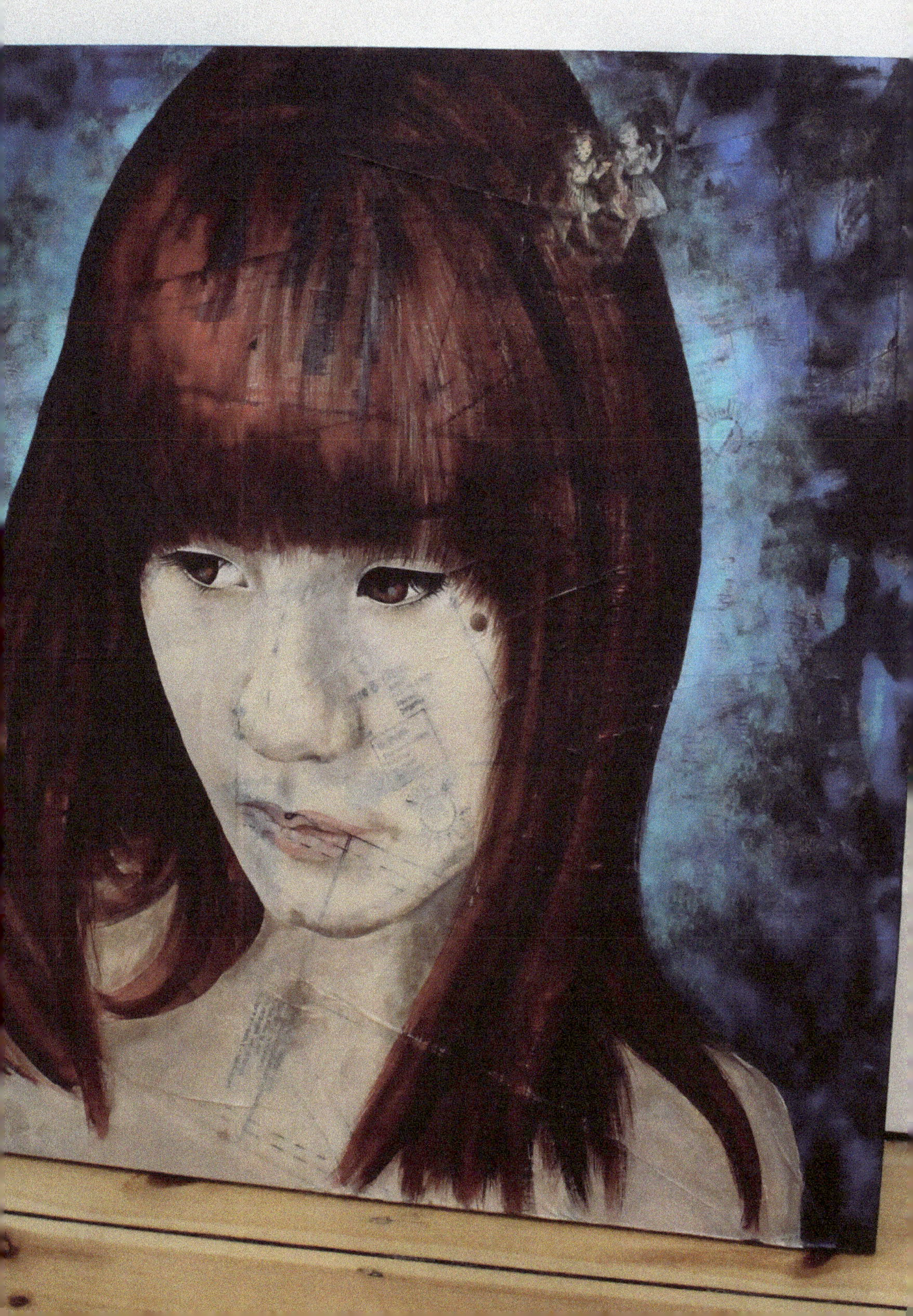

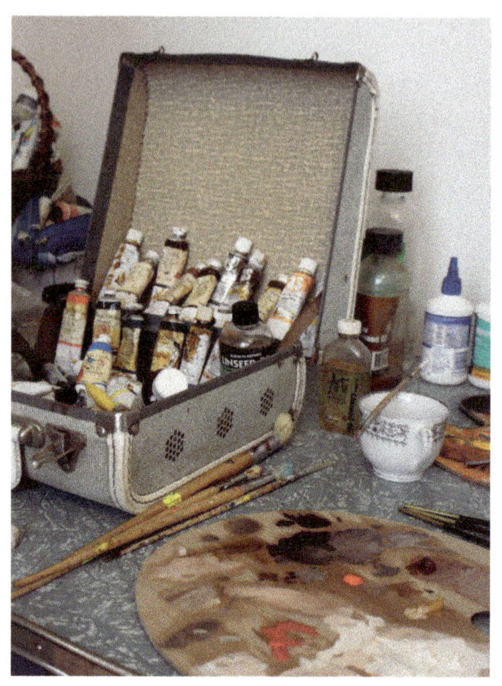

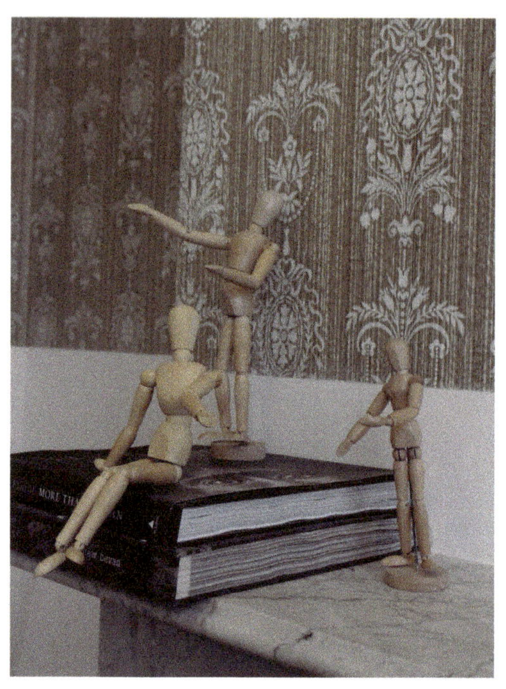

Helen's favourite paintings are still on the walls. Her art supplies are still in the room with the flocked wallaper.

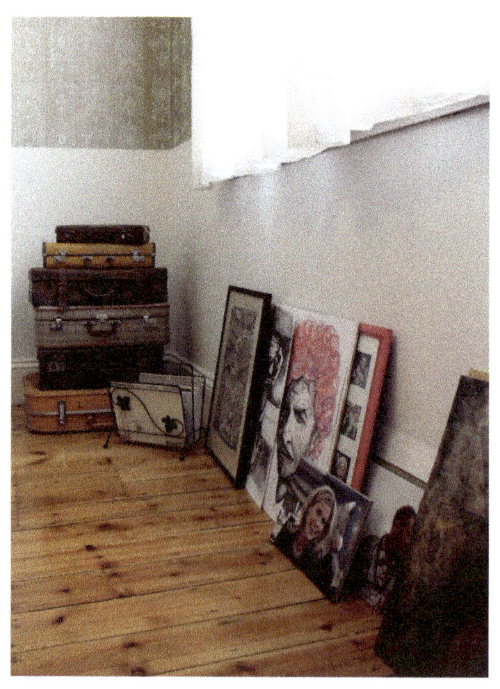

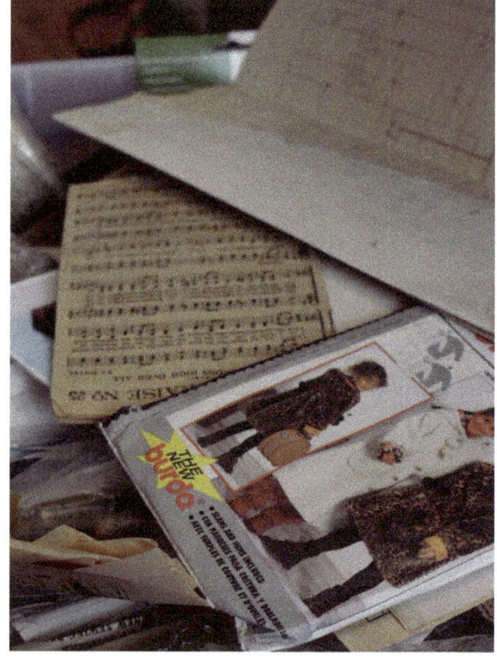

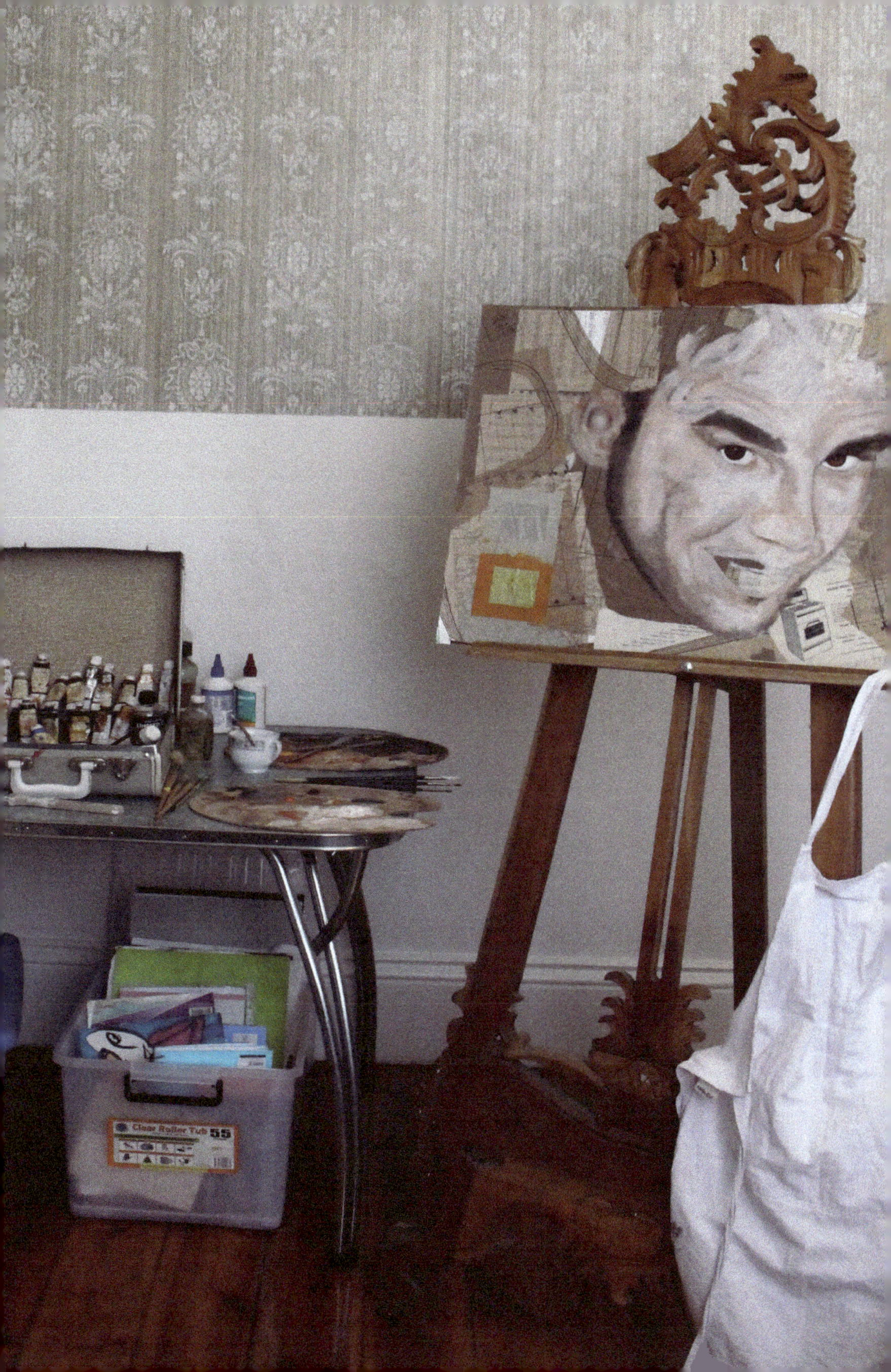
55

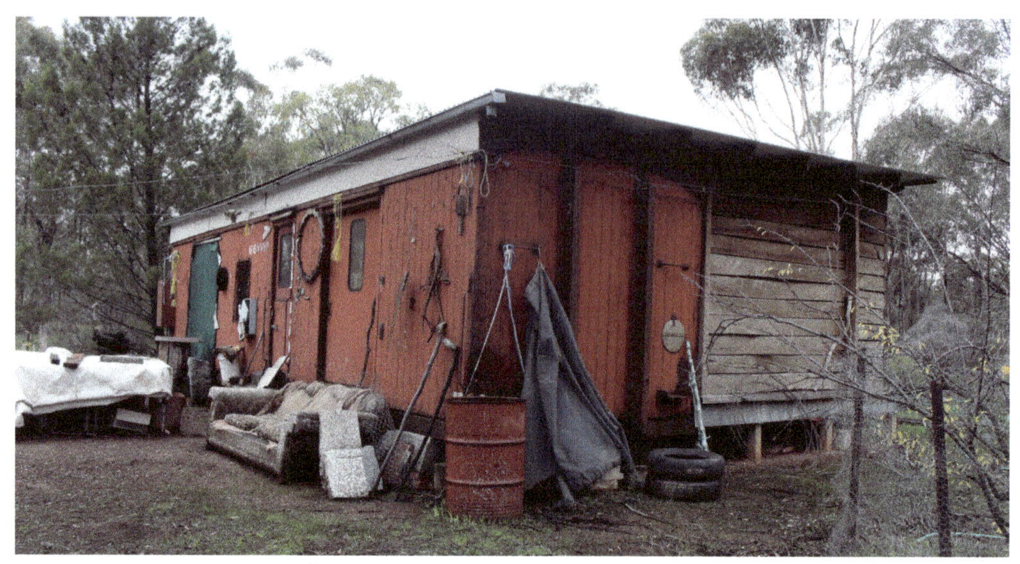

Stanley Farley

Warmth & words

You can't get much more 'goldfields' than Stanley Farley's place. The Whipstick Forest is so pecked and pock-marked with mines you've got to watch where you step. Stanley says, around here they're mostly ground scratchings; shallow diggings no more than six-feet deep. But they're right through the place. This eerie-quiet bush was once teeming with people.

For the masses of miners who came here, the only allure was gold. Beauty for many was harder to find in this forest. It was even for Stanley and his wife Lynda Newton, who bought their 20-acre Whipstick block in 1976.

"I didn't think we'd stay here. I just wanted a piece of land and to get out of Melbourne," Stanley says. "I like living in the landscape, I always have. I like being in the organic world. That's very important to me." Stanley's early years were spent around family properties to the state's north east, around the Ovens Valley and Gippsland.

"It's very different to here and I always had in mind I'd go to the north east. My idea of the country used to be lushness, thick, soft and green. We came here and it was all black and red and bare. I didn't like it at all, but I thought it'd do for a time. Turns out it grew on us and after a while, we couldn't leave.

"Now, when I look at lush country I don't like it, I've totally reversed. I see the colours and the details here. I like the extremities of heat and cold and it gets very cold here and very hot."

Right now, it's whip cold. Rain has amplified the colours. Ironbark trunks are

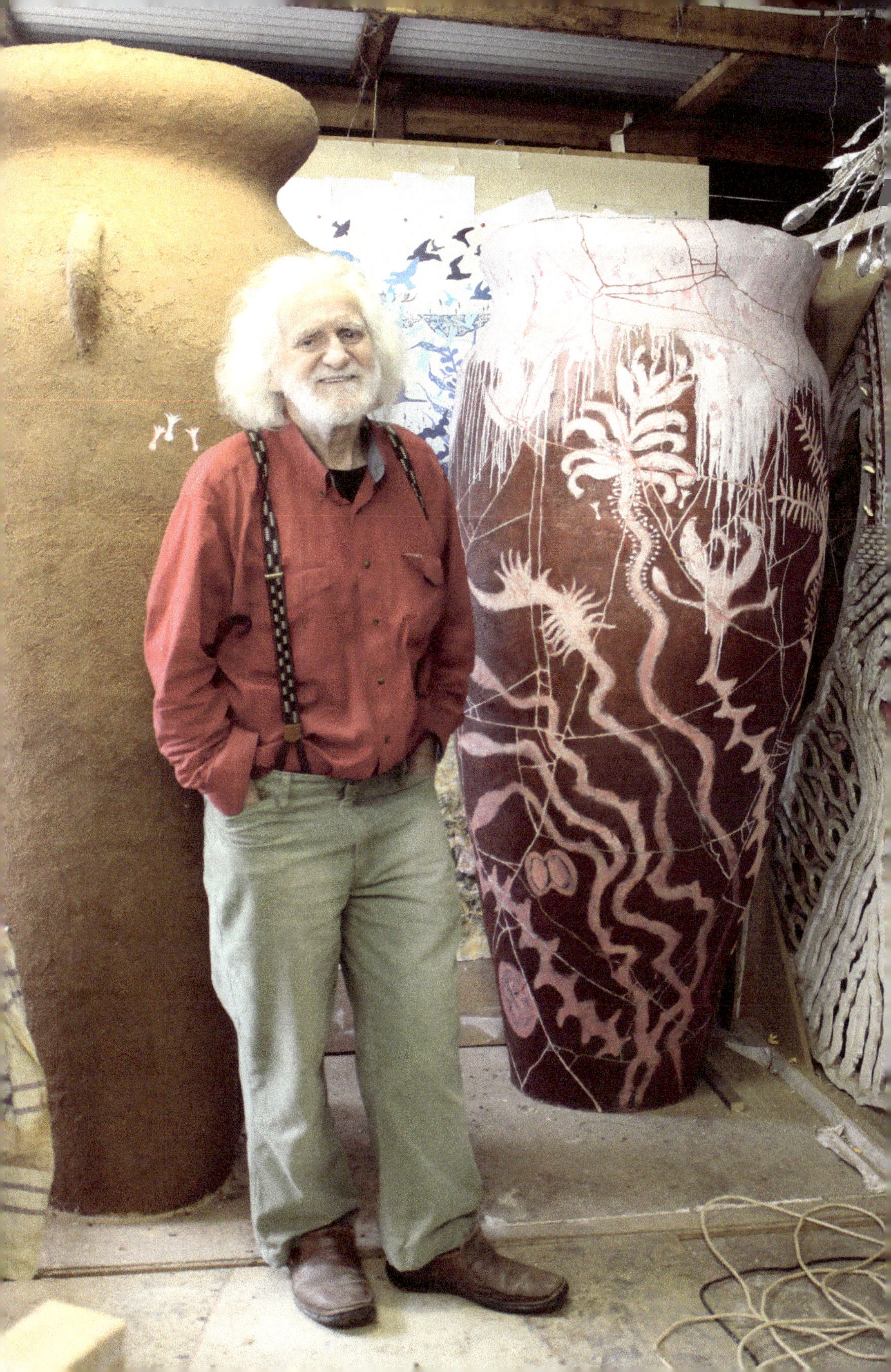

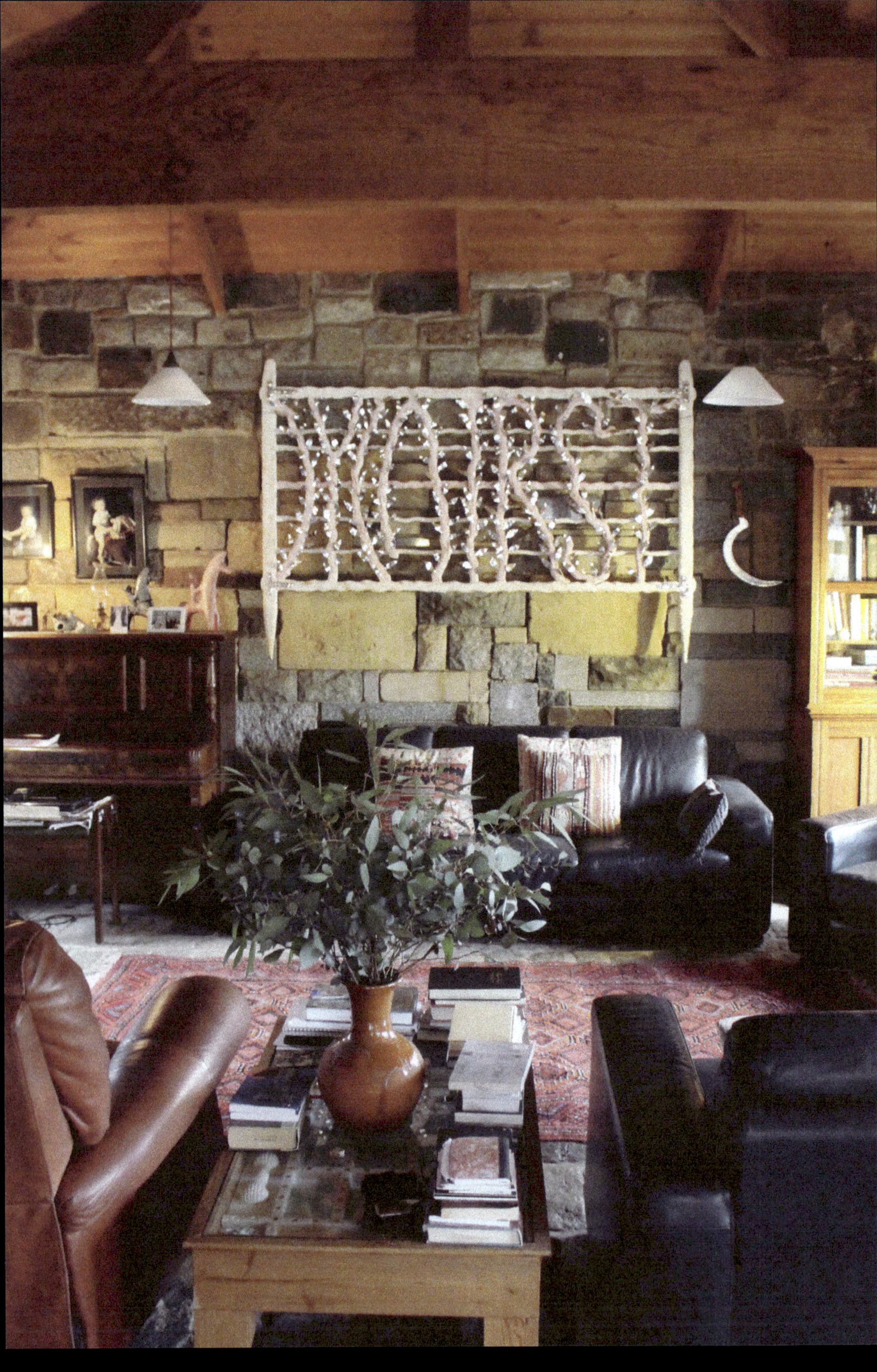

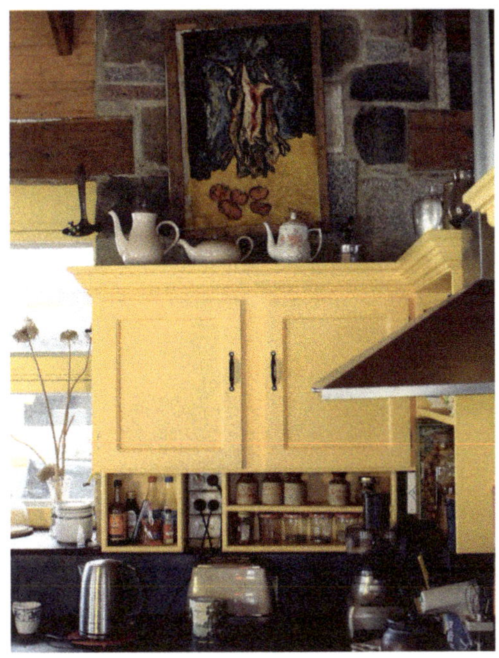

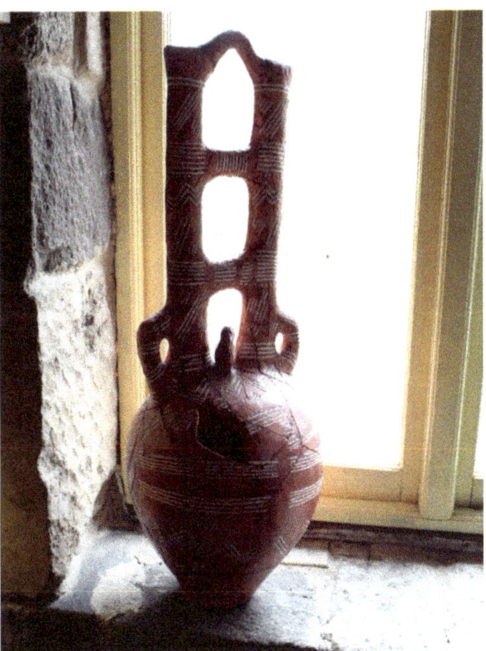

coal black. Yellow box are streaky white. Hot pink blossoms of flowering gums punctuate the green.

Inside Stanley and Lynda's home, there's nothing but warmth. Weighty stone walls radiate a woodfire's flame. There's a story in these stones. Stanley built the house using stone left over from the cathedral build in nearby Bendigo.

The English gothic Sacred Heart Cathedral is one of Bendigo's heritage treasures. The land it sits on was purchased in 1855, and construction began during the 1890s depression, giving many out-of-work miners an income. Work steadily continued until the mid-1930s, when it ceased for almost 20 years. War came and took many Bendigo sons with it. The cathedral build paled in comparison, and wasn't started again until 1953. The tall spire, with its human-sized gargoyles, finally completed the church in 1977. A year after Stanley and Lynda landed in the area.

"There were tonnes and tonnes of stone left over from the build and it was being tipped all over the place and used as fill," Stanley says. "I asked the monsignor if I could have some and he said I could take what I liked."

Stanley lifted each stone by hand and carted them by trailer and EH Holden back to the bush. For years. It was a slow, laborious, labour of love. Much like the cathedral. Stanley says this house was 20 years in the making. "And it's still not finished," he laughs. What else would you expect from a tinkerer, a maker, a sculptor?

"I just like making things," Stanley says. "Making art is all I've ever done. Not for a living, I've had to work part time. I never expected to make money out of it."

Stanley's working life here was spent teaching art at La Trobe University for nine years, then at Bendigo TAFE for 18. He's retired from the paid work now, but never from the art. "I still get just as excited as I've always done when I have an idea or I'm working on something. It's just beautiful when I'm making something, it's very fulfilling. It takes all my thought and all my presence in that time. I can't imagine not doing it."

While the house is personalised with many of Stanley's pieces, the actual work happens in his studio, reached via a skinny track by the dam bank. It's an old guards van railway carriage that was picked up for $300 from the former Bendigo Railway Workshops in the 1980s. Stanley says a heap of the carriages came to Bendigo, and were snapped up as farm sheds and make-shift homes. "They were beautifully made, the timbers in them are beautiful."

It's like the Tardis in here. Narrow carriage doorways lead to a tacked-on space filled with over-sized Greek-style urns. Ancient Greece has long inspired Stanley. The island of Crete is a place he has returned to many times. "They're very exciting things. They went up to about six foot in Crete and were used to store olives and wine in the palaces," he says of the urns. He made these from wood, coated with acrylic, then painted. "They're like a ship inside, they're ribbed. They were very difficult to make but I wanted to solve the problem of making them."

Stanley's last exhibition 'Nests in the Bronze Age' at Woodbine Gallery was developed from an artist residency at the British Archaeological School in Crete, where he became aware of Cyprian ceramics for the first time. The exhibition of drawings and sculptures, inspired by the Cyprian Bronze Age, playfully invested the antique with new life by incorporating virtual nests and eggs.

"I'm making a lot of work around the idea of books at the moment. My next exhibition will be about books." Reading is another of Stanley's loves. "Poetry is the main thing I read," he says. "It's very important to me. Reference to poets feature in a lot of the work I've done." Lovely words feature in his studio, too. Photocopied pages of stanzas are hanging by bulldog clips to catch the eye. Like *A Quiet Normal Life* by American poet Wallace Stevens.

It was here. This was the setting and the time
Of year. Here in his house and in his room,
In his chair, the most tranquil thought grew peaked

"I like to get to know them by heart and that's a good way to do it," Stanley says of the pegged-up poems on his studio walls.

Playing with words is another theme of Stanley's work. Nowhere is this more evident than in his Poetbureau. A whimsical, marvellous urn-shaped chest dedicated to poetry. Stanley was moved to make the piece after learning about the Politbureau in communist Russia; a seven-member supreme policy-making authority of feared men such as Stalin, Lenin, Trotsky and Bibnov. "I thought to counteract the Politbureau, we needed a Poetbureau. A department of poets. It contains 99 of my favourite poets." Gentle names including Pablo Neruda, Ezra Pound, Emily Dickinson and Banjo Patterson. Each tiny drawer contains a poem, gently folded.

It's a fitting place, on the whole, for the world's great creatives.

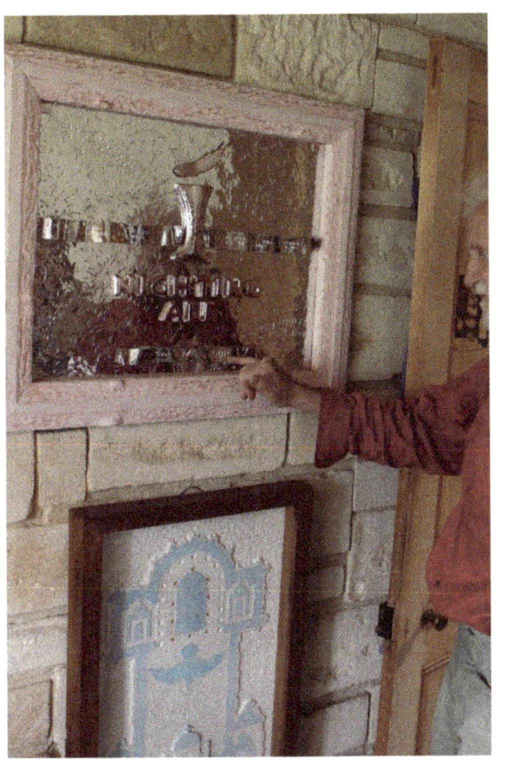

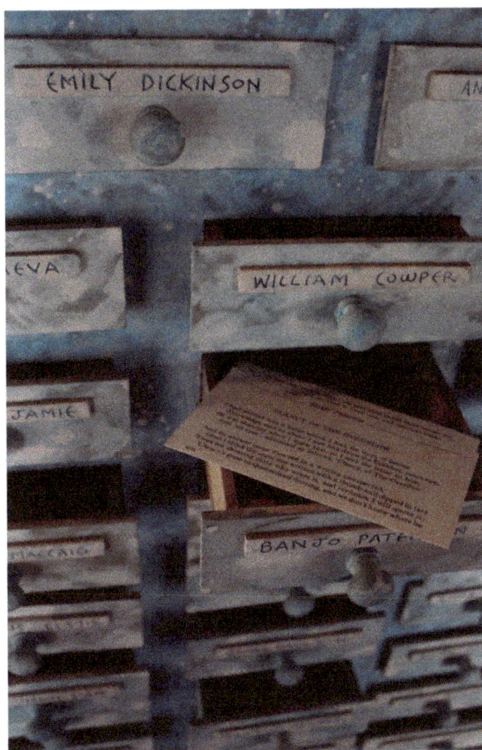
EMILY DICKINSON
WILLIAM COWPER
JAMIE

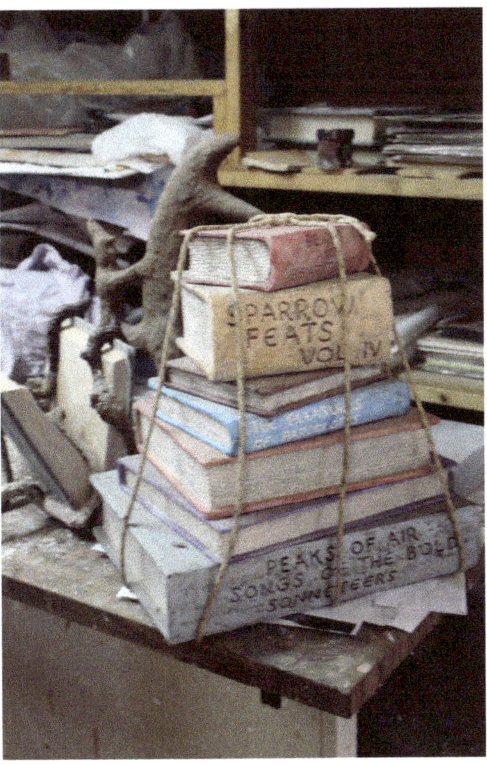
SPARROW FEATS VOL IV
PEAKS OF AIR
SONGS OF THE BOLD SONNETEERS

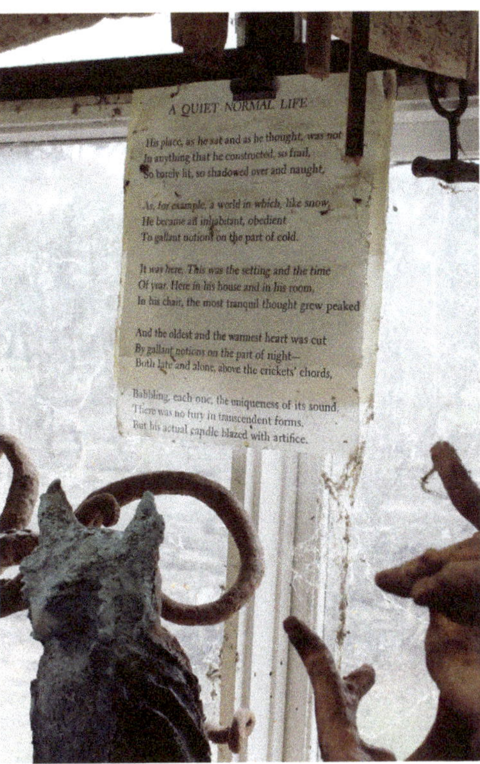
A QUIET NORMAL LIFE
His place, as he sat and as he thought, was not
In anything that he constructed, so frail,
So barely lit, so shadowed over and naught,
As, for example, a world in which, like snow,
He became an inhabitant, obedient
To gallant notions on the part of cold.
It was here. This was the setting and the time
Of year. Here in his house and in his room,
In his chair, the most tranquil thought grew peaked
And the oldest and the warmest heart was cut
By gallant notions on the part of night—
Both late and alone, above the crickets' chords,
Babbling, each one, the uniqueness of its sound.
There was no fury in transcendent forms.
But his actual candle blazed with artifice.

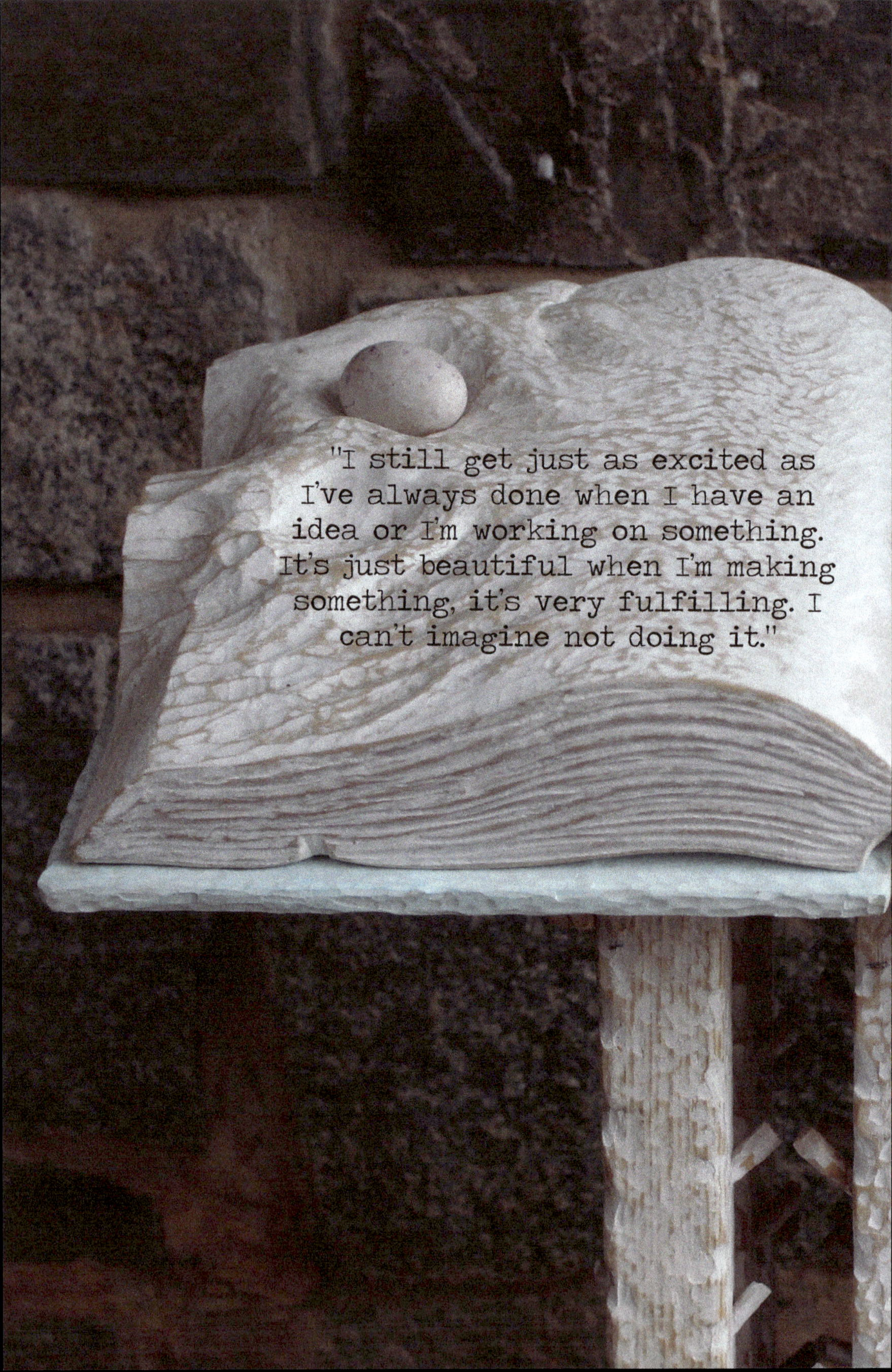
"I still get just as excited as
I've always done when I have an
idea or I'm working on something.
It's just beautiful when I'm making
something, it's very fulfilling. I
can't imagine not doing it."

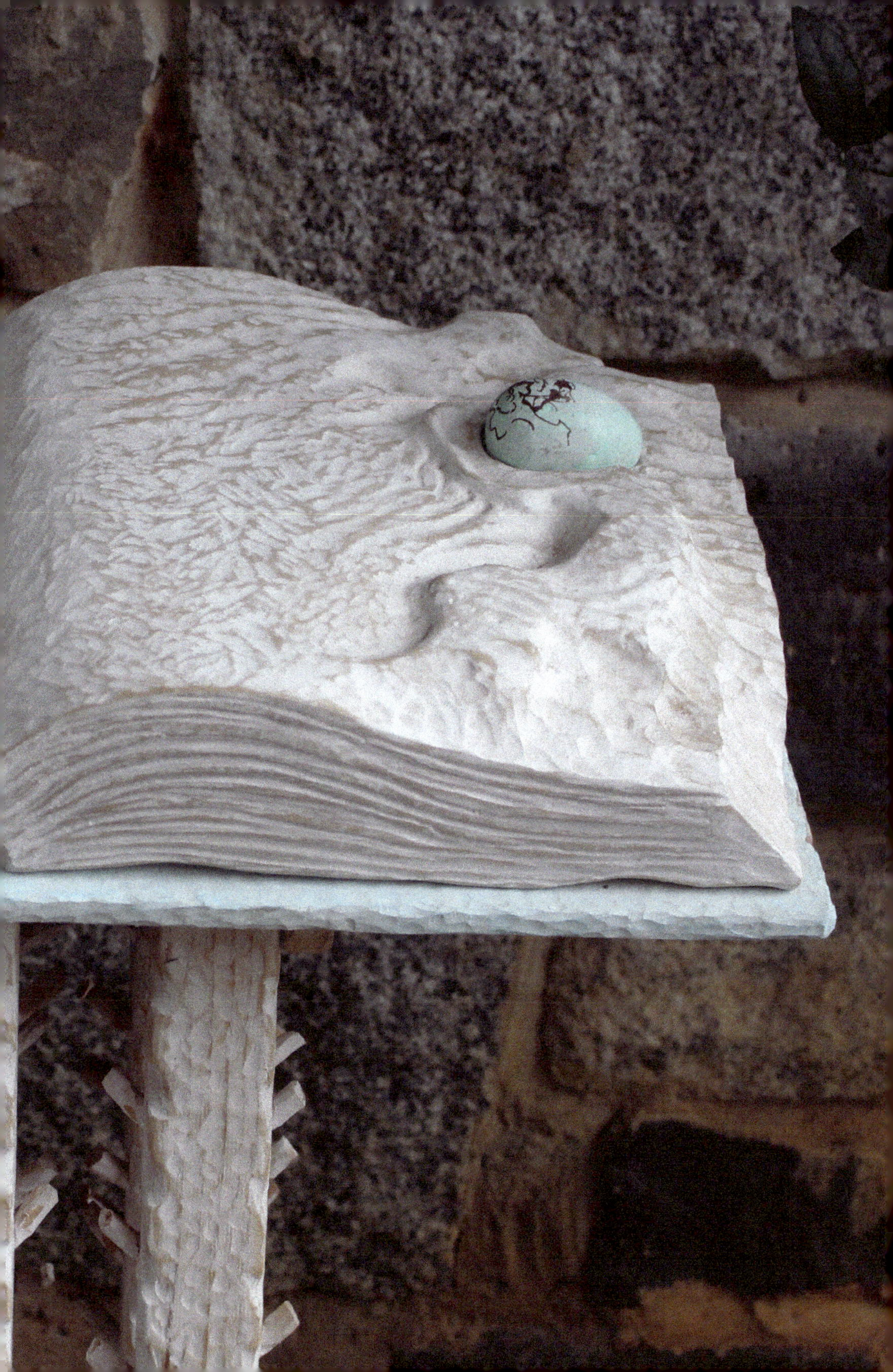

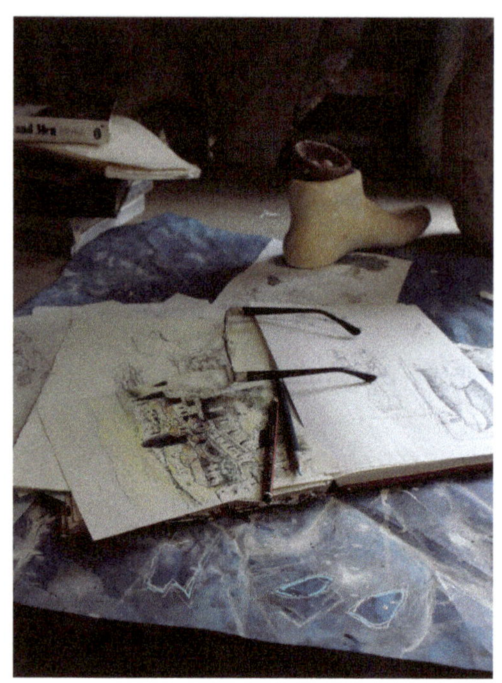

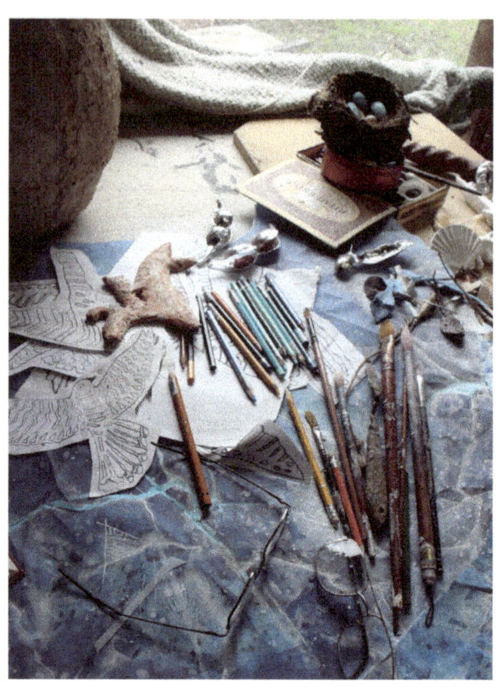

Narrow carriage doorways lead to a tacked-on space with oversized Greek-style urns.

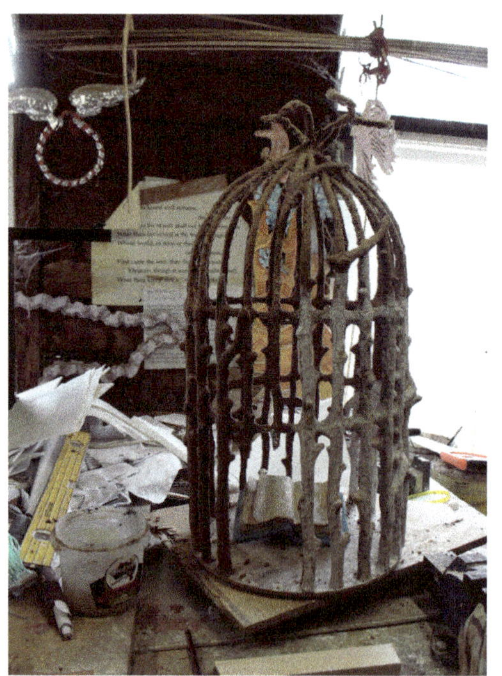

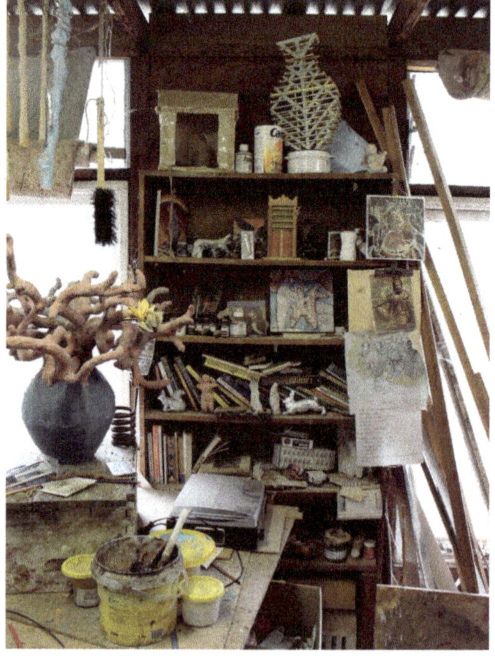

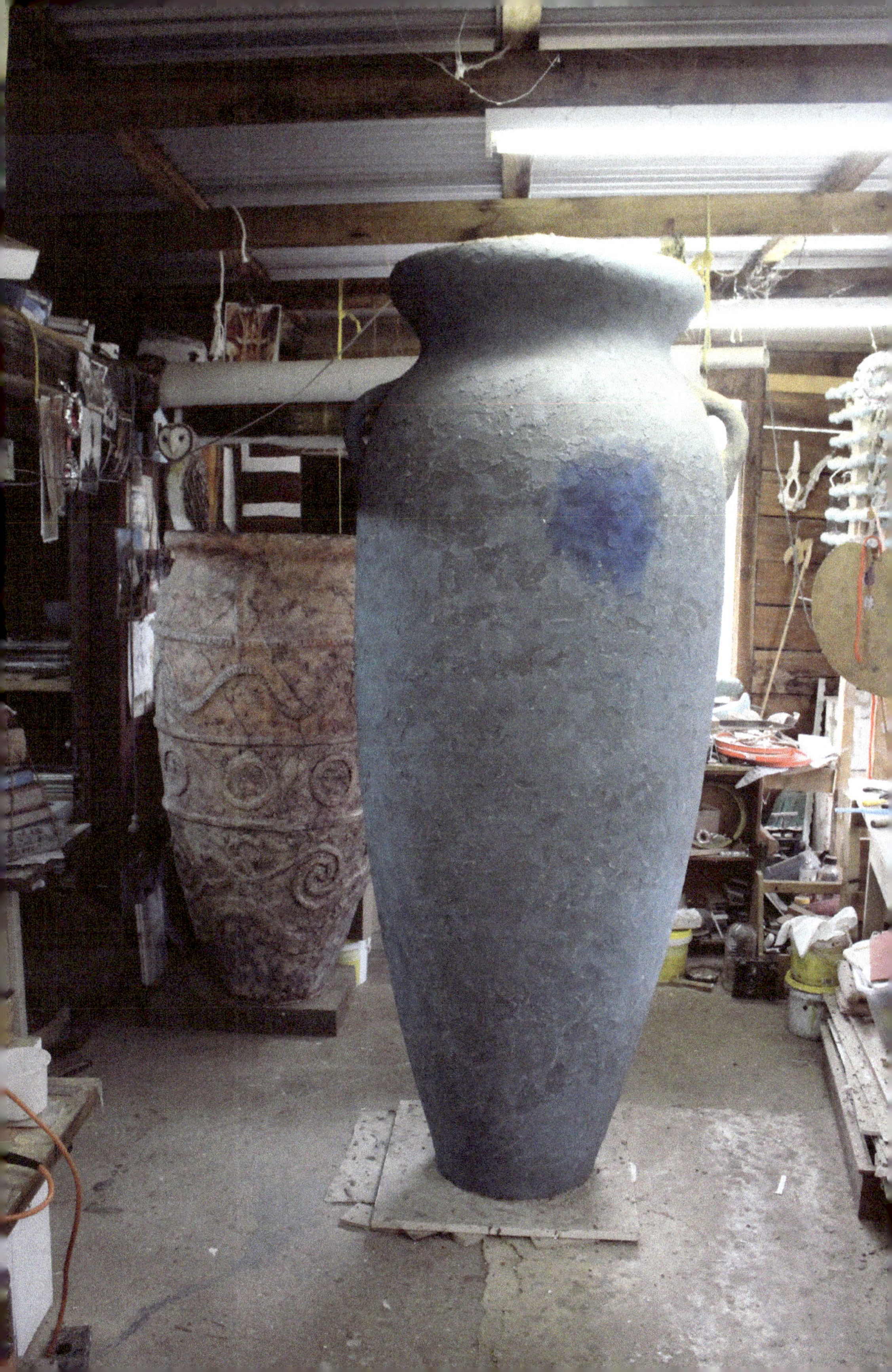

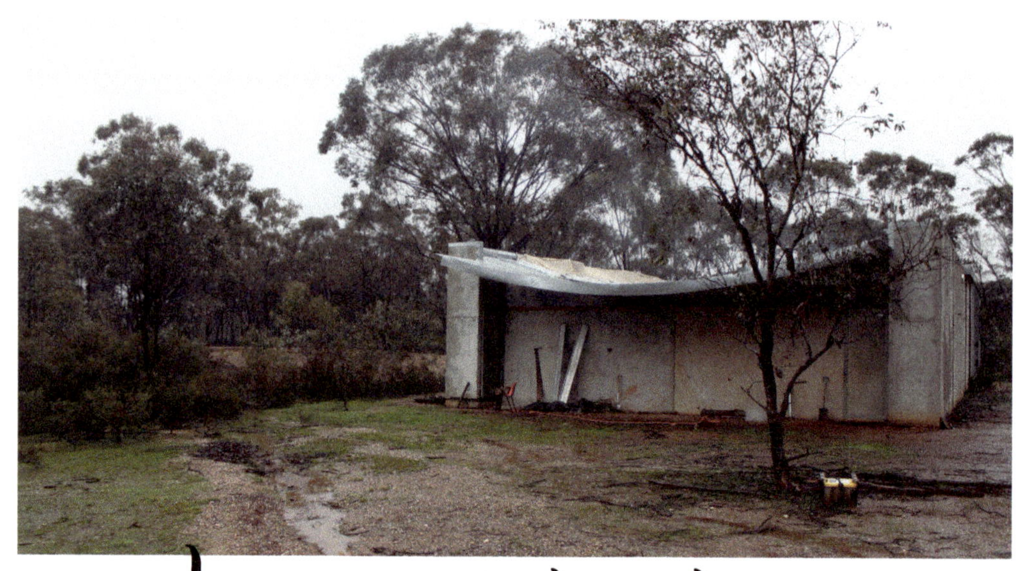

John Wolseley

The wobbly naturalist

The world is well familiar with wombats and koalas and kangaroos of Australia. But what of the mangrove worm? "Have you ever eaten one?" asks John Wolseley. "They're an absolute delicacy in Arnhem Land. It's a giant grub that makes amazing channels through wood. It's actually a batty kind of shellfish with a long, worm-like body and two shells at its head working like an excavating machine. It's such an effective creature."

Evidence of the mangrove worm's industrious ways can be found in John's Whipstick Forest studio. He picks up a curved piece of wood, the underbelly a ribbed warren of thick wriggly tracks. The wood was found in an Arnhem Land swamp on one of John's recent travels. It's a long way from home here. It's journeyed all the way from the north-east corner of the Northern Territory, down through the country in John's Landcruiser truck, to be welcomed into this concrete fold of fantastic natural wonders.

"I'm very much a wobbly naturalist," John says. "When I'm painting I see my job as an artist to show how nature works. In order to do that you have to know how all these fascinating things operate."

John takes his lessons from the source. From spending months at a time living under a canvas roof, sleeping in his truck, living among the Yolŋu people of Arnhem Land. The gifts of his travels are everywhere here. Map drawers house collected specimens. Wasp and termite nests, kingfisher and pardalote corpses lie

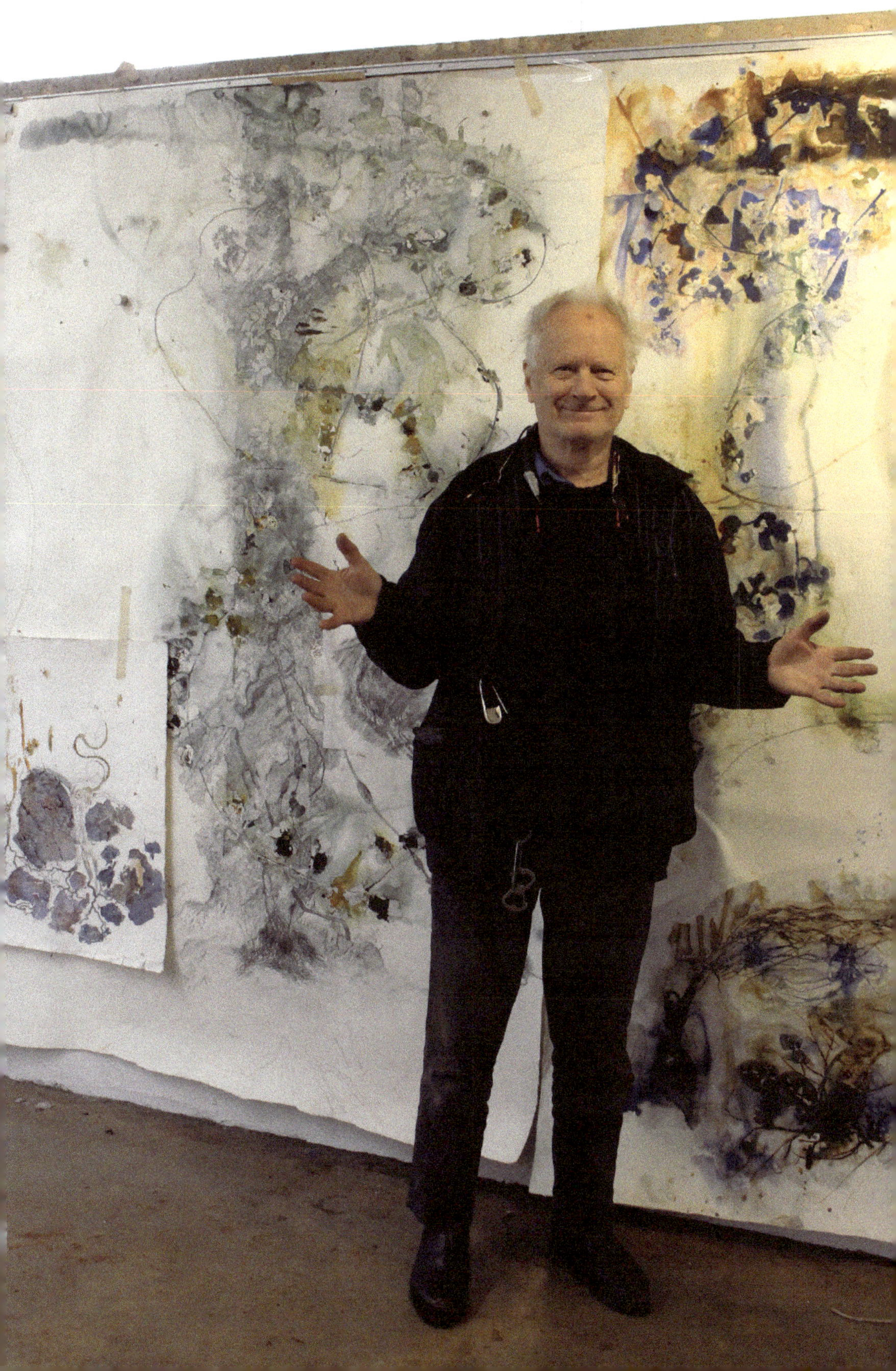

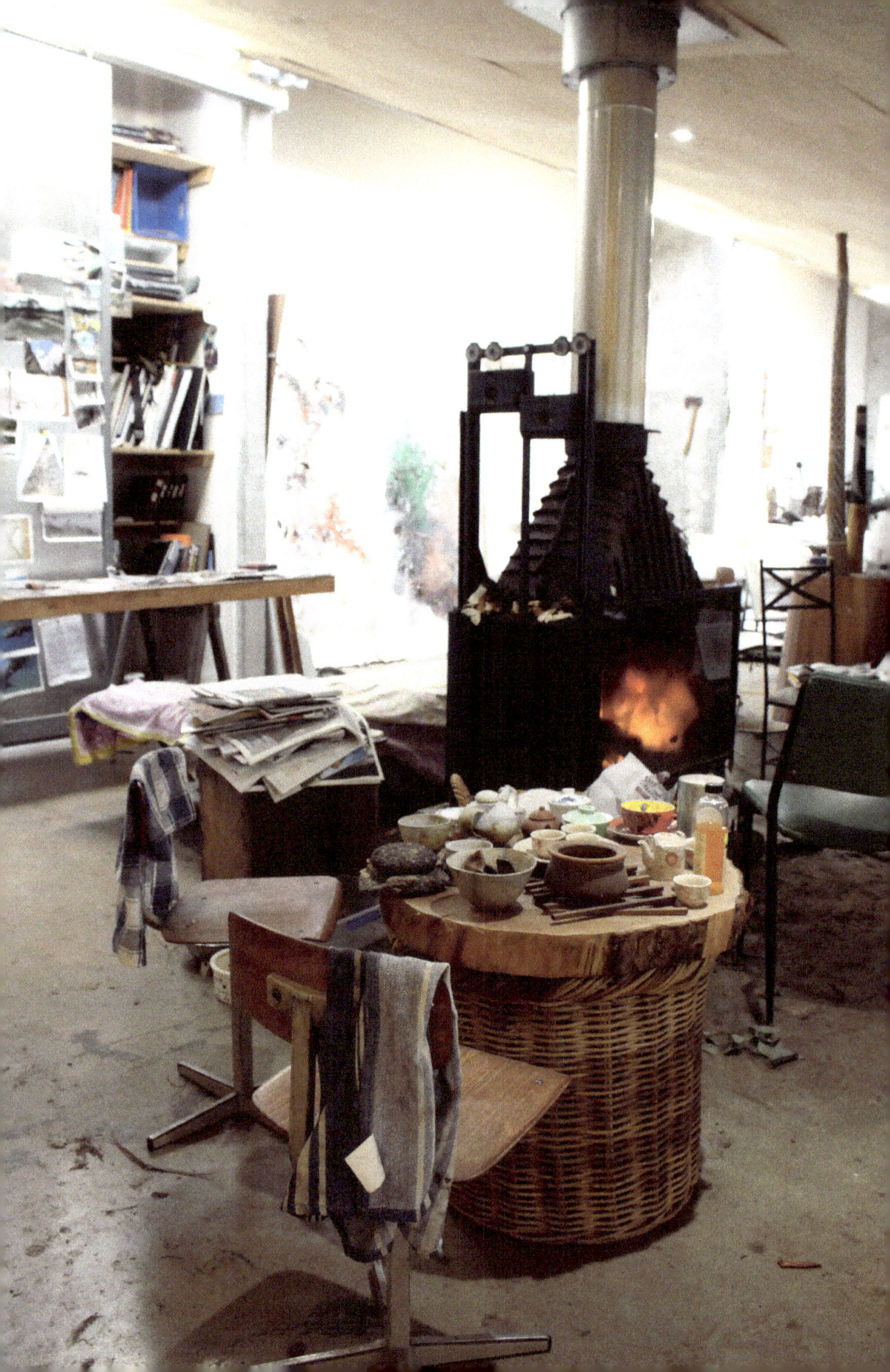

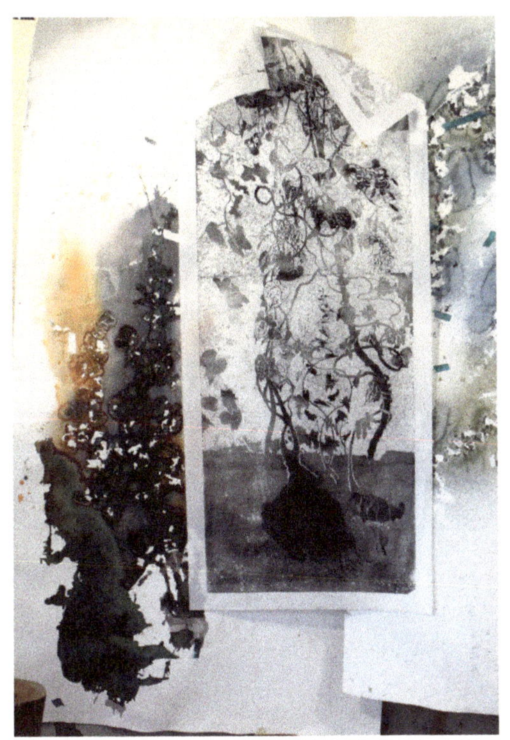 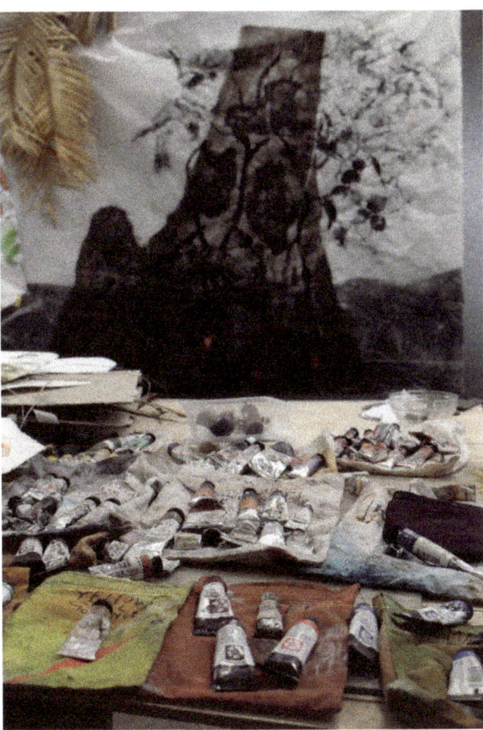

among pots of paintbrushes. Some Indigenous funerary poles lean against a wall. A living yam vine borrows warmth from the glass wall of a central atrium. "It's slightly mad," John says of the space.

This studio was purpose-designed for him more than 20 years ago. "I got the slowest builder in the world to make this. It took him 20 years. It was designed by a famous architect and that's why it's sort of amazing. That's also the trouble. If you get a bloody famous architect, you don't get it on time."

He was a mate of John's, and he had free rein. "Because I knew he was rather amazing I said, what would you do?" To the untrained eye, he designed a massive concrete bunker, with a dramatic low slung ceiling. "The shape refers to the fact that I've spent a lot of my life under canvas," John says.

"It's given me a place where I can bring back huge sheets of paper I've been doing art on from far flung places. It's given me wonderful walls which I can assemble them on. It's also given me a kind of base in what I call the 'other end of the mallee'. The mallee is my home and the chief thing I paint in a way. This is a wonderful base in my favourite country."

John was born in England in 1938. He studied art in London, then worked at print workshops in London and Paris. In the 1960s he moved to his ancestral home in the west of England and founded Nettlecombe Studios, a collective for artists and farmers. After travels through Spain and Borneo, he made his way to Australia, in 1976.

John first came to Bendigo in the 1980s as an artist-in-residence at the local arts college. "I visited Stanley Farley next door, who was teaching there at the time. He took me on a walk through the forest and I found this shack. Stanley said he thought it was for sale, so I bought it. I sort of fell in love with the Whipstick. I realised it's an incredibly unusual, beautiful forest if you know how to look at it."

John agrees not everyone does. "Some call it bush burial country," he says. Bendigo author Dianne Dempsey committed its views and vices to paper in the novel *Girls in Our Town*. She writes; "The Whipstick is harsh, sandstone country with little water, covered by a dense mass of box-ironbark, mallee eucalyptus, wattle and dodder-laurel vines. In the early days of the gold rush, these parasitic vines were so pervasive they created huge webs in which the diggers would often become lost and caught like flies, they suffered desperate, lonely deaths.

"But before the diggers there were the Dja Dja Wurrung people, and before them there were the spirits – ghost creatures – who were disturbed when the miners sunk their shafts and dug their tunnels."

John's goldfields-themed artwork features on the book's cover. His words feature on the back. "...the Whipstick Forest is full of toughness and beauty. It is harsh, rich and resilient – hard to get to know and impossible to leave." He feels its spirit.

Capturing the energy of the natural world is at the heart of his work. "I start off by going to a place and trying to find my way into it. I collaborate with the actual plants and rocks and sometimes animals to make the painting."

The works-in-progress stuck to lofty steel walls with magnets show the process, in a medley of watercolour, collage, drawing and nature printing; some works have actual plants still clinging to paper. "I'm saying to the plant, 'let's you and I try to narrow the gap between the artist and plant and let's go and make these things'. The physical nature of the plant, aided by curious stuff called 'retention fluid', makes the paper accept the gift from the flower. Then I do lots and lots of drawings. Traditional drawings. You might even say it's anal retentive."

The finished pieces John calls "abstracted things about energy and the way plants and animals work". One of the works on the walls here incorporates Charles Darwin's diagram to explain power and movement in plants. It's no surprise to hear Darwin is somehow distantly related to the artist.

As he speaks John is working on a new body of work with his 'sister', the great Yolŋu artist Mulkun Wirrpanda, in which they are both painting the same plant species from different perspectives. Part of John's 20-metre contribution is taking up one wall in the studio. Once finished, it will be shown in the National Museum in Canberra, with Mulkuns' 130 bark paintings. "It's all about the flood plain in Arnhem Land, and features all the edible plants," John says. Such as the yam, a tropical plant precariously growing by the window here in a Victorian winter.

"Here is a yam," John says. "It has huge sacred significance to the Yolŋu people and is absolutely delicious and here is a lino cut of it." He points out a picture stuck up beside the plant, no longer than a ruler. This tiny microcosm of a John Wolseley artwork says it all really.

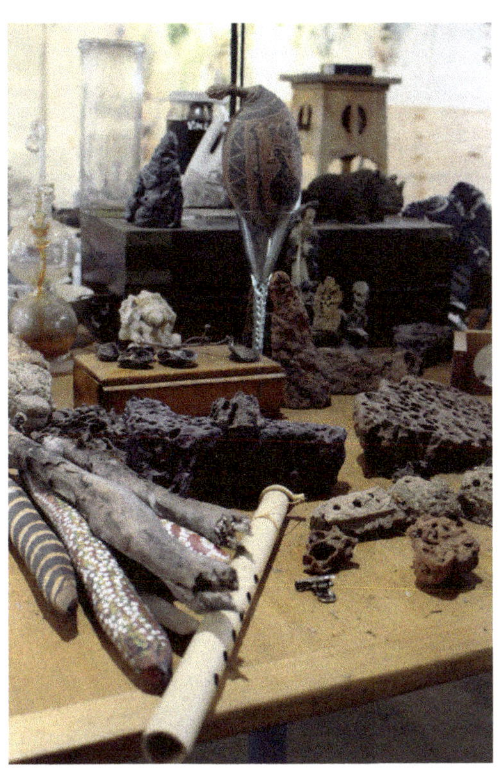

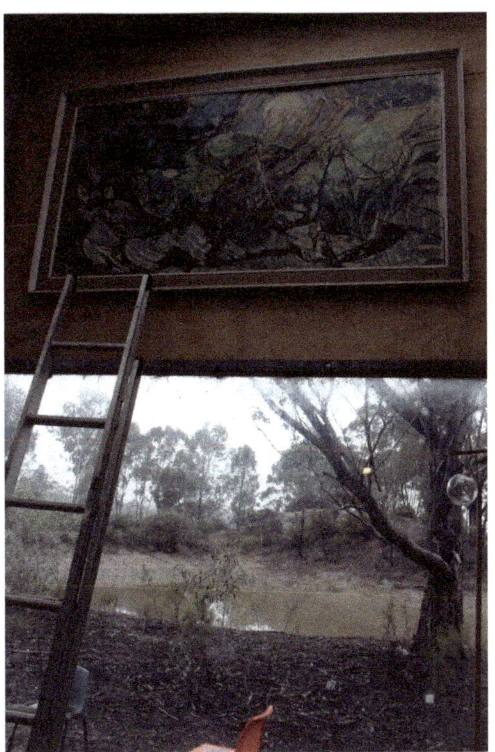

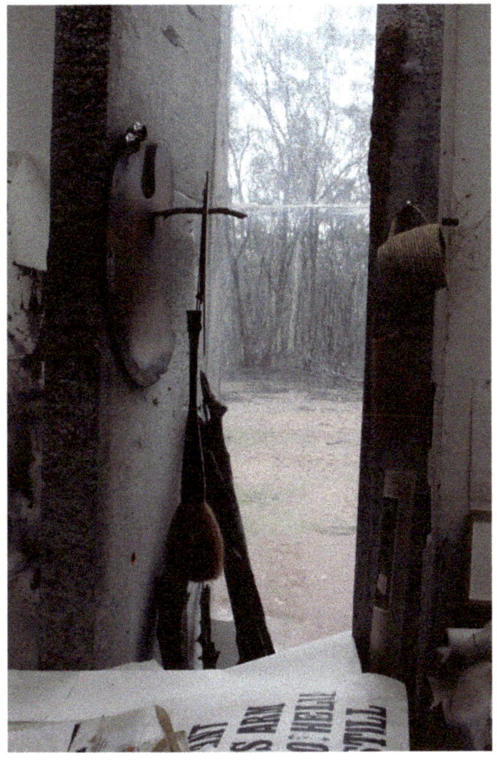

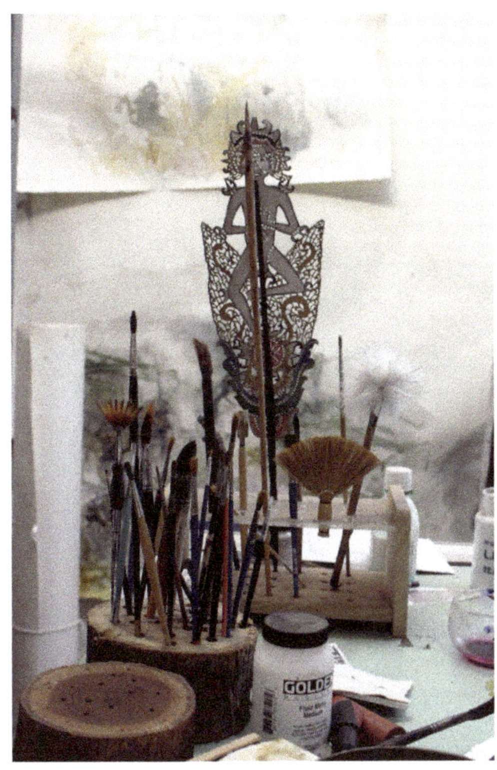

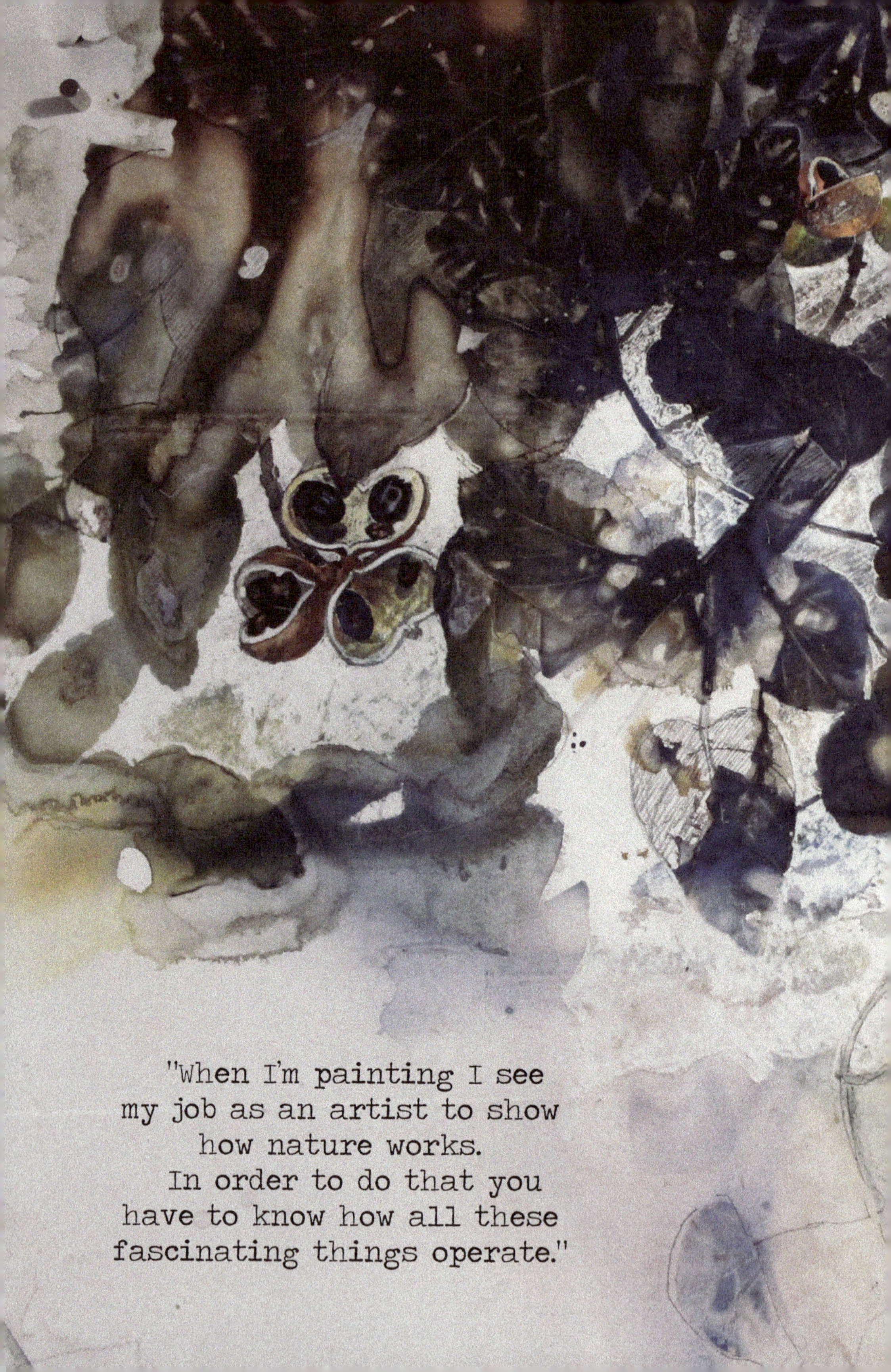

"When I'm painting I see
my job as an artist to show
how nature works.
In order to do that you
have to know how all these
fascinating things operate."

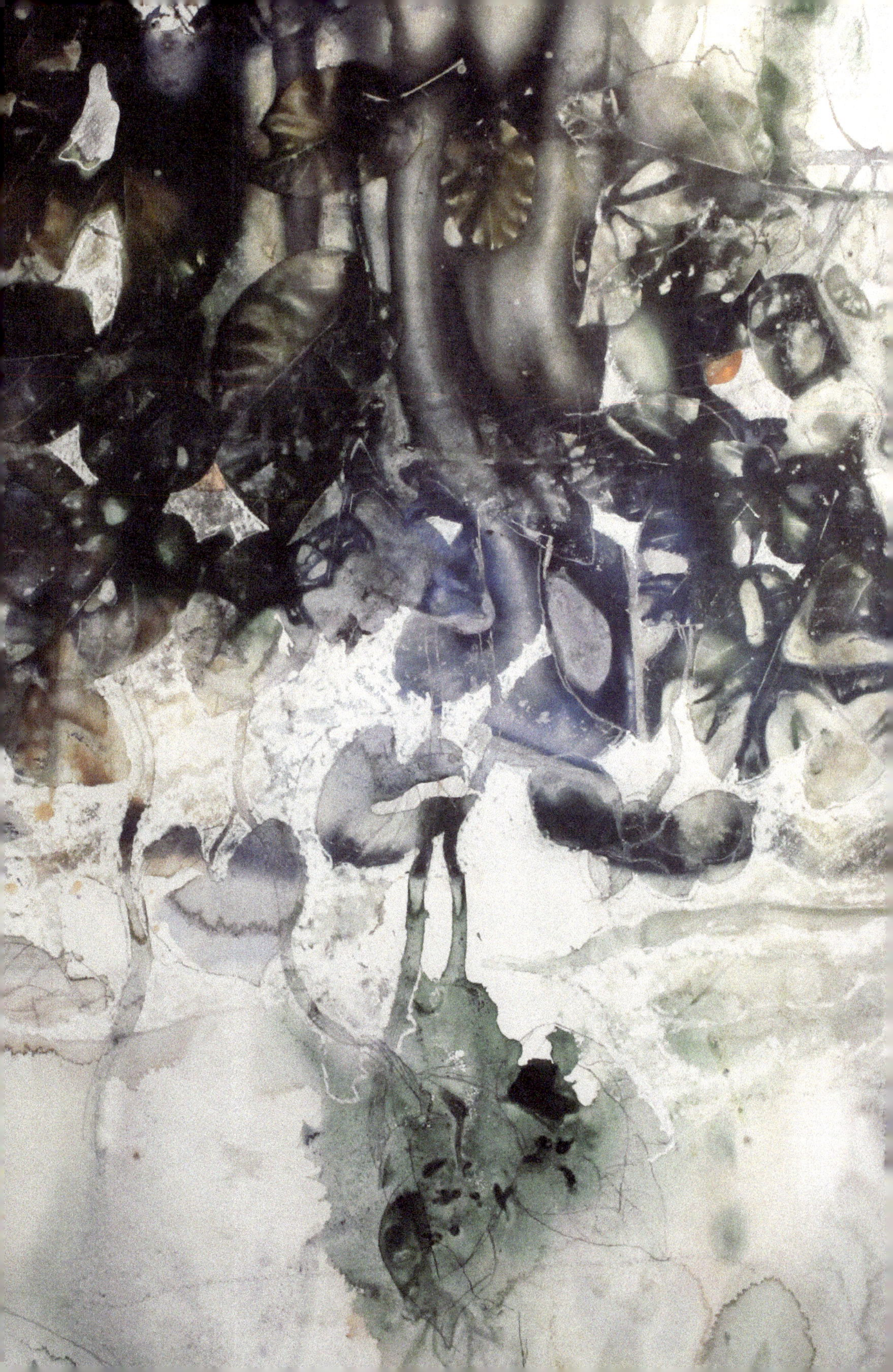

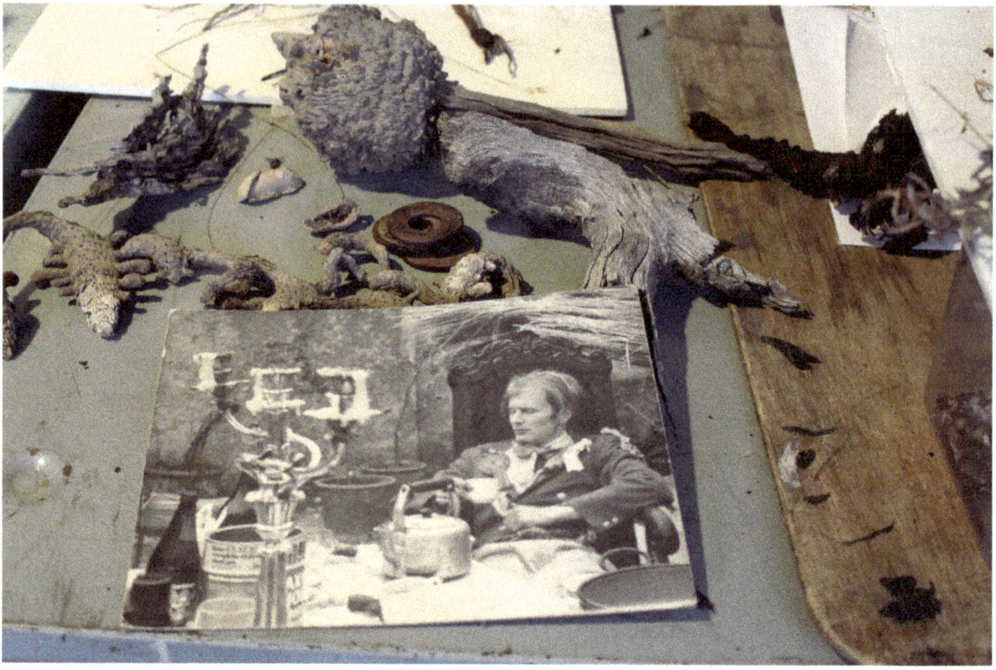

A living yam vine borrows warmth from the glass wall of a central atrium.

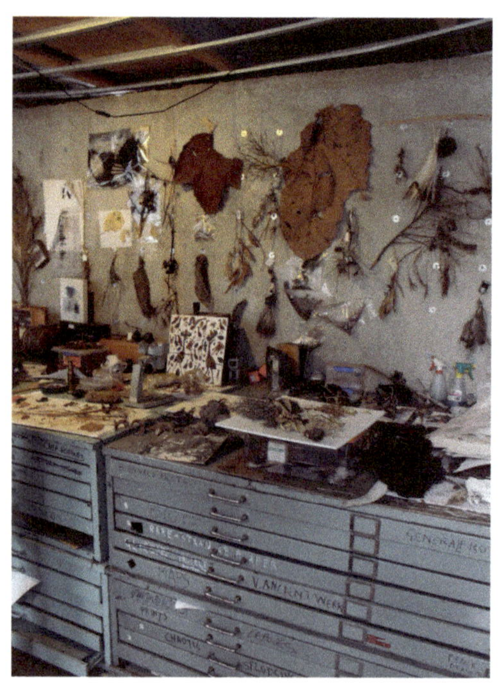

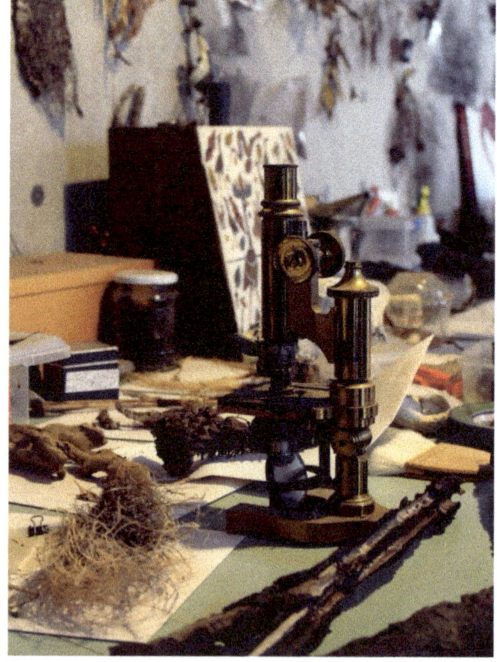

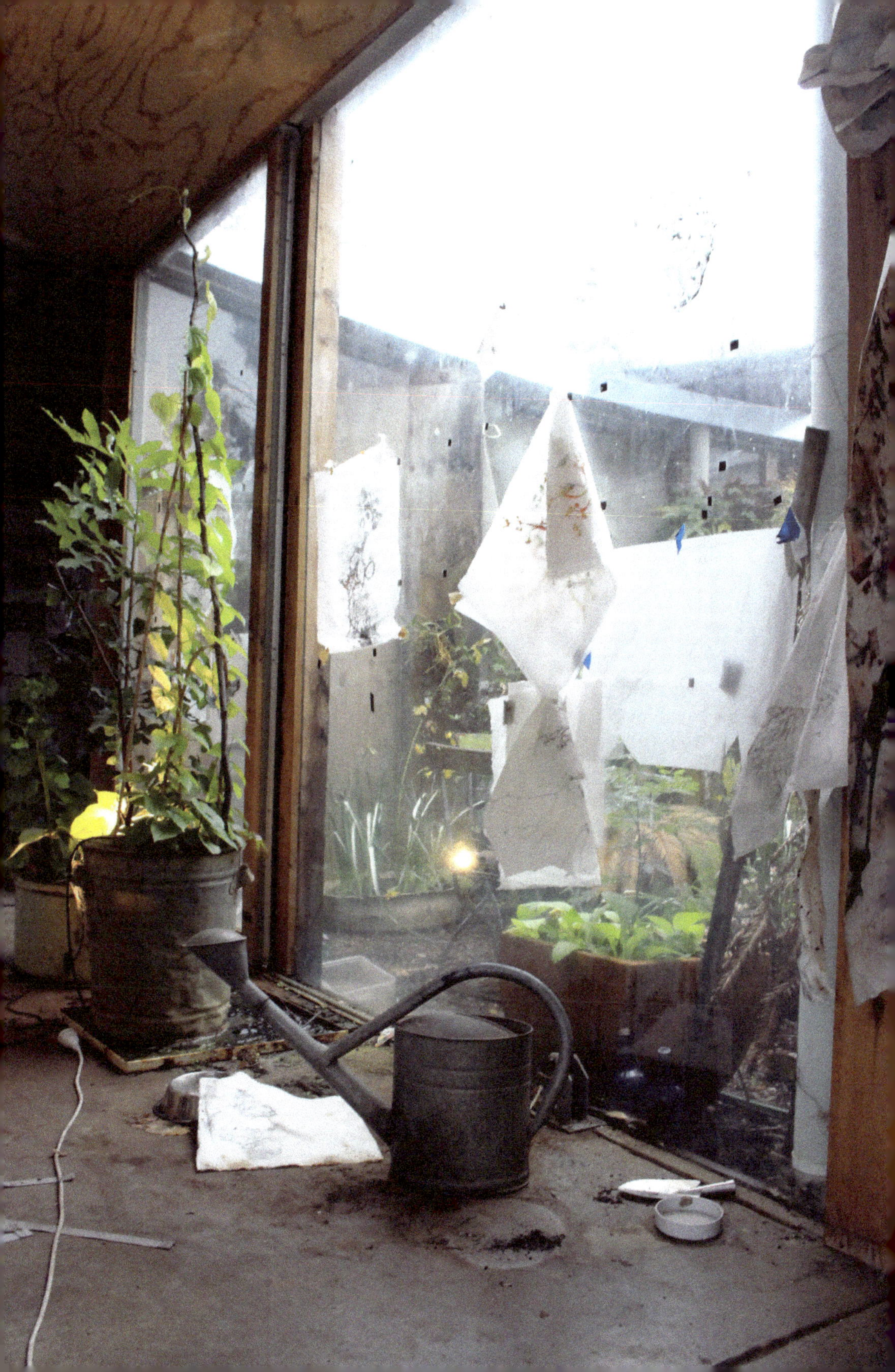

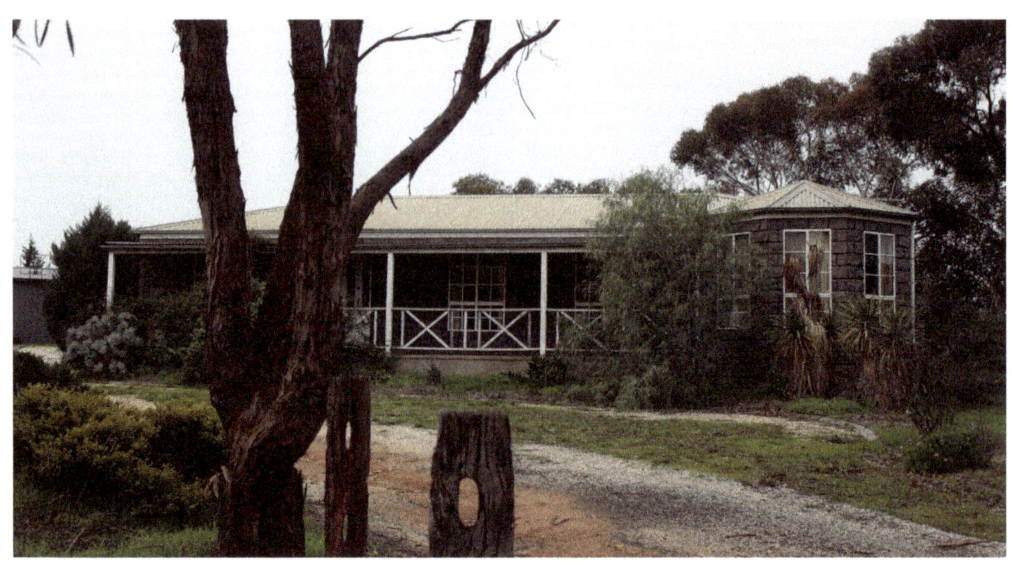

Carl Rolfe

Luck, fate & family

You've got to wonder; how much of life is guided by fate, and how much by design? How much by those who came before us, and how much by the elements?

Consider the horrific Black Saturday fires of summer 2009. The Bendigo fire started in bushland behind Carl Rolfe's bluestone house in Maiden Gully, then raged its way across suburbs to lick the city's edge. There but for the grace of a wicked easterly, Carl's lovely home would have been counted in the 50 lost that day. Not forgetting the one fatality. Instead, he watched it roar straight past him.

"It was 46 degrees and so, so windy," Carl says. "The speed at which the fire moved was incredible. I realised you can't outrun a fire. It tore up the gum trees and they exploded."

The drive to Carl and his wife Zerin's place passes by clusters of new homes, replacing those lost, and stands of defiant gums, sprouting anew. Those tough old ironbarks being engineered to burn, then regenerate.

Maiden Gully is often touted as lizard country. It's hard to get a thing to grow. But those trees prove otherwise. You've just got to know how to adapt out here.

For Carl and Zerin, it wasn't hard at all. "We're escapees from Melbourne," Carl says of their move in 2000. "One of the nice things about moving to the country was we could afford to buy a place. We didn't need to be at the mercy of landlords anymore. I'd never been to Bendigo before then, so it was a bit of a novelty turning up to this place with a truck-load of furniture.

"We're glad we moved. I think when we were in the city we tended to be much

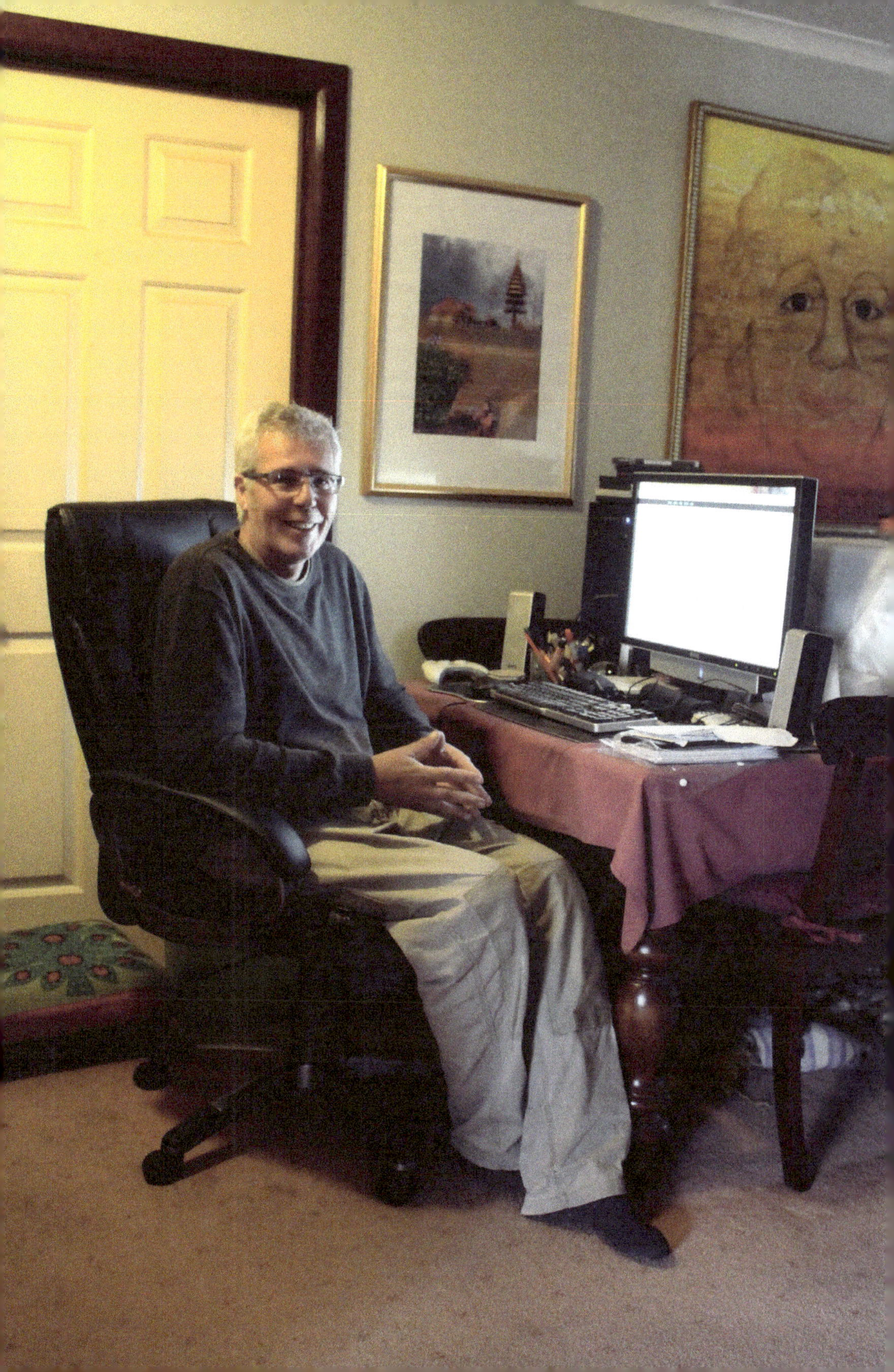

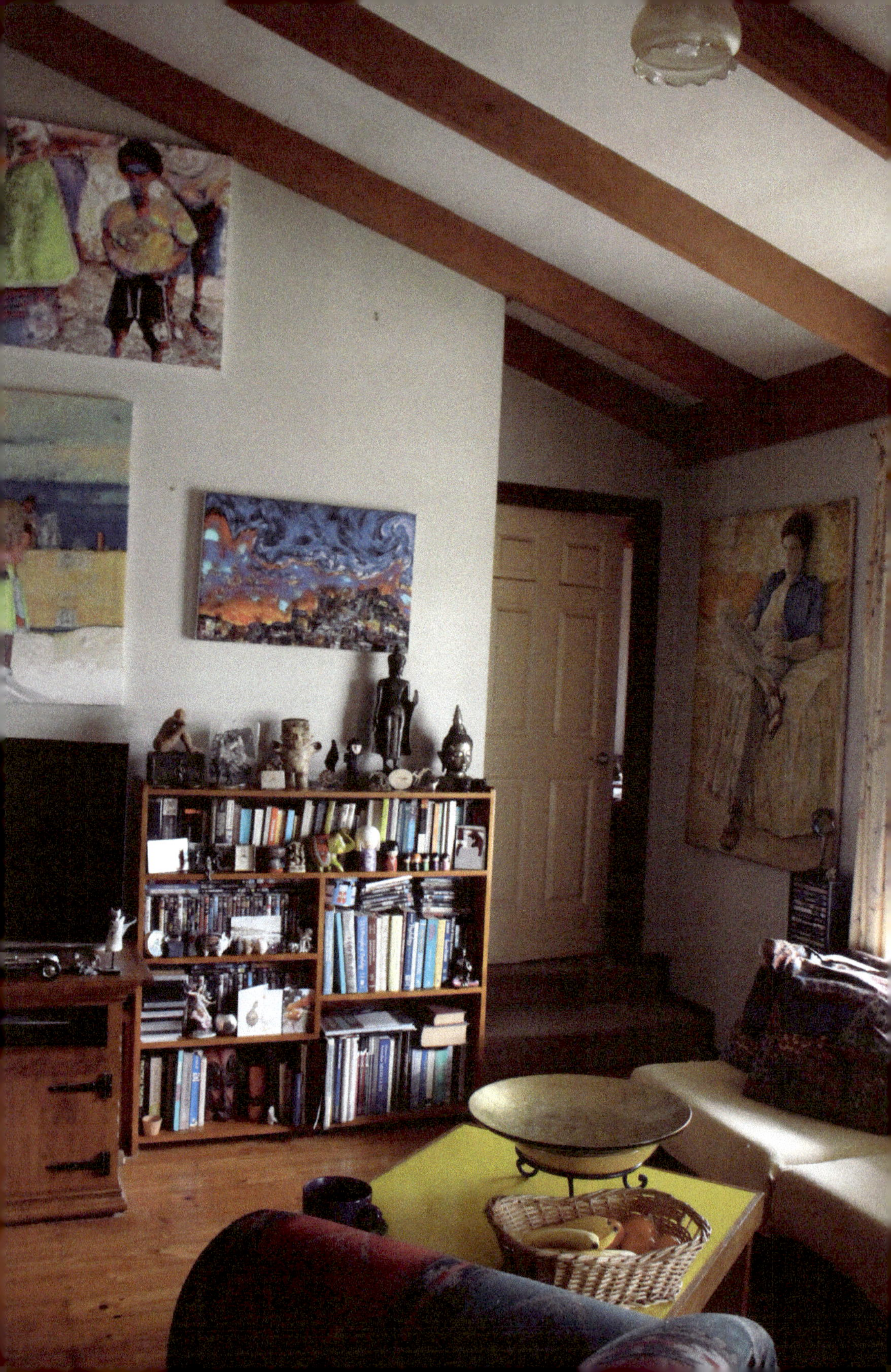

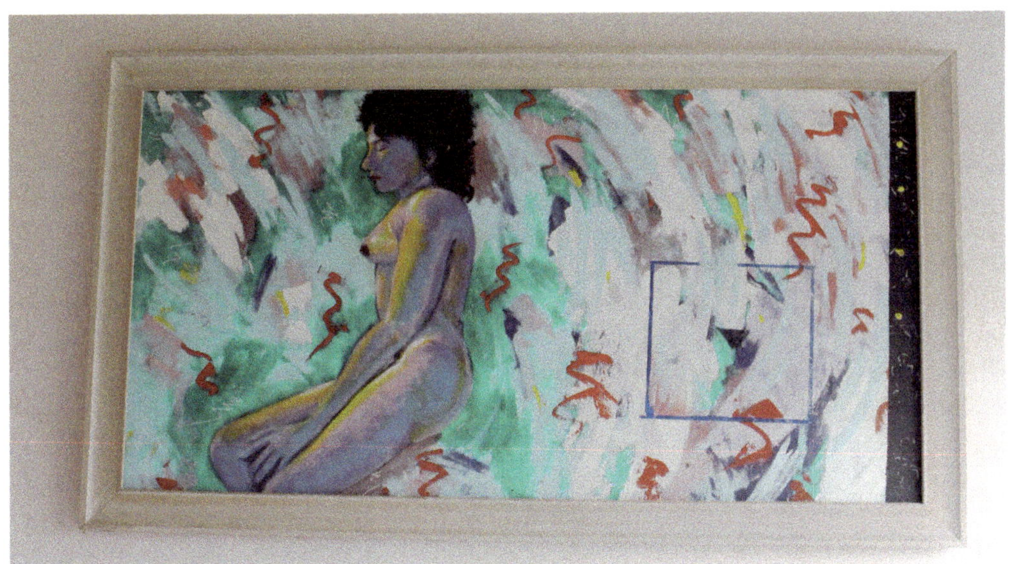

more stressed about everything. It's much easier to be relaxed here. It hasn't just changed my artwork, it's changed our whole lifestyle."

The couple went from a boxed-in life, surrounded by city chaos and views of neighbouring apartments, to the stone walls and soaring timber ceilings of this place. And beyond that, the Milky Way, weaving right across the top of the house. There's no light pollution here to mar the stars.

The works of art on the walls tell a story of Carl's progression as an artist. It's all he ever wanted to be, and given his family background, was wholeheartedly encouraged.

Carl's great-grandfather directed, wrote, acted in and produced early Australian films including what is considered the first feature film, *Robbery Underarms*. His mother is a respected and sought-after portrait painter who won the prestigious Portia Geach Portrait Prize in 1985. Carl says she has had the greatest influence on him. Today, her works hang alongside his in this home. Most notably the portrait she painted of Carl when he was 17 years young, all graceful limbs and completely at ease with posing for his mother.

"She's entering the Archibald again this year," Carl says. "She's 93. I've no doubt the thing that keeps her mind active is painting. Her body is frail but her brain works perfectly. One of the things about painting is you're constantly trying to solve little problems.

"My mother instilled in me a love of art and an endorsement of art as a valid way to live your life. As a child, I was supplied with the raw materials to create paintings and sculptures. I was also given an old Kodak Box Brownie, which was a wonderful camera for the time. I still have and treasure that little metal box.

"My father's parents forced him to be a teacher when he always wanted to be an architect. His attitude was he wasn't going to force his children to do anything we didn't want to. If I wanted to be an artist I should do it and believe in it. I was a lucky one. I was allowed to be free." His brother is a musician and his late sister was also an artist.

Carl studied fine art painting, photography and printmaking at the Canberra School of Art. "I started off with the obvious, going to art school and trying to support myself by painting. I found that difficult, as many artists do." He says he quickly discovered he needed to be a realist, so began working in graphic design by day, and painting by night.

Zerin describes him as being driven by art. She recalls her early years with Carl, in the late 1980s. They met when she was editing a magazine, and he was working on the graphics. "He'd work all day, get home, have dinner, then paint until two or three in the morning. He was driven. He was driven to say something..."

Many of his earlier works carried a message. "I've become less heavy-handed with environmental things," Carl says. "I kind of want to see the beauty in the world now. We see enough of the darker side of life. A lot of my early work was critical of society and it was much darker. But there's no need for me to express it now. Ultimately I'd like to do the most beautiful work possible. I like to show some part of human nature, but it's much brighter now."

His medium has changed, too. "The biggest change for me was going from using oils and acrylic on canvas to computer art. I just found it exciting again. I use lush rich colours on contemporary hand-painted digital canvasses. The unique methods I use have been developed through a love of experimentation.

"There is a resistance to computer graphics being considered fine art, but things are gradually changing. It's still making something by hand, it's just the medium has changed from canvas to computer screen."

Carl treats the finished works like screen prints, which are numbered, and the plates used to create them destroyed. He keeps an archival copy of his work, but often only one is ever produced. Finishing a work, placing an order and waiting for the canvas to arrive brings a feeling of anticipation often lacking in our world of convenience. But the wait is always worth it. "Before I open the package there's fear. But mostly, once I see the work, I feel wonderment. At what can be produced. At the colours."

It's a way of looking at the world that Carl carries with him. As he speaks, he has just returned from a trip to South America where he trekked in Peru and explored Machu Picchu. His life-affirming photographs of local people will serve as fodder for more artwork.

"I am mostly an optimist who loves to travel. Nature and man have created some truly magnificent sights in the world. At times I do battle to prevent myself from being overwhelmed by the negatives of the world – corruption, racism, injustice and greed. It's then that I force myself to refocus on beauty or use my art to express a burden of thought I carry. I've learnt that the common man is inherently good, and the less people have, the more generous they can be."

A quote comes to mind from the American Leo Burnett: "Curiosity about life in all of its aspects, I think, is still the secret of great creative people." Perhaps that is the greatest guide of all?

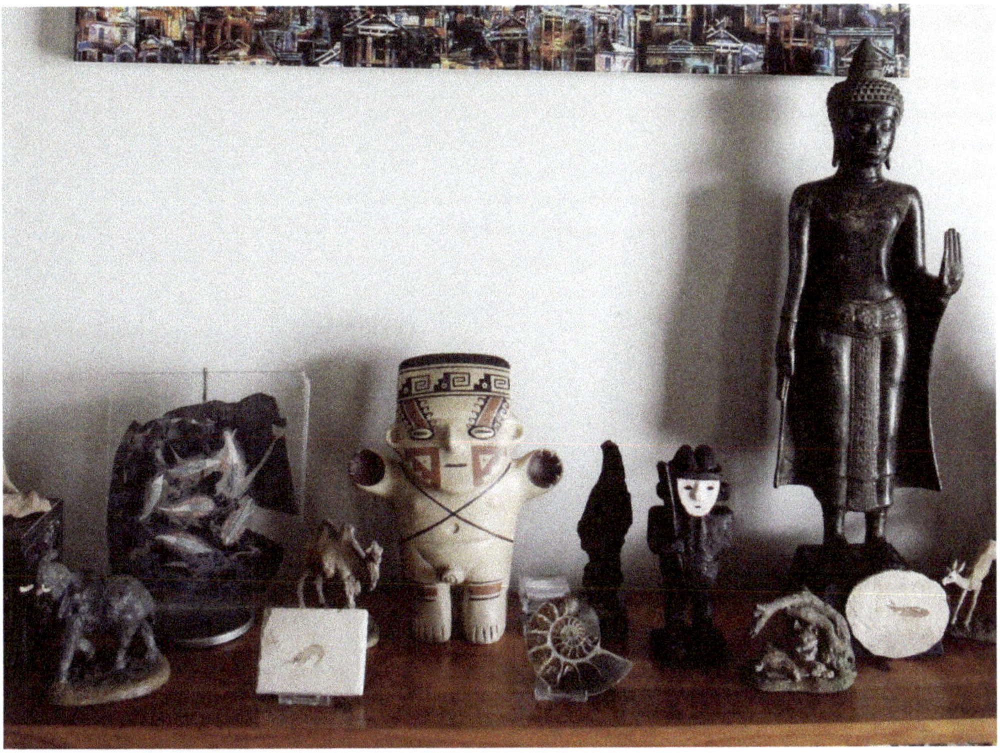

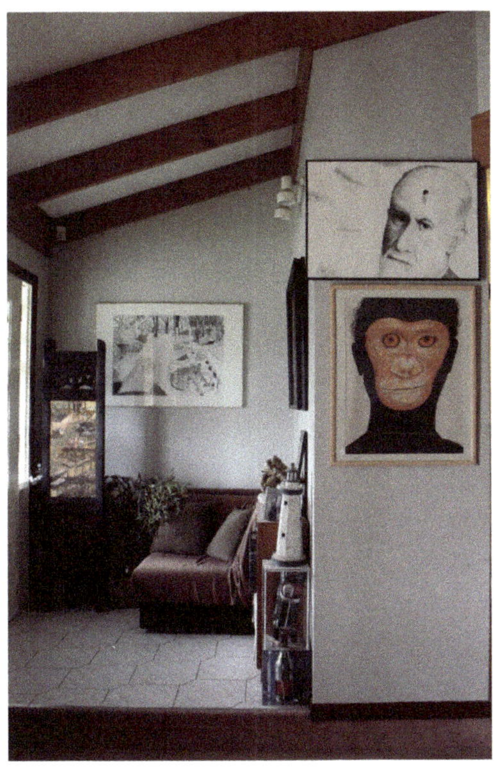
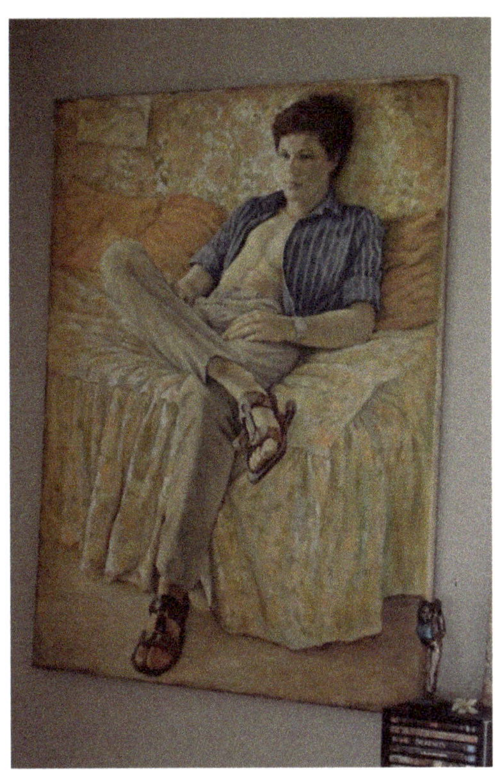

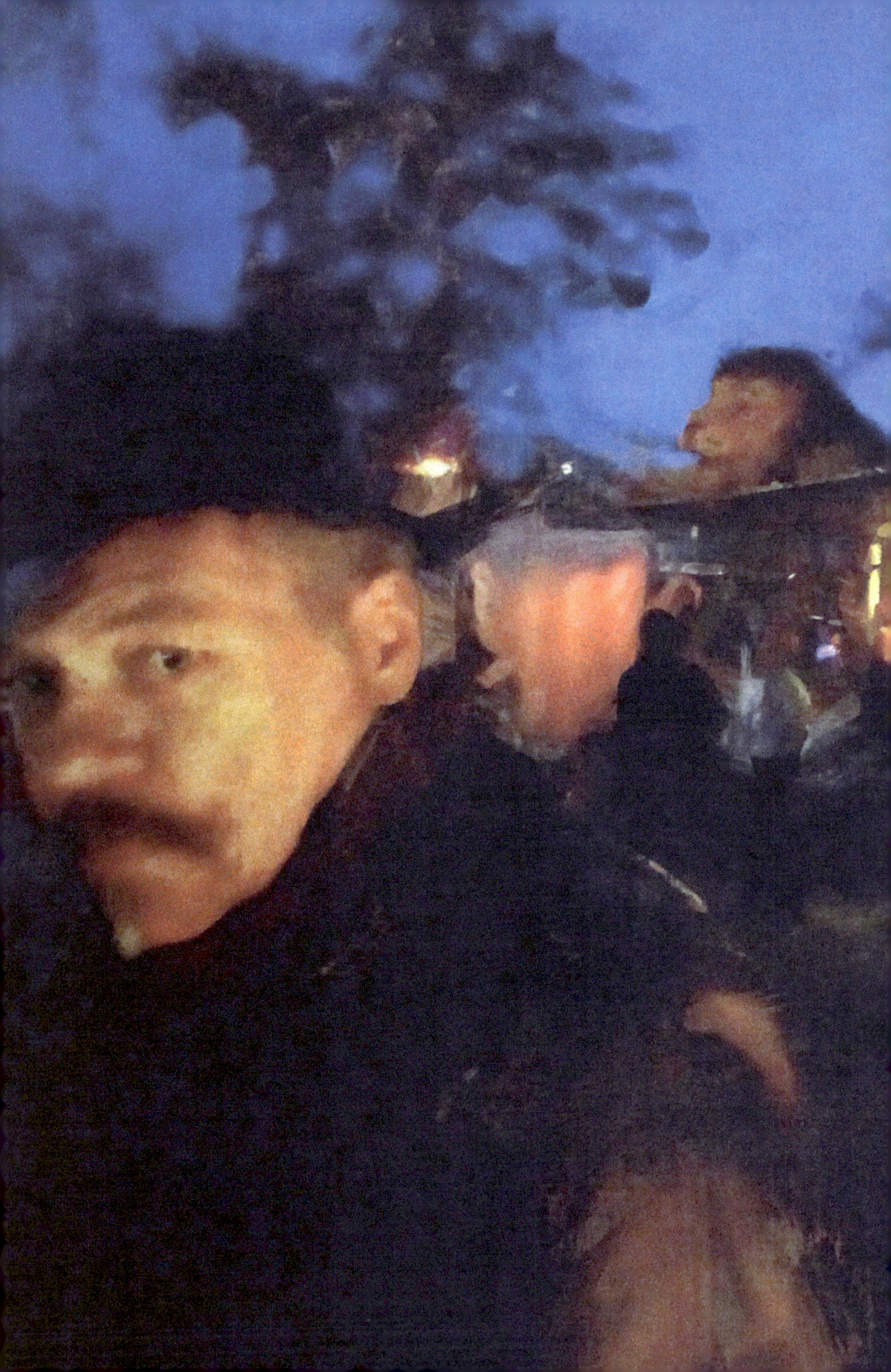

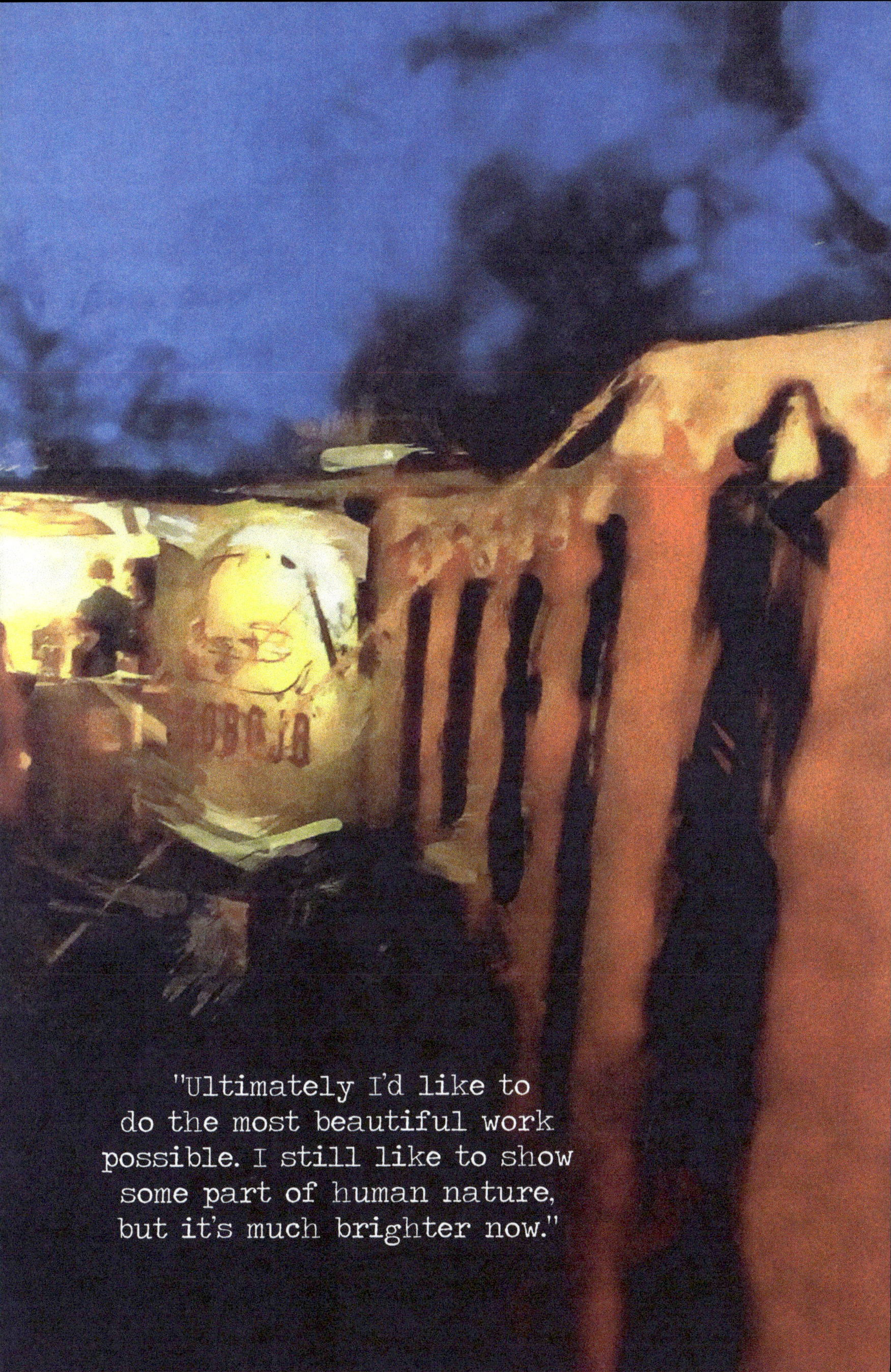

"Ultimately I'd like to do the most beautiful work possible. I still like to show some part of human nature, but it's much brighter now."

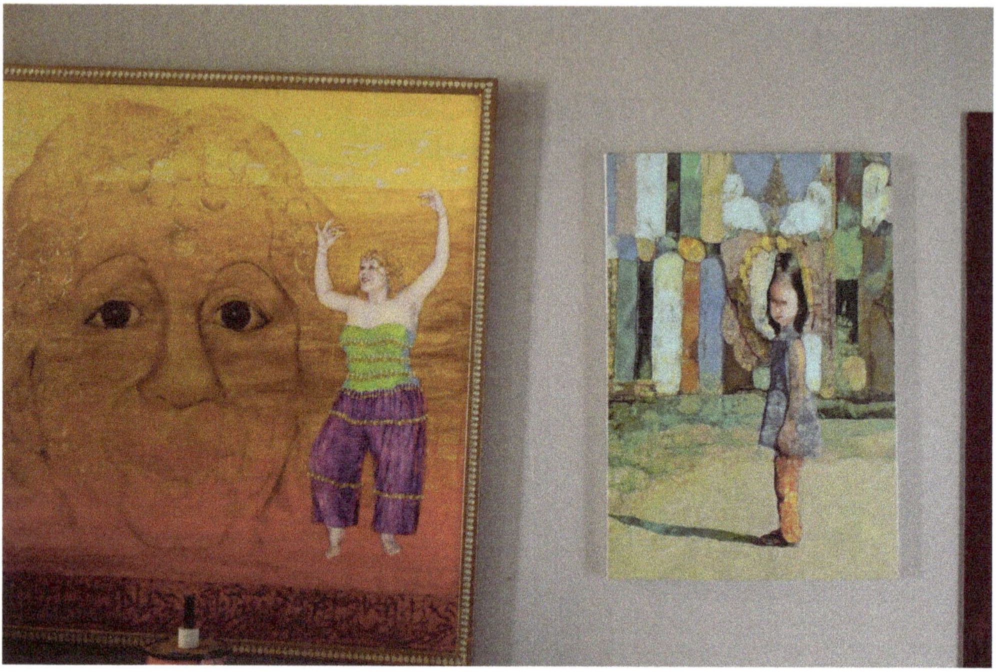

The art on the walls tell a story of Carl's progression as an artist. It's all he ever wanted to be.

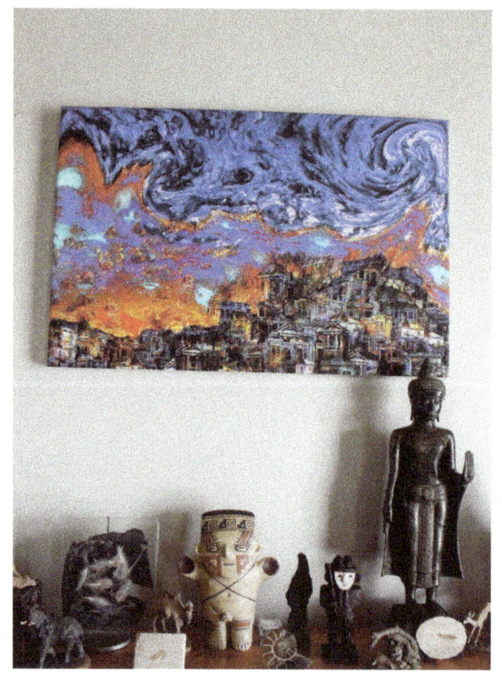

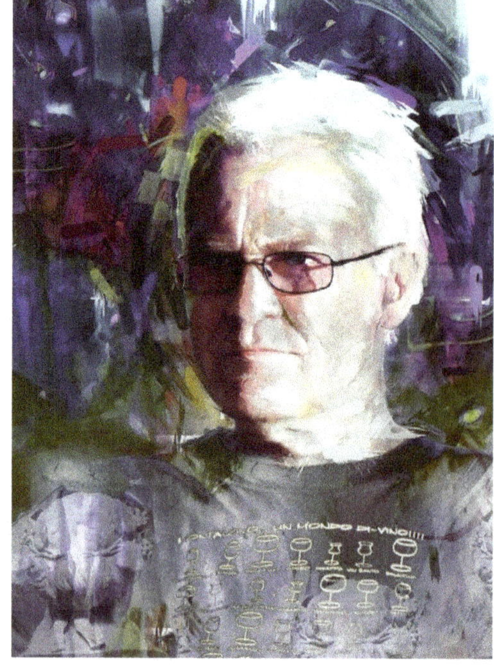

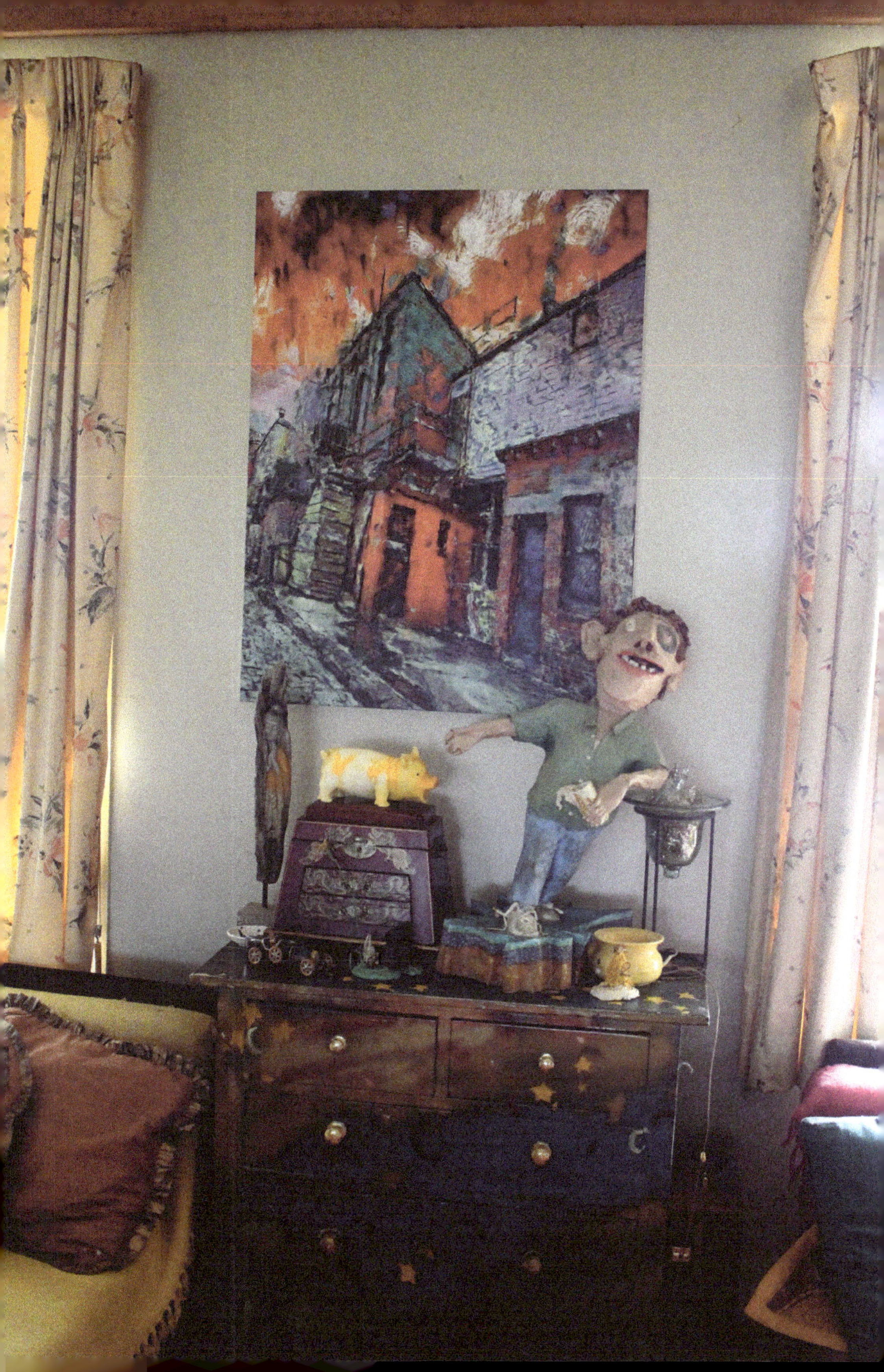

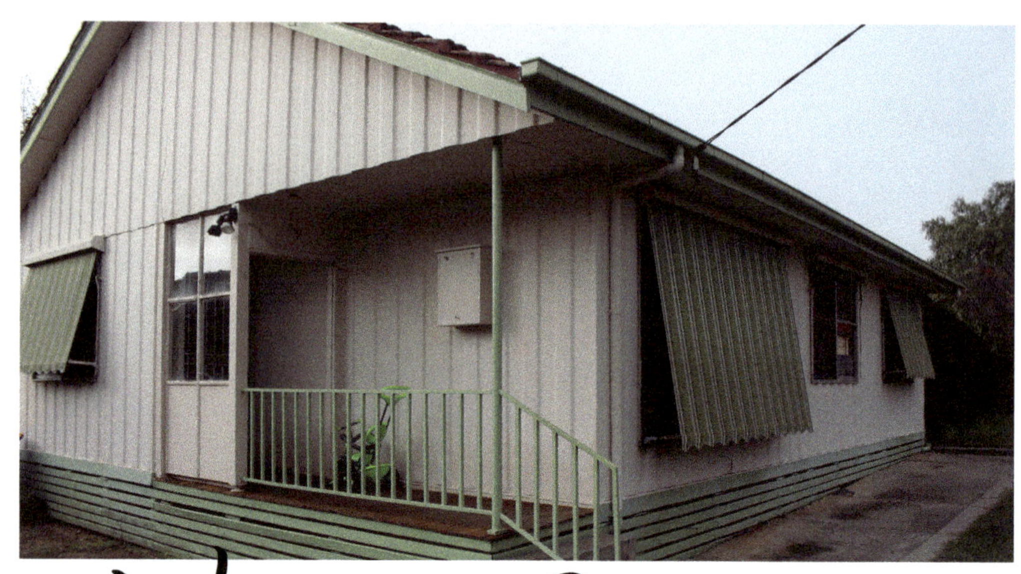

Arkeria Rose Armstrong

Colours of country

When the Australian ambassador in Rotterdam, Netherlands, opened Arkeria Rose Armstrong's first exhibition in 2015 he invited the audience to look around at the works. "You can see Australia in the colours," he said.

There in South Holland hung the hues of Australia's red centre, the turquoise waters of Broome, the purple opals of Lightning Ridge. Arkeria knows these colours and more. She grew up around and within them, as she travelled the breadth of the country as a kid in her family's caravan.

Arkeria is a Gamilaraay artist, born in 1988 in Ceduna, South Australia, to a school teacher mother and fisherman father. Her early years were spent growing up with her little sister in the tiny seaside community, until her dad caught gold fever. "He decided he'd pack us up and travel around Australia looking for gold," Arkeria says. "I was seven and my sister was five."

"It was just us and that little caravan in the middle of nowhere. At the time we didn't think we were any different from anyone else. We met a lot of kids in caravan parks who had the same sort of lifestyle. We didn't realise until we started going to a mainstream school how different our lives were."

Looking back now, Arkeria can see it was a charmed childhood. Plus, it provided a deep vein of truth to draw upon for her art. "It opened my eyes to all different

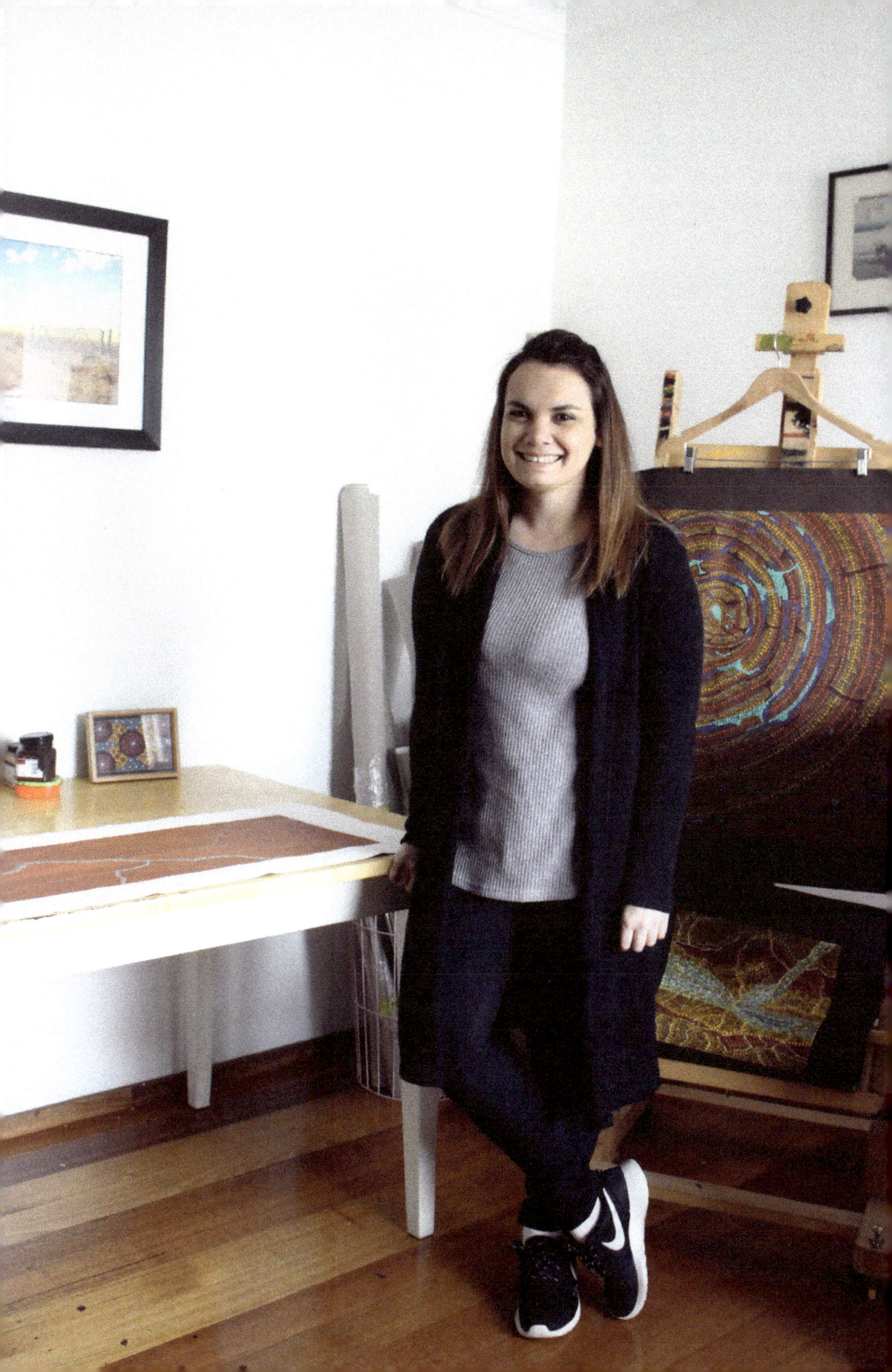

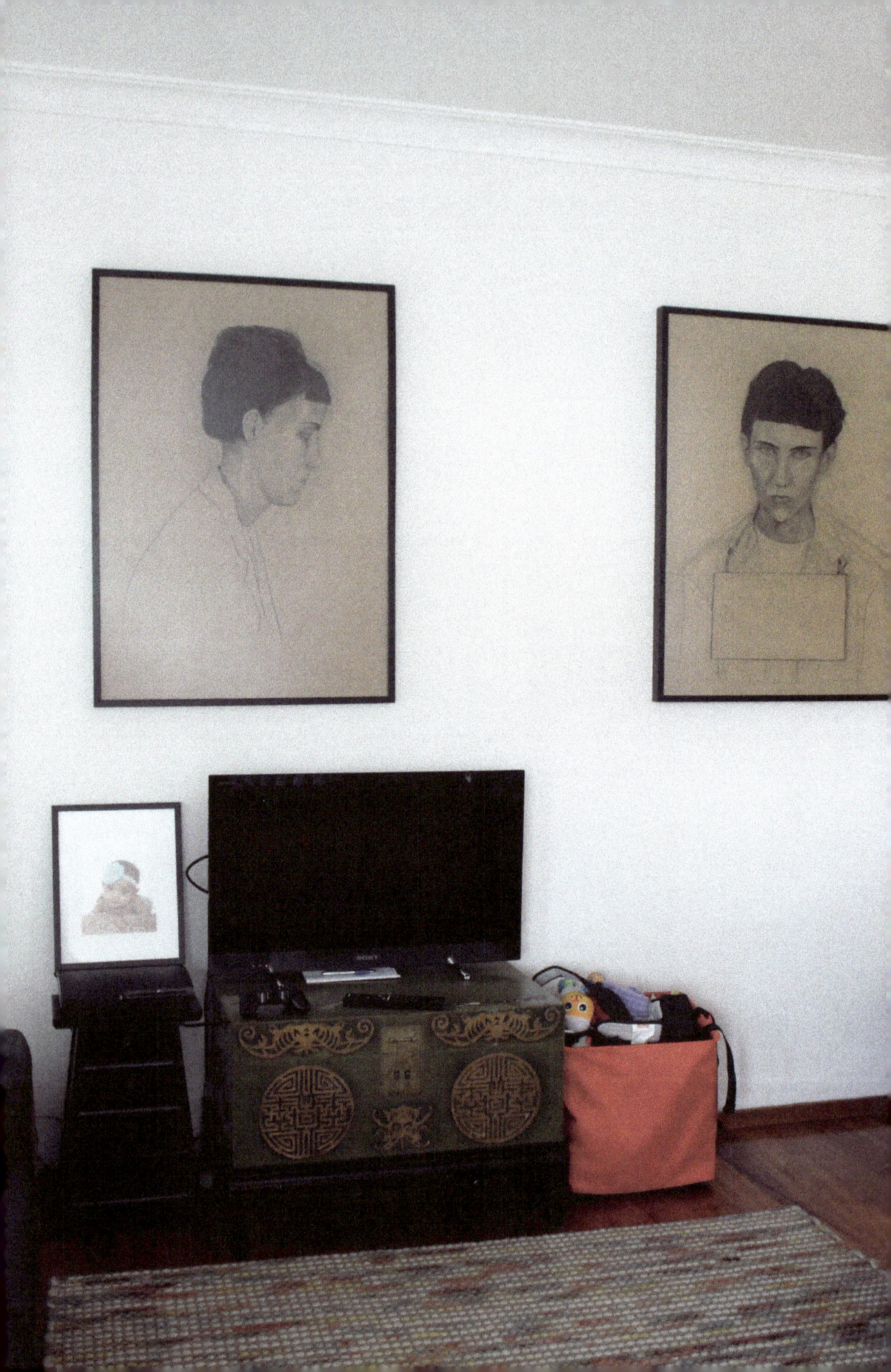

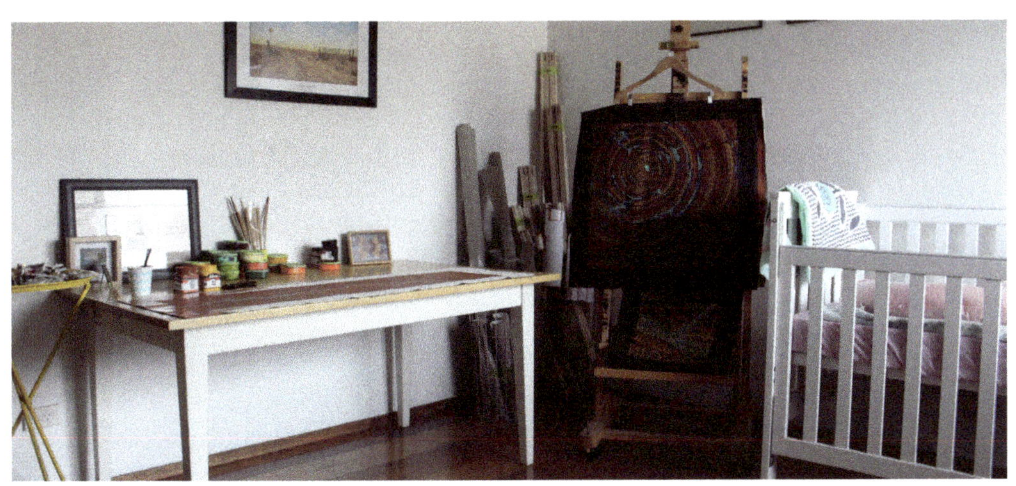

sorts of possibilities for me, creatively, and now that I can reflect on it I realise that some of the experiences we had were priceless."

It's the places she's seen and the Indigenous communities she's spent time in that influenced her first show. "We had all sorts of experiences with Aboriginal women all around Australia," she says. Such as finding flecks of gold between the cracks of dry river rocks with Indigenous women in Halls Creek.

Gold was a constant presence in Arkeria's childhood. She remembers her dad's first big find. It was in central Victoria, not too far from where she now lives in Eaglehawk. "We were staying in a mud hut left over from the old goldfields days. Mum had candles lit in there and we were doing school work. I can just remember Dad running through the bush, screaming, he'd found some."

The quest took the family all the way to Marble Bar, in the Pilbara; that other famous mining region in Western Australia. There Arkeria's mum began teaching at the local school, and there they stayed for four years. "It's one of the hottest places in Australia," Arkeria says. It also has a strong Indigenous culture.

"At the high school we attended it was 60 per cent Aboriginal kids. Mum always made us aware of our Aboriginality and it's never been something that's not there in our day-to-day lives. In most of the towns we lived in the Aboriginal population was quite prominent."

In central Victoria it's less so. The traditional owners of this region are the Dja Dja Wurrung people. They are part of the world's oldest living culture, yet non-Indigenous Australians are only just coming to realise the significance of this heritage, the stories and customs and spiritual places. Artists like Arkeria are helping bridge the gap.

"Aboriginal art all over Australia is seen differently depending on where it comes from, the traditions of that place and the way they traditionally paint," she says. "I suppose I'm trying to find a balance between what's traditional and what's contemporary. If you're living on Country and with your community, you have those older generations to guide you through the process. I have a strong enough connection to culture to know I'm doing the right thing. It's just finding that balance between being an artist and being an Indigenous artist."

Arkeria's grandfather, Don Briggs, is a Yorta Yorta Elder in Shepparton. He paints with traditional ochre pigments, hand ground. Her late grandmother, Rose Fernando, was a Gamilaraay Elder and one of the last sand painters in northern New South Wales. Rose had a significant influence on Arkeria growing up, and now art is a way to keep her spirit close.

Arkeria says she was always a creative kid. Making things was a big part of their home schooling. They made do, made up games and plays and stories. She always knew art would be a part of her life, but never predicted how much so.

Not long after she came to Bendigo with her family, Arkeria began studying to be a teacher at La Trobe University. She opted for the arts electives, thinking that would equip her to teach art. During her final exams, she met the owner of the Aboriginal Art Gallery in Rotterdam, who'd come to Australia looking for Indigenous art. He asked Arkeria if she would paint a few pieces for a group show.

"I thought, I've almost finished exams, I've got time to do a few pieces, why not? After that he said, 'what about a solo show?'" And life hasn't been the same since. Mid-way through painting the 24 works for the exhibition, Arkeria and her partner Chris became pregnant with their daughter, Harriet.

Four days after mum and bub came home from hospital, Arkeria resumed painting. Harriet was just three months old when the young family flew to the Netherlands for the show. "I don't think I really got it until I went to Rotterdam. Not until I walked into the gallery and saw my work hanging up. I just thought, oh my gosh, I actually am an artist. I hadn't seen the work for months, since it was un-stretched and hanging around my house. I'd forgotten what it looked like."

Now, her paintings are in demand. "I wasn't expecting it take off the way it has. I'm quite young for an Aboriginal artist. Most are in their 40s when they get an opportunity to do a solo exhibition."

Regardless of the success, Arkeria is well-grounded here in this suburban street of fibro houses in historic Eaglehawk. "I live in Eaglehawk because it's very community-orientated. You've got everything you need in the little main street and you do have the bush just out there. Mum and Dad live here too, and they were pushing Harriet in the pram in the Whipstick today."

Arkeria is now represented in galleries in Alice Springs and Kununurra. And she's receiving commissions from Rotterdam. Harriet's cot had been pulled into the living room, right beside the easel and paints, so Arkeria can work between her toddler's day-time naps. Her fluid dot paintings defy the stop-start nature of the work.

"The dots have their own movement. It's not like a brush stroke. I start by painting a brown canvas, in three or four tones. So the dots also change colour depending on where they go on the canvas. It's expressive of how the country is too; changing colours and movement." The paintings represent a bird's eye view of the landscape. "Aboriginal artists have been doing that for thousands of years."

Arkeria continues the tradition in Eaglehawk, surrounded by family mementos, the artwork of her friends, and a slumbering daughter. As well as pale baby pink, this lovely, light-filled room houses all the colours of the country. It's beautiful.

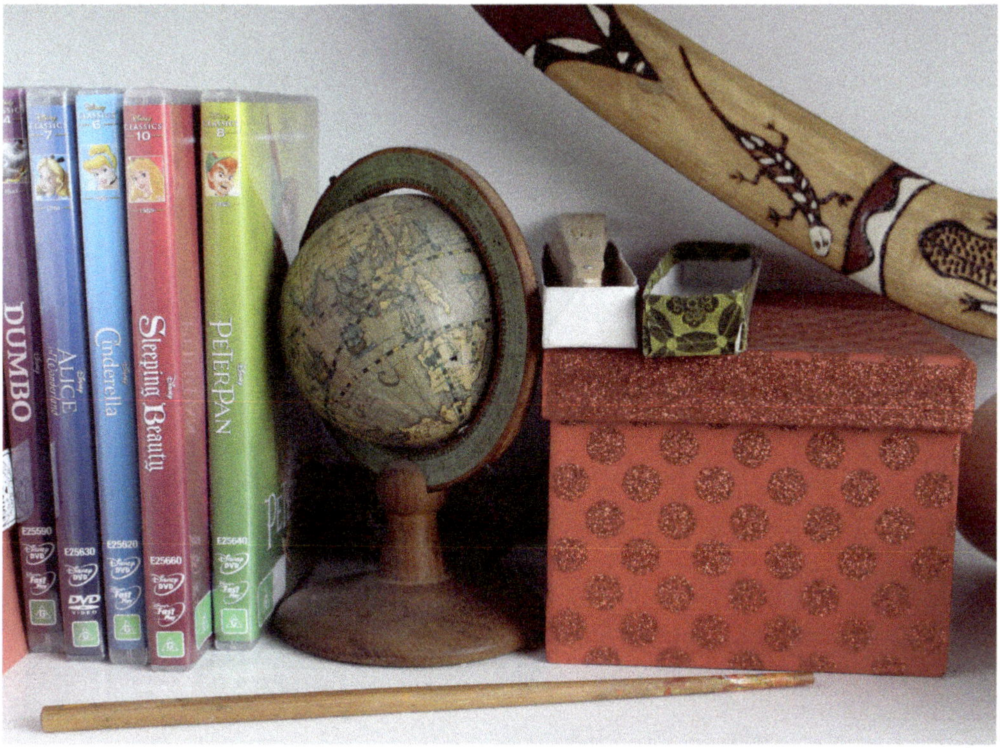

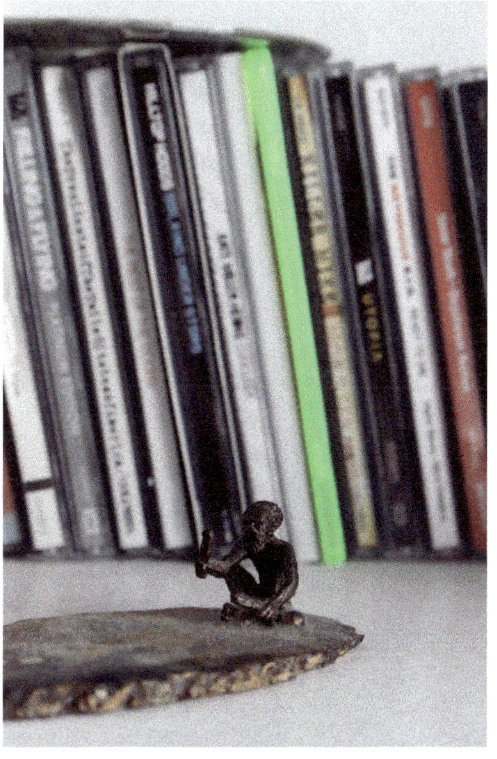

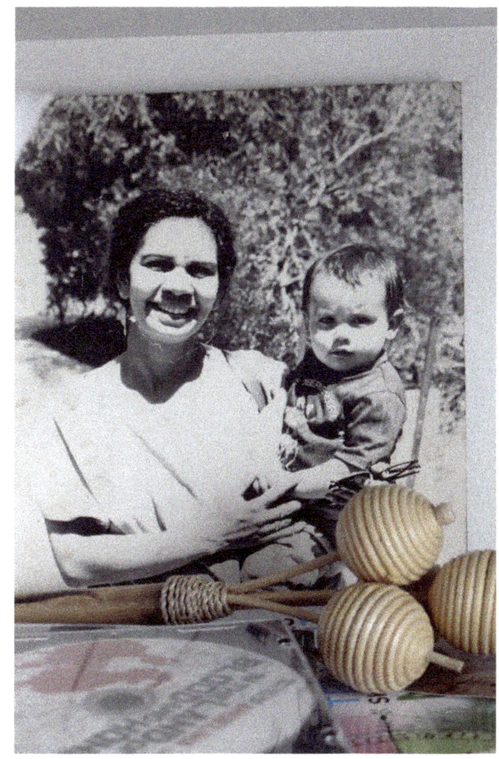

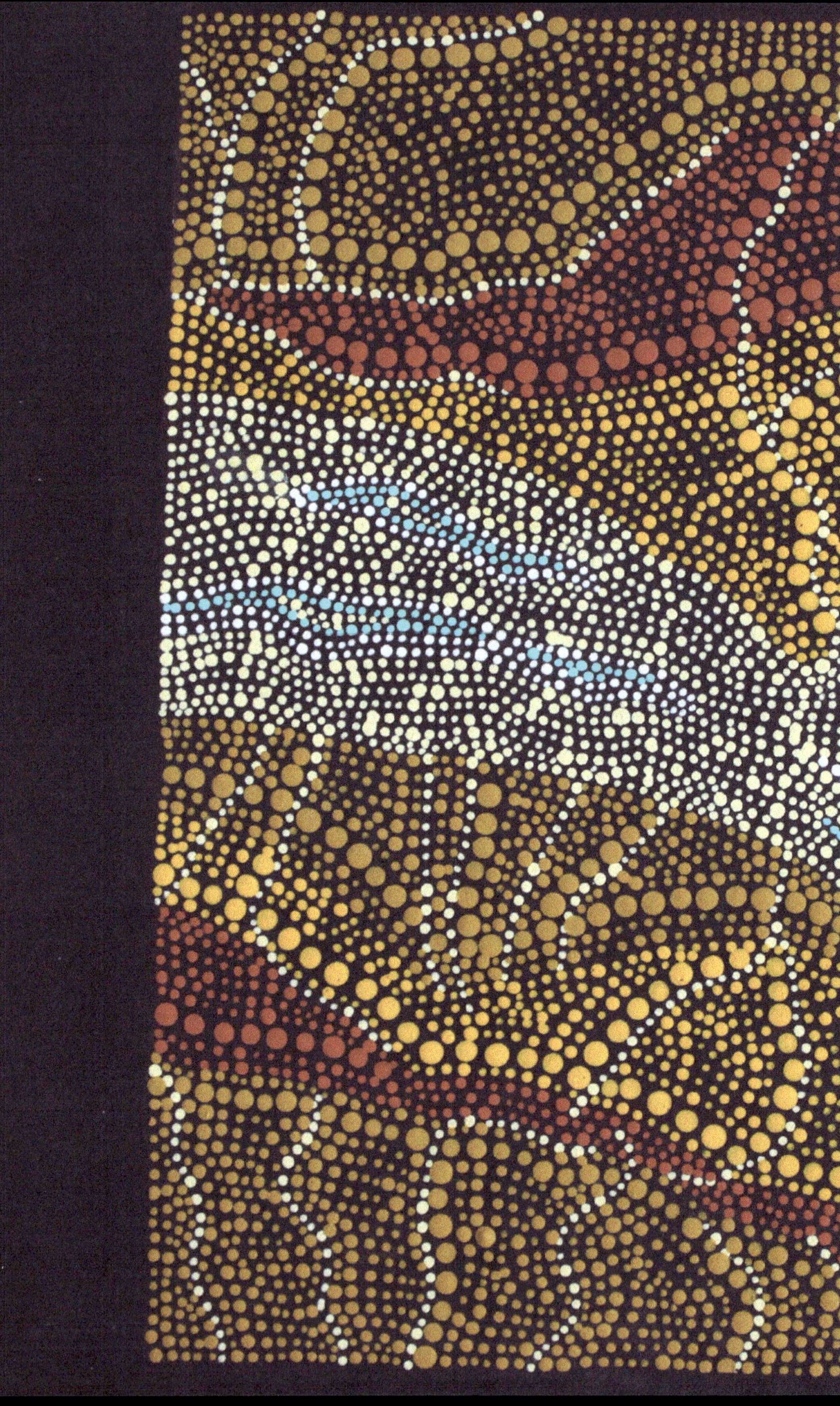

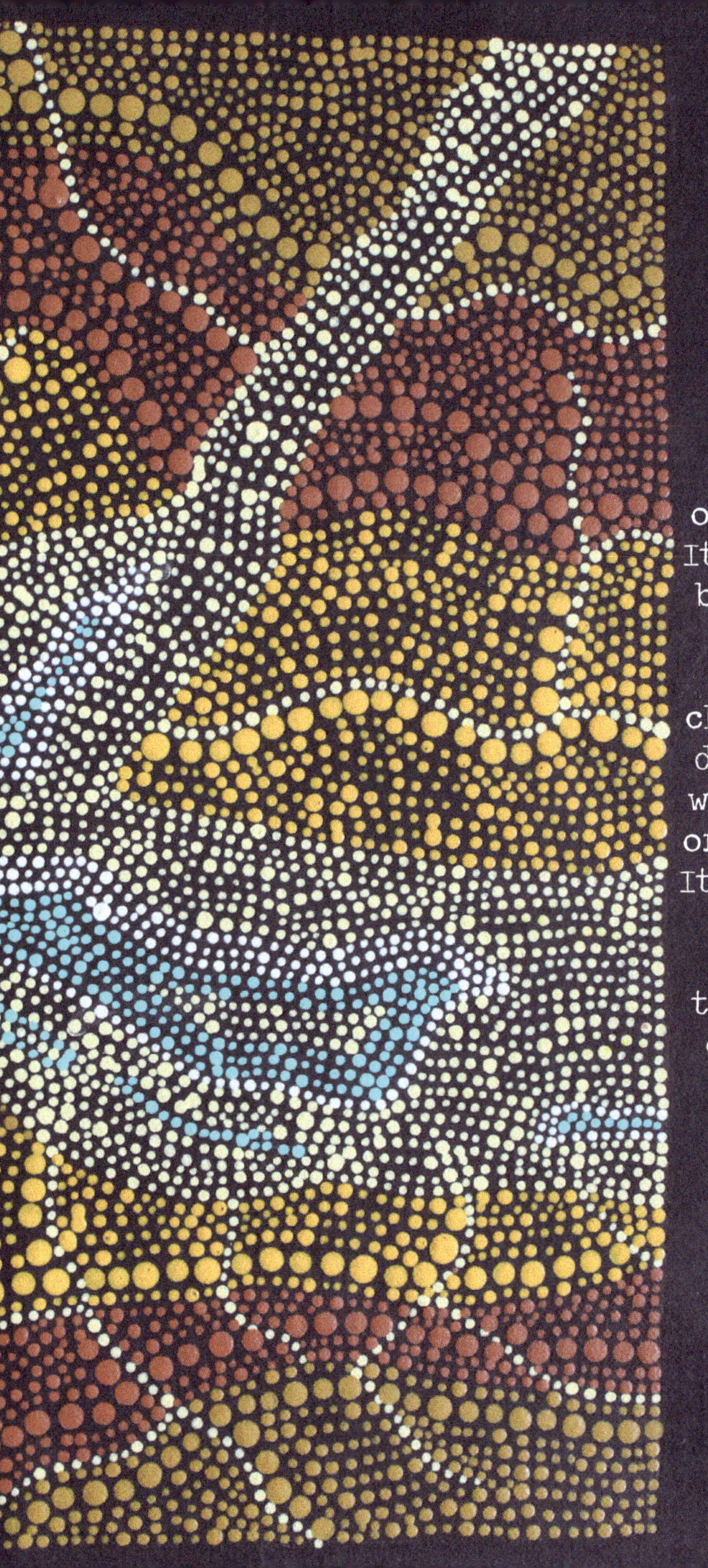

"The dots have their own movement. It's not like a brush stroke. So the dots also change colour depending on where they go on the canvas. It's expressive of how the country is too; changing colours and movement."

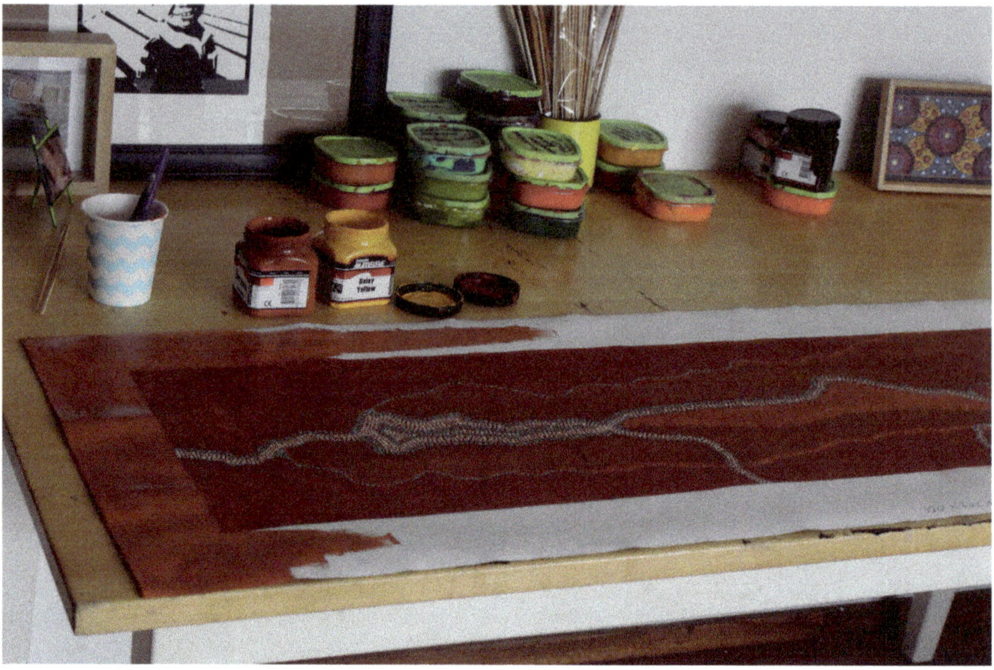

This lovely light-filled room houses all the colours of the country. It's beautiful.

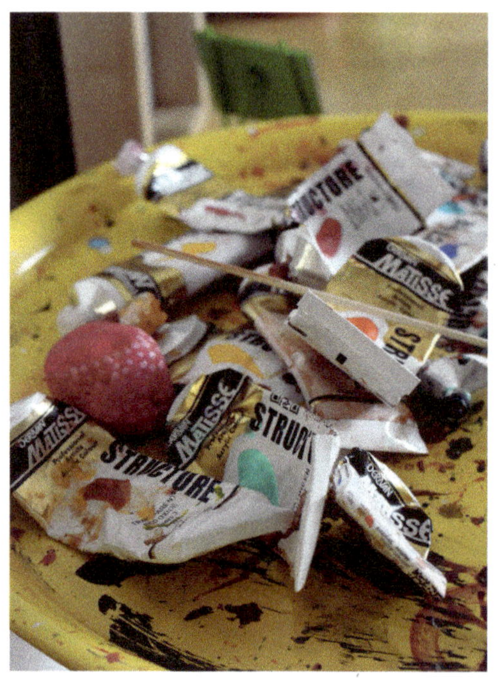

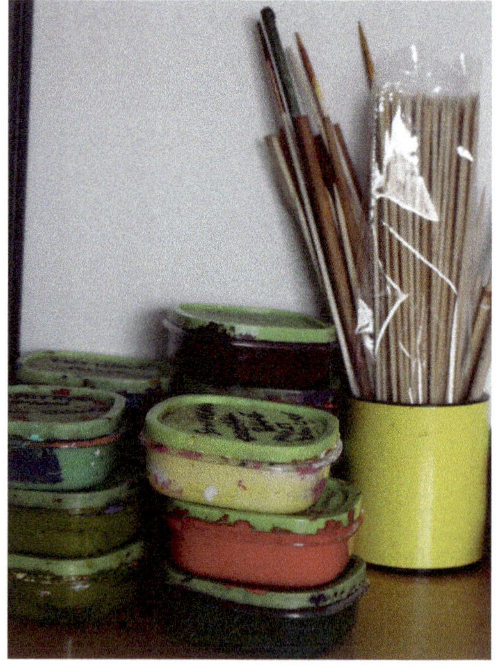

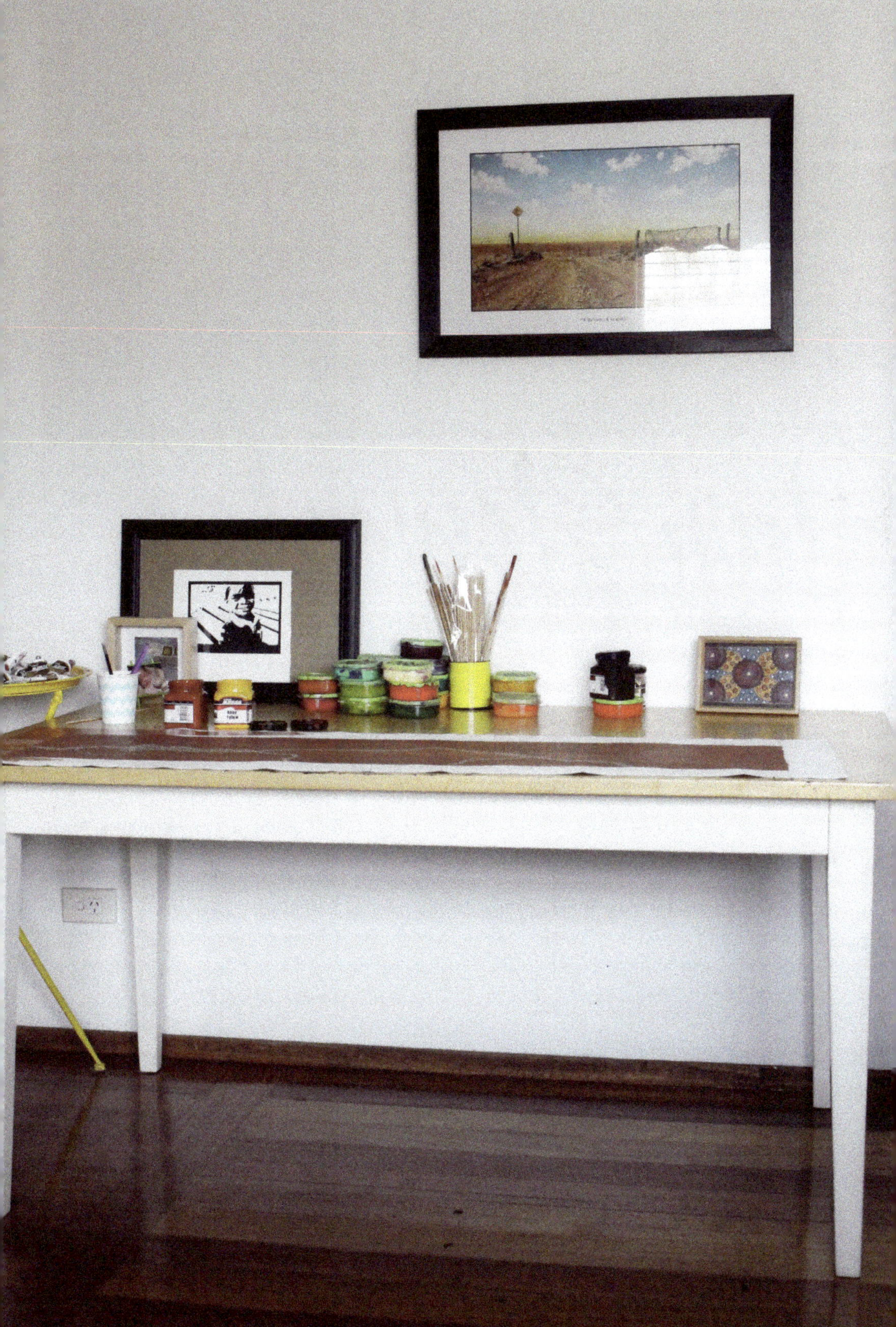

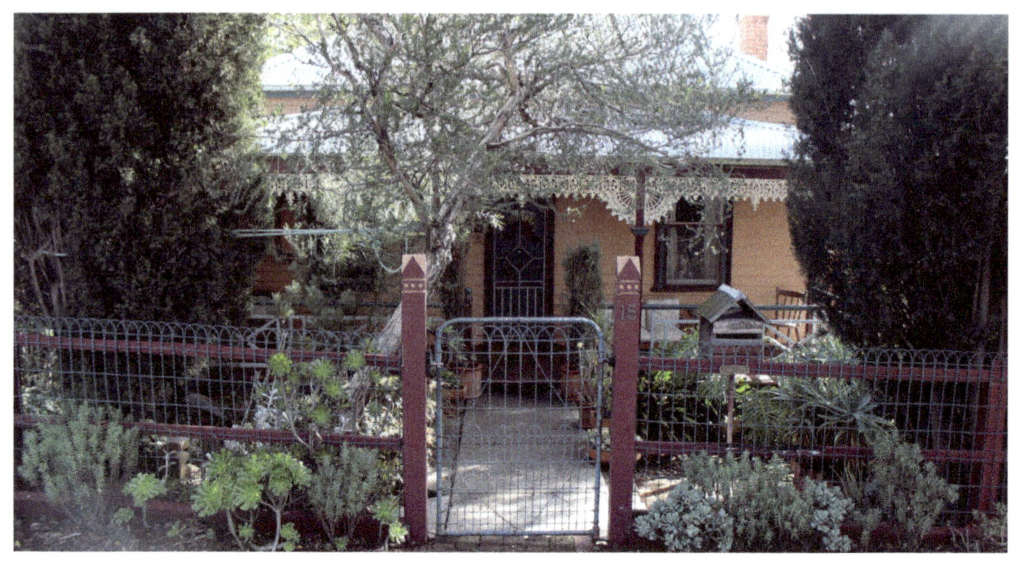

Iain Stewart

Where the art is

The stories in this book come like nuggets. They come as whiffs of Chinese whispers as to who should be approached next. Iain Stewart's story comes like that. Another artist mentions he has a great dig. A quirky backyard studio. That he's a great person. Golden.

"This is a family home," Iain says on the welcome to his quintessential cottage; a timber Victorian in one of Bendigo's first gazetted streets, on the blood boundary of working-class Long Gully. "This whole house is full of art, even the kitchen. And most of my collection is by locals."

Iain and his wife Regina are the fourth owners of this historic house. It was built for a mine foreman. The mine owners being further downhill towards the city, in Italianate and Georgian mansions. For every timber house in Long Gully in the gold days, there were at least two canvas tents called home. "The mines went all the way from here to Eaglehawk," Iain says. "The stamps were going day and night, day and night."

With mining companies came employment and an emerging middle class in Bendigo, and camps of temporary huts were replaced with these practical symmetrical cottages, with a hallway down the centre, four rooms either side, and a lean-to kitchen out the back. Classic, coveted features include timber floors and ceilings, open fireplaces and double hung sash windows. Just gorgeous.

They're in demand now, but when Iain and Regina arrived in Bendigo in the

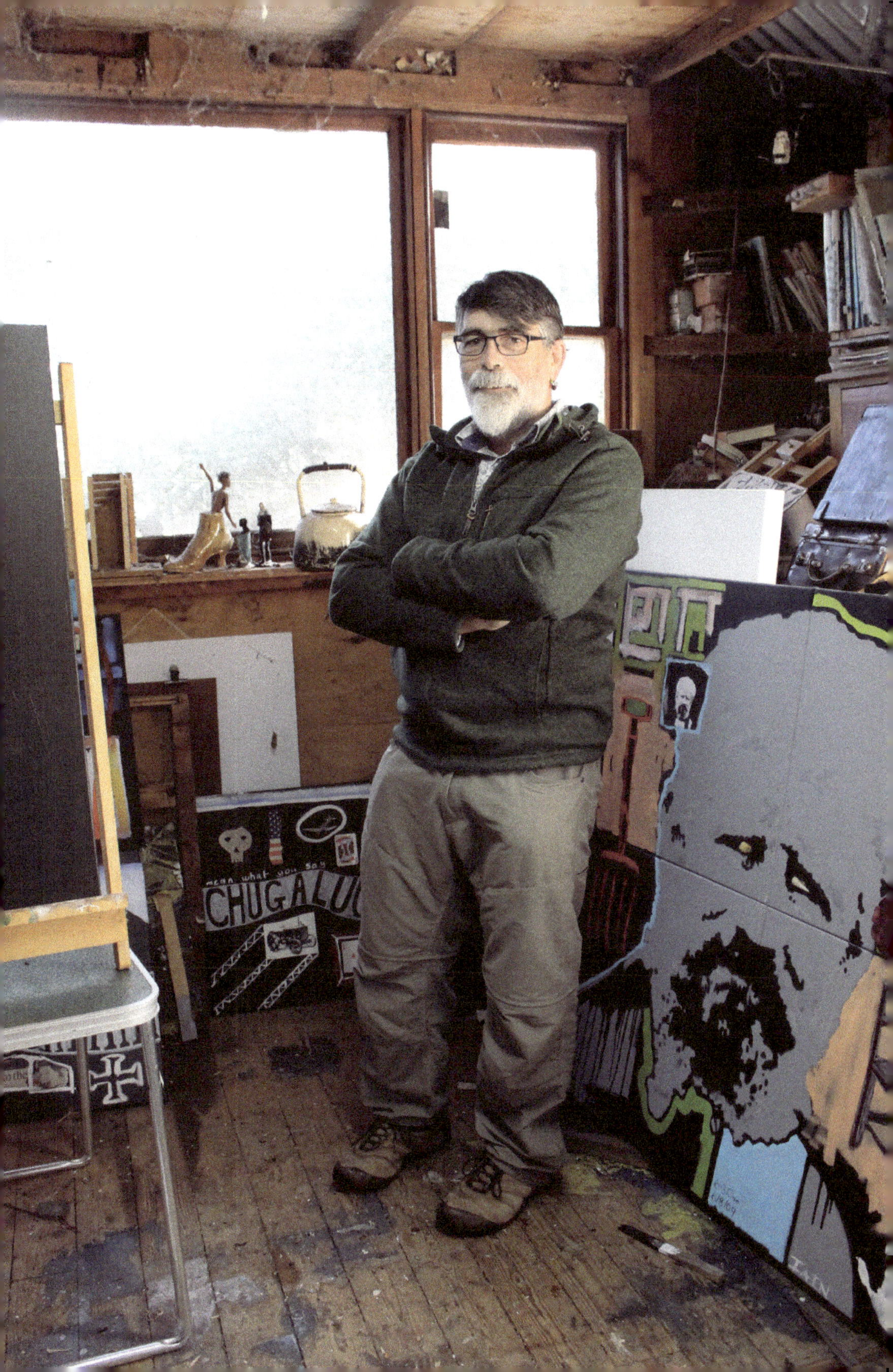
mean what you say
CHUGALU

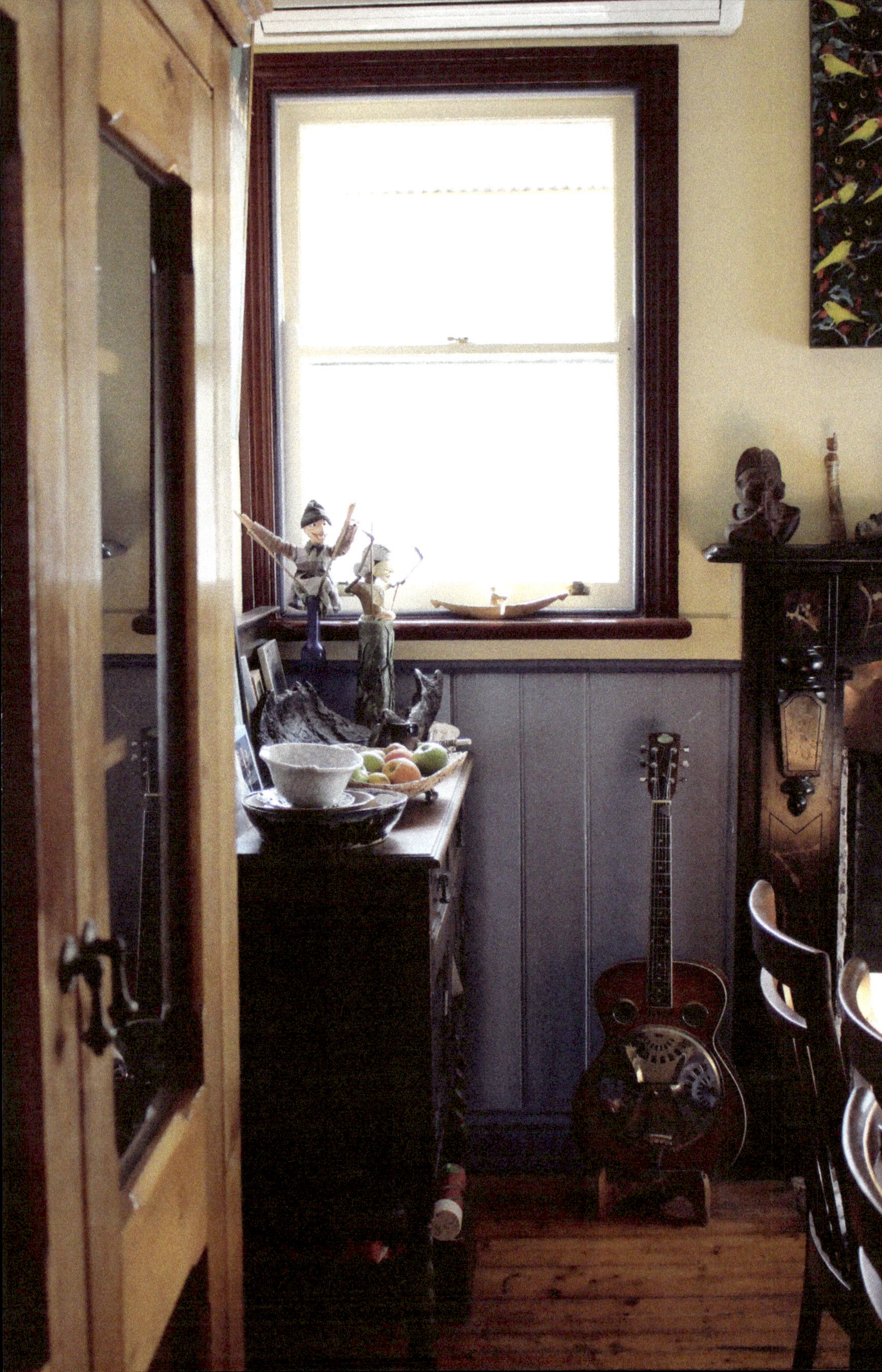

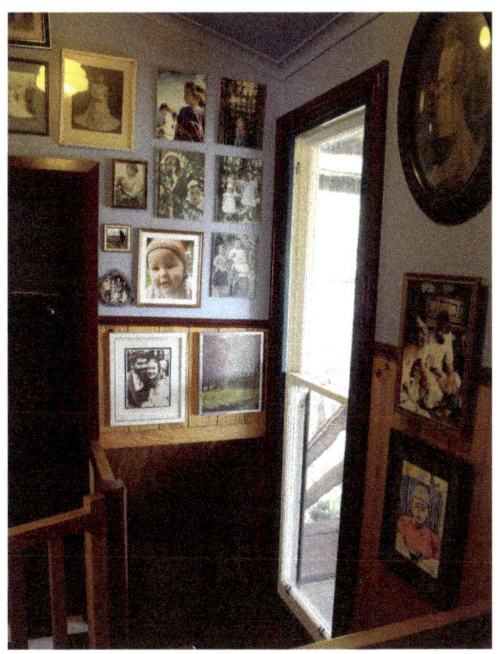

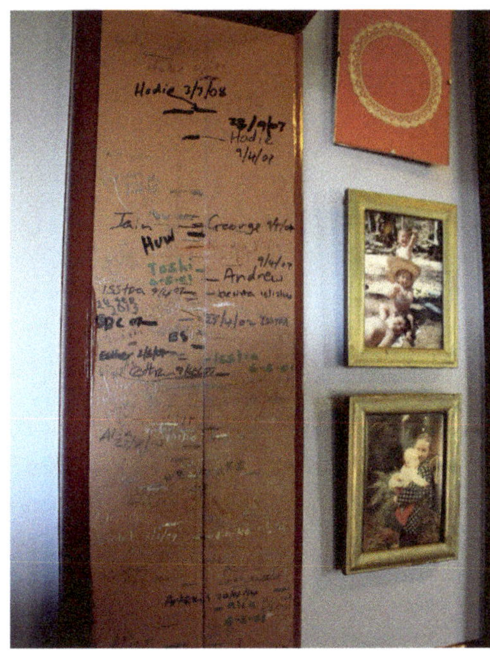

late 1970s, prices were just right. "We thought, yeah, this is a funky old town with lovely old buildings, and we could probably buy a house here. The affordability of Bendigo meant people who were arty minded could come and settle."

Iain was a qualified carpenter and aspiring artist. Regina had just finished medical school and was working as an intern at the Bendigo Hospital. Here, Iain found the sense of home he'd long sought.

"I grew up in Ferntree Gully. It was an outer suburb of artists. I was an immigrant and everything was new to my family. We came to Australia from Scotland when I was 18 months old.

"Growing up, I was interested in how other people saw things and artists saw things in an interesting way. Gough Whitlam was Prime Minister and everything was about art. Art gave life meaning and purpose and it's always been that way with me."

Ironically, the now high school art teacher didn't find purpose at high school. "I figured education wasn't purposeful for me. I just felt like there were so many things I had to find out about before I got educated."

He dropped out of Boronia High, began working the odd carpentry gig, moved from place to place, slept on couches. He hitched his way around the state. The country. Eventually, at 19, all the way back to Scotland, via Pakistan, Afghanistan, Iran and Iraq. "I thought, my god, this world is so huge. And everywhere I went people were warm and friendly and full of humanity."

While Iain says he'd never felt 100 per cent Aussie, when he got to Scotland, his birth country didn't feel like home either. "I couldn't have lived there permanently," he says. "It was impossible to get work and at that stage people were just really down and out.

"I did feel different here. But art was a good way to be different. And I discovered I actually had a talent for it at about eight years of age."

In Bendigo Iain enrolled in the local university's fine arts course. At that stage, in the early 1980s, the studios were above the famous Gillies Pie factory. A red brick, saw-toothed beast beside the railway tracks. "The space was really, really good," he says. "You could get a slab of Boston bun and share it 'round."

The Gillies branded pies are no longer made in Bendigo. But many of the artists are still here, still making great work. Others will never be forgotten. "I met Brian at art school. We shared the Boston bun," Iain says.

He's referring to his great mate, Brian Lunt, who passed away from cancer in 2011. The pair made history in Brian's suburb of Eaglehawk, for the quirky films they made under the label Two Blues Productions. Two blues being the colours of the local footy club. The films, featuring local identities, oddities, scenes and a brilliant original music score, launched the Eaglehawk Dahlia and Arts Festival ten years running. Eaglehawk's historic town hall is also the arthouse Star Cinema. It was the perfect venue for their annual screening.

After uni, Iain got together with some other alumni to open The Art Space in an old hardware supply shop in central Bendigo, which sustained them with studio and gallery space for eight years.

Running parallel to Iain's growing practice was a growing family. Not long after moving into their home, Iain built a second story underneath the stumps, added a couple of bedrooms, and he and Regina filled the house up with three kids. Grown up and off in the world now, their son and two daughters are still a constant presence in the house. Iain's illustrations of them as babies, their photographs and marks to measure their growth take pride of place alongside the art.

Iain's art is a bit like his home. It's made up of objects and materials found and loved. It's made of mementos. "I see opportunities in things and I find stuff," he says. "If I want to make a piece of art, I find the pieces for it."

Like the "trophy to end all trophies" in the middle of the downstairs, homemade coffee table. "I never got a trophy for sport, but I can make my own. I saw this box of trophies at the recycling yard and I went, wow, all those memories, waiting to be liberated. So I liberated a few of them." Gaudy gold limbs jostle for recognition in a piece made for fun. "You can have a laugh at art. It doesn't have to be all that serious. I don't take art any more seriously than gardening, or reading, or drama, or riding my bike. All of those things are just as important."

Being creative has helped Iain through some tough patches though. He made art to reconcile cancer treatment in 2001, the near-loss of Regina when their third child was born, the death of his mate Brian. Some of these works he keeps in the home, some in the chook shed-cum-studio at the back of his lovely leafy garden. Iain says his memories are tightly interwoven with his work.

"I can't remember stuff without them. I remember things because of the paintings. I remember what was going on when I painted them. I have lots of emotions in them. I can feel what was happening at the time. They're stories."

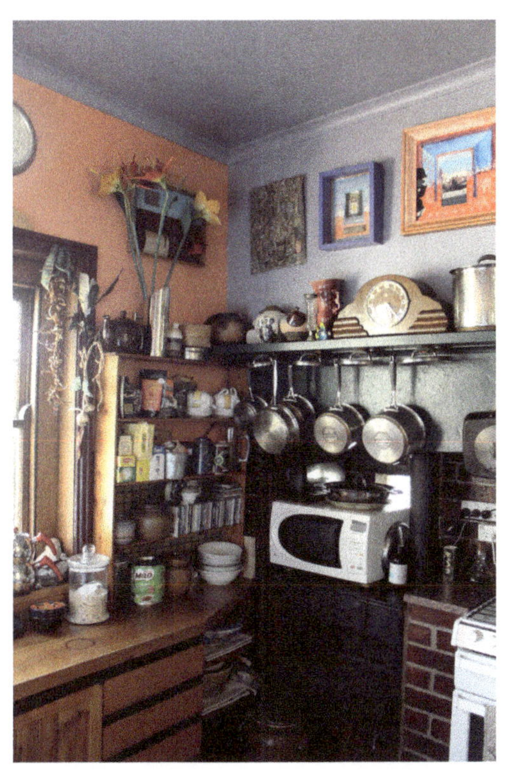

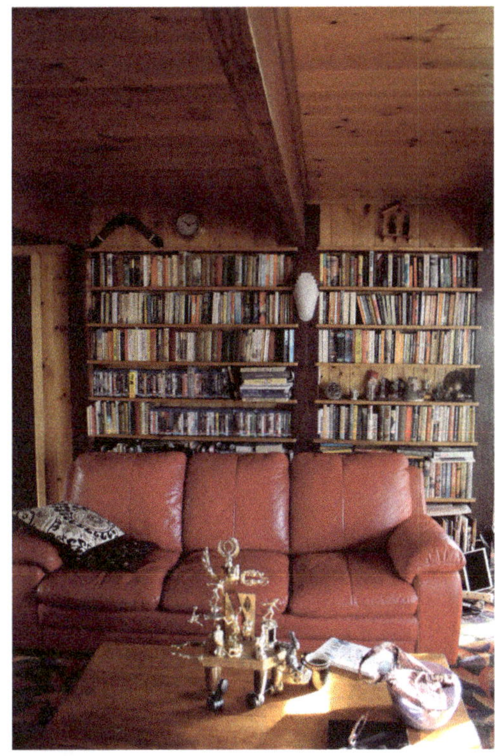

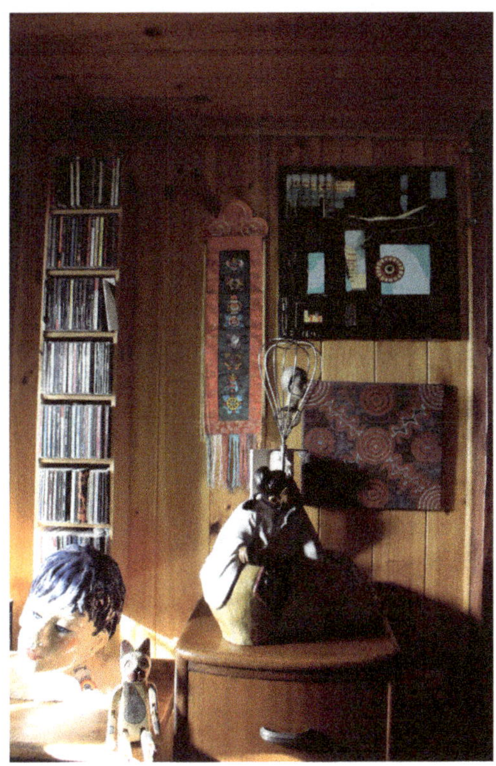

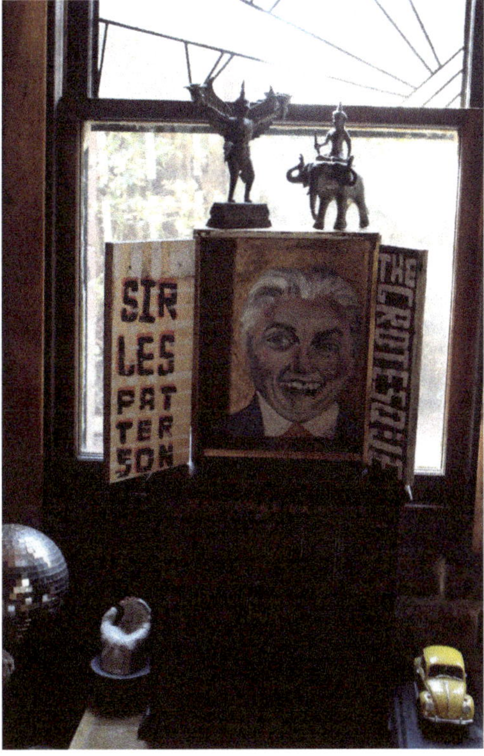
SIR
LES
PAT
TER
SON
THE

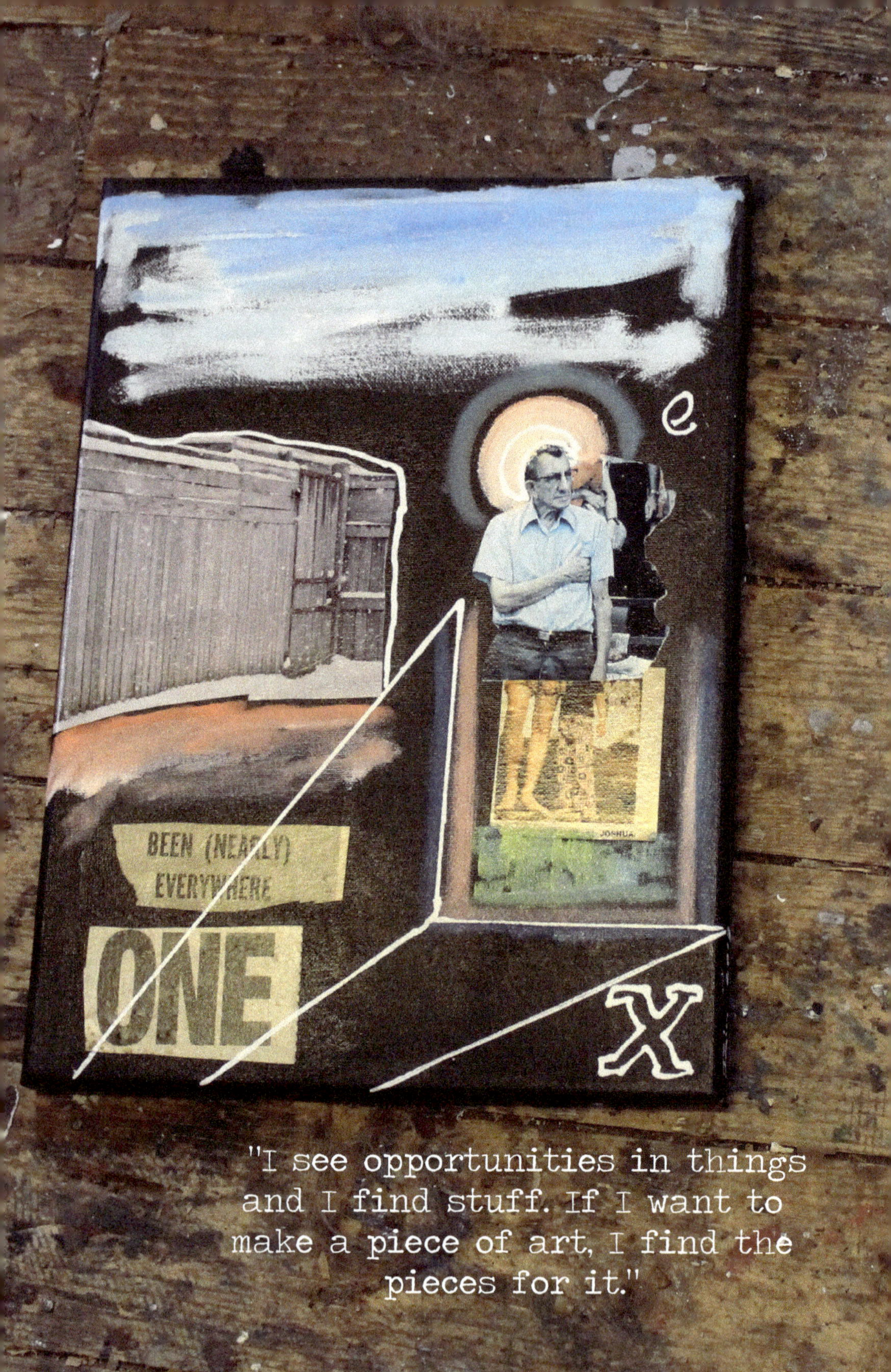

"I see opportunities in things and I find stuff. If I want to make a piece of art, I find the pieces for it."

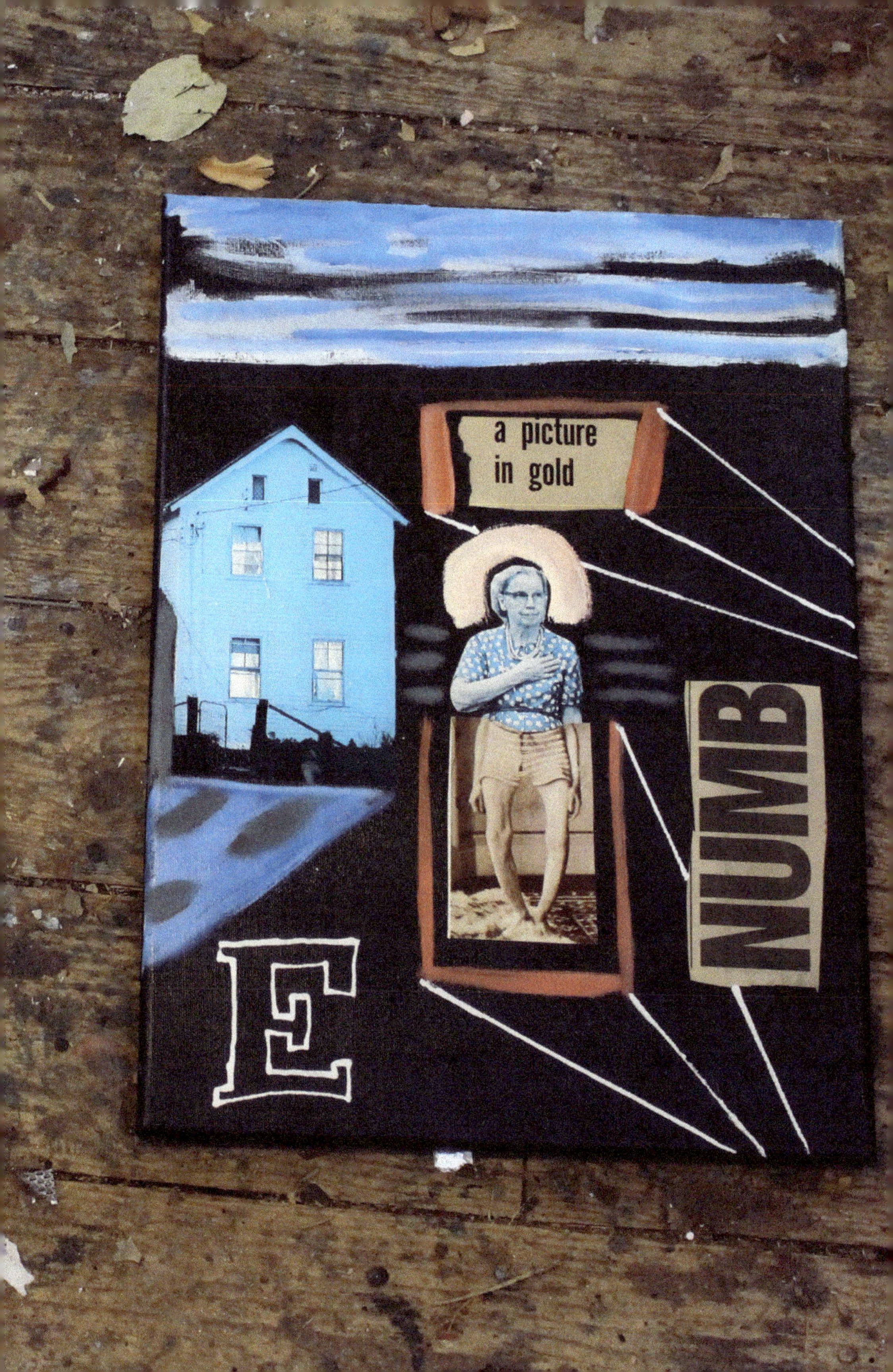
a picture
in gold
NUMB
E

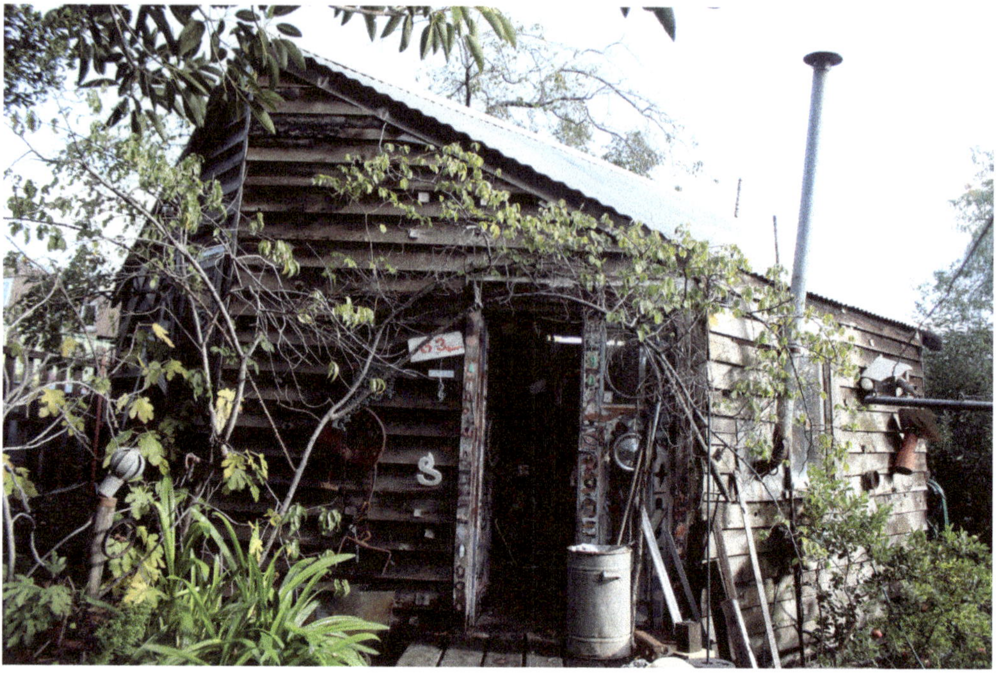

Some works he keeps in the home, some in the chook shed-cum-studio at the back of the garden.

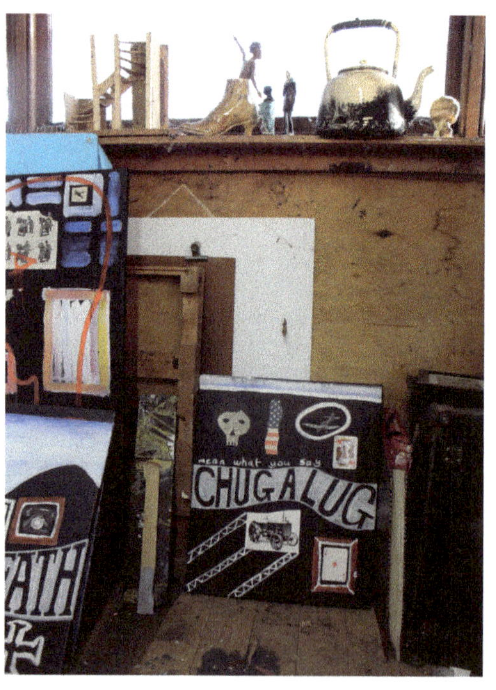

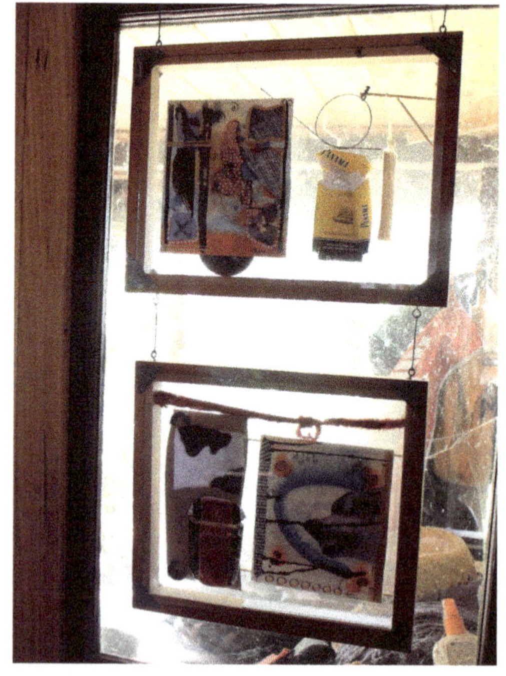

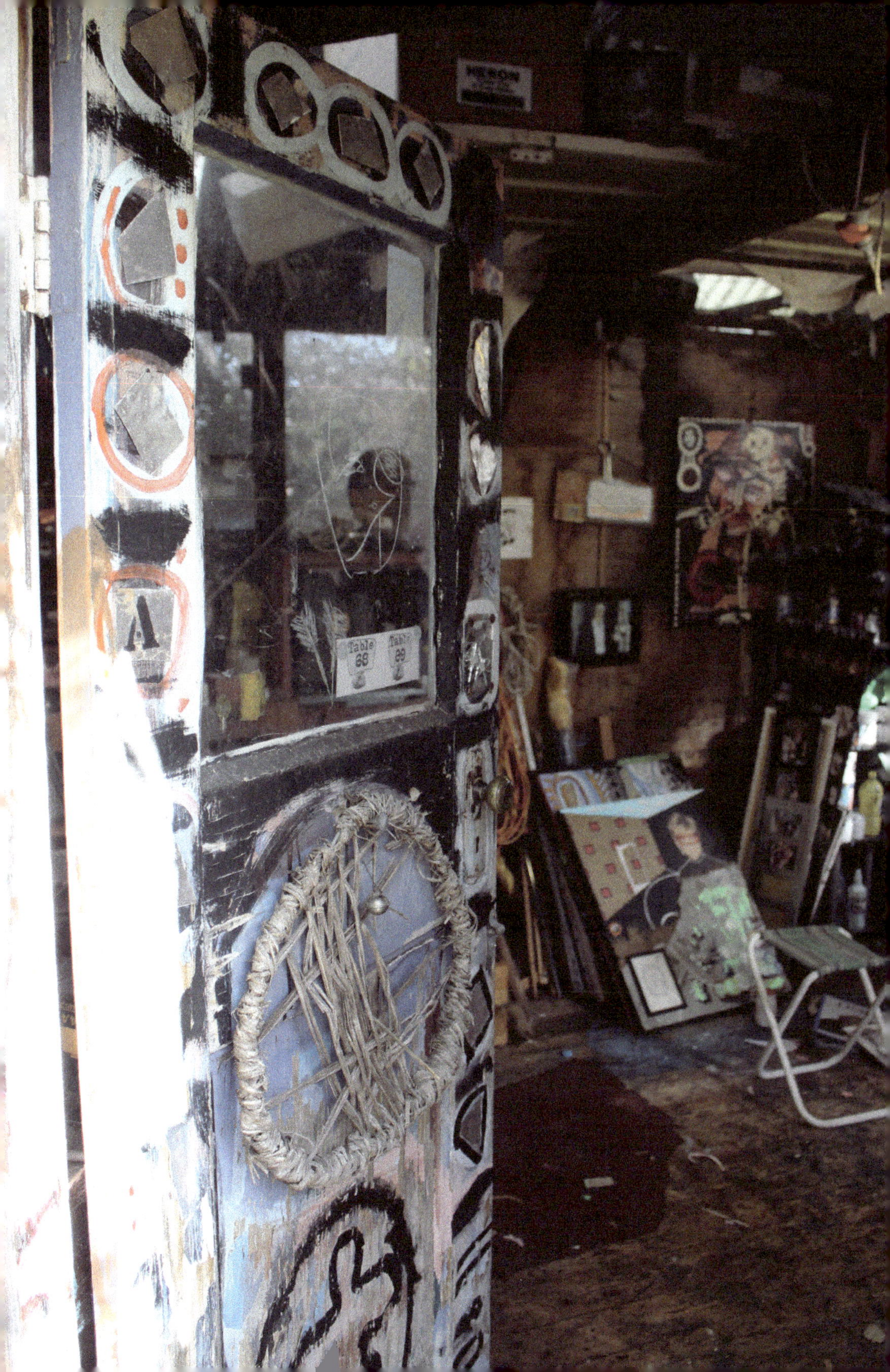
A
Table 68
69

www.ingramcontent.com/pod-product-compliance
Ingram Content Group UK Ltd.
Pitfield, Milton Keynes, MK11 3LW, UK
UKHW062313290726
14090UKWH00018B/1041